T0332483

EPISTEMOLOGY AND COGNITION

STUDIES IN COGNITIVE SYSTEMS

VOLUME 6

The titles published in this series are listed at the end of this volume.

EPISTEMOLOGY AND COGNITION

Edited by

JAMES H. FETZER

Department of Philosophy,
University of Minnesota, Duluth, U.S.A.

KLUWER ACADEMIC PUBLISHERS

DORDRECHT / BOSTON / LONDON

Library of Congress Cataloging-in-Publication Data

Epistemology and cognition / edited by James H. Fetzer.
      p.   cm. -- (Studies in cognitive systems ; 6)
    Includes indexes.
    ISBN 0-7923-0892-1 (alk. paper)
    1. Knowledge, Theory of. 2. Languages--Philosophy. 3. Semantics
  (Philosophy) I. Fetzer, James H., 1940-   . II. Series: Studies
  in cognitive systems ; v. 6.
  BD161.E62 1990
  121--dc20   90-42217

ISBN 0-7923-0892-1

Published by Kluwer Academic Publishers,
P.O. Box 17, 3300 AA Dordrecht, The Netherlands.

Kluwer Academic Publishers incorporates
the publishing programmes of
D. Reidel, Martinus Nijhoff, Dr W. Junk and MTP Press.

Sold and distributed in the U.S.A. and Canada
by Kluwer Academic Publishers,
101 Philip Drive, Norwell, MA 02061, U.S.A.

In all other countries, sold and distributed
by Kluwer Academic Publishers Group,
P.O. Box 322, 3300 AH Dordrecht, The Netherlands.

Printed on acid-free paper

Printed in the Netherlands

To
Loren E. Lomasky

TABLE OF CONTENTS

TABLE OF CONTENTS

EPILOGUE

SERIES PREFACE

This series will include monographs and collections of studies devoted to the investigation and exploration of knowledge, information, and data-processing systems of all kinds, no matter whether human, (other) animal, or machine. Its scope is intended to span the full range of interest from classical problems in the philosophy of mind and philosophical psychology through issues in cognitive psychology and sociobiology (concerning the mental powers of other species) to ideas related to artificial intelligence and computer science. While primary emphasis will be placed upon theoretical, conceptual, and epistemological aspects of these problems and domains, empirical, experimental, and methodological studies will also appear from time to time.

The present volume reflects the kind of insights that can be obtained when research workers in philosophy, artificial intelligence, and computer science explore problems of common concern. The issues here tend to fall into two broad but varied sets, namely: those concerned with content and concepts, on the one hand, and those concerned with semantics and epistemology, on the other. The collection begins with a prologue that focuses upon the relations between connectionism and alternative conceptions of nativism and ends with an epilogue that examines the significance of alternative conceptions of the Frame Problem for artificial intelligence. Because these papers are rich and diverse, they ought to appeal to a wide and heterogeneous audience.

J. H. F.

ix

FOREWORD

This collection of papers has been derived from a special triple-issue of SYNTHESE devoted to epistemology and cognition. About two-thirds of those contributions are reprinted here in a somewhat different sequence, which is intended to highlight and to reinforce their relationship to one another. By way of introduction, a few words concerning each might prove to be helpful. The Prologue provides a searching analysis of the relations between connectionism and varieties of nativism, in which Stephen Stich and William Ramsey distinguish three positions – minimal rationalism, anti-empiricism, and rationalism – suggesting that connectionism cannot defeat the first but might defeat the third, where most of the interesting cases seem to fall in between.

Part I begins with a critical exploration of Fodor's "language of thought" hypothesis in which David Braddon–Mitchell and John Fitzpatrick argue that, when correct views about the nature of psychological explanation are considered, the theoretical necessity for a language of thought tends to disappear. Their position does not dictate that Fodor's hypothesis cannot be true, but instead suggests that a *prima facie* case on its behalf has not yet been made. Charles E. M. Dunlop examines the version of this hypothesis that is implied by Roger Schank's theory of conceptual dependency, implying that Schank's approach encounters serious difficulties when it is viewed as an effort to afford "a psychologically valid computer model of human mental processes".

David Cole contends that *a priori* arguments against functionalism, such as those advanced by Hilary Putman, cannot possibly be sound. The relevant empirical evidence, moreover, actually tends to confirm rather than to refute the functionalist position. Paul Thagard explores the complex nature of conceptual change, contending that belief revision cannot be understood without taking into account its consequences for conceptual change, precisely because they are extricable intertwined. William Bechtel and Adele Abrahamsen survey various nonpropositional techniques for representing knowledge, hinting that the emergence of connectionism tends to reinforce the benefits that may yet be derived from alternative approaches to problems within this domain.

Part II begins with an examination of William J. Rapaport's sophisticated efforts to defend purely syntactical conceptions of semantics from Searle's

Chinese Room example, in which Neal Jahren contends that this defense depends upon assuming what he wants to prove, namely: that humans implement natural language "the way it would be on a computer". Yorick Wilks focuses upon another formal approach – the logic-based tradition in knowledge representation, in general, and Drew McDermott's work, in particular – suggesting that it is rooted in the mistaken belief that networks of inferential relations might be sufficient for something to qualify as having in mind.

William Edward Morris undertakes a systematic assessment of the conception of knowledge as information-produced belief that Fred Dretske has advanced, contending that gaps between "information-caused beliefs" and "knowledge" can only be bridged by employing a theory of justification of the kind it was intended to avoid. George Graham offers a subtle analysis of relationships between emotional and cognitive states, with concern for the possibility that specific states of emotion, such as states of depression, might not only be rationally warranted but possess cognitive significance.

Eddy Zemach differentiates between "internalist" accounts of understanding (found in the work of Fodor, Dennett, and other functionalists) and "externalist" accounts (associated with the work of Davidson, Burge, and other semantic theorists) in defense of a Wittgensteinian conception of mentalistic semantics, which he applies to meanings, sentences, and beliefs. In the Epilogue, finally, Eric Lormand turns attention to the Frame Problem by comparing accounts advanced by Dennett, by Haugeland, and by Fodor to the original problem envisioned by McCarthy and Hayes, suggesting that these alternatives are not crucial obstacles to success in Artificial Intelligence.

J. H. F.

ACKNOWLEDGEMENTS

The selection of papers reprinted here were drawn from the following sources;

William Ramsey and Stephen Stich, "Connectionism and Three Levels of Nativism", *Synthese* **82** (1990), pp. 177–205.

David Braddon–Mitchell and John Fitzpatrick, "Explanation and the Language of Thought", *Synthese* **83** (1990), pp. 3–29.

Charles E. M. Dunlop, "Conceptual Dependency as the Language of Thought", *Synthese* **82** (1990), pp. 275–296.

David Cole, "Functionalism and Inverted Spectra", *Synthese* **82** (1990), pp. 207–222.

Paul Thagard, "Concepts and Conceptual Change", *Synthese* **82** (1990), pp. 255–274.

William Bechtel and Adele A. Abrahamsen, "Beyond the Exclusively Propositional Era", *Synthese* **82** (1990), pp. 223–253.

Neal Jahren, "Can Semantics Be Syntactic?", *Synthese* **82** (1990), pp. 309–328.

Yorick Wilks, "Form and Content in Semantics", *Synthese* **82** (1990), pp. 329–351.

William Edward Morris, "Knowledge and the Regularity Theory of Information", *Synthese* **82** (1990), pp. 375–398.

George Graham, "Melancholic Epistemology", *Synthese* **82** (1990), pp. 399–422.

Eddy Zemach, "Human Understanding", *Synthese* **83** (1990), pp. 31–48.

Eric Lormand, "Framing the Frame Problem", *Synthese* **82** (1990), pp. 353–374.

PROLOGUE

WILLIAM RAMSEY AND STEPHEN STICH

CONNECTIONISM AND THREE LEVELS OF NATIVISM

ABSTRACT. Along with the increasing popularity of connectionist language models has come a number of provocative suggestions about the challenge these models present to Chomsky's arguments for nativism. The aim of this paper is to assess these claims. We begin by reconstructing Chomsky's "argument from the poverty of the stimulus" and arguing that it is best understood as three related arguments, with increasingly strong conclusions. Next, we provide a brief introduction to connectionism and give a quick survey of recent efforts to develop networks that model various aspects of human linguistic behavior. Finally, we explore the implications of this research for Chomsky's arguments. Our claim is that the relation between connectionism and Chomsky's views on innate knowledge is more complicated than many have assumed, and that even if these models enjoy considerable success the threat they pose for linguistic nativism is small.

1. INTRODUCTION

About 25 years ago, Noam Chomsky offered an argument aimed at showing that human beings must have a rich store of innate knowledge, because without such innate knowledge it would be impossible for children to learn a language on the basis of the data available to them. This "argument from the poverty of the stimulus" has had an enormous impact in linguistics, cognitive science, and philosophy. Jerry Fodor has described it as "the existence proof for the possibility of cognitive science ... [and] quite possibly the only important result to date".[1] Hornstein and Lightfoot have urged that the argument serves as the foundation for most current work in linguistics.[2] And a number of authors, including Chomsky himself, have maintained that the argument from the poverty of the stimulus shows that empiricist theories of the mind are mistaken and that "the only substantive proposal to deal with the problem of acquisition of knowledge of language is the rationalist conception . . . ."[3]

During the last few years, however, a new research program, often called 'Connectionism' or 'Parallel Distributed Processing' (PDP), has attracted considerable attention in cognitive science. Connectionist

3

J. H. Fetzer (ed.), Epistemology and Cognition, 3–31.

models of cognitive processes differ in many ways from earlier accounts commonly adopted by Chomskians. What makes them important for our purposes is that they employ powerful new learning techniques that enable systems to acquire complex and subtle skills in a wide variety of domains, without the assistance of large amounts of pre-programmed information. Very early on it was clear that the existence of these strikingly powerful learning strategies was a *prima facie* challenge to Chomsky's nativism. One observer, for example, comments that connectionism "sustains the vision of larger machines that are built on the same principles and that will learn whatever is learnable *with no innate disposition to acquire particular behaviors*" (italics ours).[4] If connectionist models invoking 'back propagation' or other learning algorithms can quickly acquire a large variety of complex skills without the help of 'innate' knowledge, it is natural to wonder whether they might not be able to acquire linguistic skills of the sort Chomsky argued could only be acquired by systems richly endowed with linguistic information at the outset. Motivated in part by just such anti-nativist suspicions, a number of investigators have begun to explore the possibility that connectionist models might acquire natural language syntax, phonology, semantics, and other features of linguistic ability. These efforts to build connectionist networks that learn aspects of natural language are very recent, and the results to date are both fragmentary and controversial. It is too early to venture a prediction on how successful they ultimately will be.

In this paper, our aim will be to explore the relation between connectionism and Chomsky's arguments for the existence of innate knowledge. Along the way, we propose to defend a pair of interrelated conclusions. The first is that there are actually three versions of Chomsky's poverty of the stimulus argument, which make increasingly strong claims about the nature of the cognitive endowments required for learning language. Though the three versions of the argument are often run together in the literature, it is essential to pull them apart if we are to be clear on the bearing that connectionist research might have on nativism. Our second conclusion is that the relation between connectionism and nativism is considerably more complex than many have assumed. There are various connectionist research programs which would, if successful, undermine all three versions of the Chomskian argument. However, the weakest version of the argument, whose conclusion is a doctrine that we will call *minimal nativism*, is easy to reconstruct in a way which will withstand any findings that may be forthcoming from connectionist research. A second version of the argument, aimed at establishing a stronger claim that we will call *anti-empiricism*, can also readily be reconstructed in the face of any foreseeable connectionist successes. However, both Chomsky's formulation of this argument and the reconstruction we will sketch require some sophisticated linguistic data. There has been a fair amount of linguistic research aimed at assembling the sort of data Chomsky's formulation of the argument requires. It is plausible to suppose that if the data needed in Chomsky's formulation are forthcoming, then linguists will be able to find an analogous body of data of the sort required by our reformulation. But, of course, there can be no guarantee on this point until the work is done. The third version of Chomsky's argument seeks to establish the strongest of the three nativist claims, the one we will call *rationalism*. Here there are indeed imaginable connectionist achievements that would show the conclusion of the argument to be false. However, there are also many ongoing connectionist explorations of language learning whose success would be fully compatible with rationalism. The bottom line, then, is that while connectionism challenges Chomskian nativism in a variety of ways, it may well turn out that even the strongest version of nativism is compatible with spectacular connectionist successes in the modeling of language acquisition.

The remainder of the paper will be organized as follows. In Section 2 we will set out the three versions of the poverty of the stimulus argument. In Section 3 we will offer an introductory overview of recent connectionist research and a quick survey of ongoing efforts to get connectionist devices to learn aspects of natural language. In Section 4 we will explore the ways in which the success of these efforts would bear upon the three versions of Chomsky's argument.

2. THREE VERSIONS OF THE POVERTY OF THE STIMULUS ARGUMENT AND THREE LEVELS OF NATIVISM[5]

What changes occur when a child learns a language? The answer, of course, is that there are many changes. The most conspicuous is that the child is able to understand the language, to communicate with it, and to use it for all sorts of purposes. There are also less obvious changes. Once a child has mastered a language, he is capable of making a wide range of judgments about the properties and relations of expressions in the language. Thus, for example, speakers of English are normally capable of judging whether any arbitrary sound sequence constitutes a grammatical sentence of English, and if it does, they are capable of judging whether or not it is ambiguous; they are also capable of judging whether two arbitrary sentences are related as active and passive, whether they are related as declarative and yes-no questions, whether one is a paraphrase of another, whether one entails the other, and so on for a number of additional linguistic properties and relations. These sorts of judgments, or 'linguistic intuitions' as they are more typically called, have played a central role in generative linguistics since its inception.

It is, Chomskians maintain, a perfectly astounding fact that ordinary speakers of a language can make a practically infinite number of judgments about the grammatical properties and relations of expressions in their language. The most plausible explanation of this ability, they urge, is that speakers have a generative grammar of their language – an explicit system of rules and definitions – stored somewhere in their mind or brain. On Chomsky's view, "the mature speaker has internalized a grammar with specific properties . . . [and] in understanding speech he makes use of this grammar to assign a precept to a signal".[6] "To know a language . . . is to be in a certain mental state . . . consisting of a system of rules and principles".[7] This system of internally represented rules guides the complex and prolific linguistic judgments that the speaker is capable of making. It is also used, in various ways, in the more ordinary processes of language production and comprehension. If there is no internally represented grammar, Chomsky and his followers urge, then it is something of a mystery how speakers are capable of having the linguistic intuitions they have. The mentally stored grammar that is posited is not, of course, accessible to consciousness. Speakers cannot tell us the rules of the grammar represented in their brains any more than they can tell us how they go about recognizing faces or recovering salient information from memory. But if speakers do have an internally represented grammar, then a natural goal for the generative grammarian would be (and has been) to discover that grammar – the grammar that is 'psychologically real'.

The argument for the thesis that speakers have an internally represented generative grammar of their language has the form of an inference to the best explanation:

I know of no other account that even attempts to deal with the fact that our judgments and behavior accord with and are in part explained by certain rule systems . . . .[8]

Later, we will explain why many connectionists believe their models call this thesis into question. For now, however, let us assume that Chomsky is right and that speakers do indeed have a mentally stored grammar of their language. We can then develop the three versions of the poverty of the stimulus argument against the background assumption that the mechanisms subserving language acquisition must be able to produce the grammar that the child comes to internally represent.

2.1. *The Argument for Minimal Nativism*

The weakest version of the poverty of the stimulus argument begins with the observation that, during the time span normally required to learn a language, a child is exposed to only a very impoverished sample of often misleading linguistic data. This 'poverty of the stimulus' is due to three important aspects of the 'primary linguistic data':

(1) The set of sentences that a competent speaker of a language can use, comprehend, and offer linguistic intuitions about is vastly larger than the idiosyncratic set of sentences to which children are exposed in the course of learning a language.

(2) While learning their language, the speech children hear does not consist exclusively of complete grammatical sentences. Rather, they are typically exposed to a large assortment of non-sentences, including slips of the tongue and incomplete thoughts, samples of foreign languages, and even intentional nonsense. Thus, the data the child has available for learning to tell sentences from non-sentences are remarkably messy.

(3) Children, unlike linguists, are rarely given any indication that certain queer and complex sentences are ungrammatical, that certain pairs of sentences are paraphrases of one another, and so on. Hence, many sorts of data that linguists rely upon heavily in deciding between competing grammars – such as data derived from speakers' linguistic intuitions – are not available to the child.

That children can acquire a grammar at all on the basis of this sort of data requires that they have a learning mechanism of some sort in place before the acquisition process begins. A video recorder exposed to the primary linguistic data that a child is exposed to does not end up with an internally represented grammar. Nor, for that matter, does a puppy or a young chimpanzee. The cognitive system which the child brings to the task of language learning must be able to go from a limited and messy sample of data to a grammar that generates most of the sentences in the data, and a huge number of additional sentences as well. And any cognitive system capable of projecting beyond the data in this way is going to be reasonably sophisticated. So, given our assumption that children do in fact end up with an internally represented grammar, the 'poverty of the stimulus' seems to require that children come to the language learning task with an innate learning mechanism of some sophistication. Moreover, despite exposure to significantly different samples of data, different children in the same linguistic community end up having essentially the same linguistic intuitions, and thus, it is plausible to suppose, essentially the same internalized grammar. Nor is there any evidence that children have any special predisposition to learn the language of their biological parents. Chinese children raised in an English-speaking environment learn English as easily as English children do. All of this suggests that the innate learning mechanisms that enable children to internalize the grammar of the language spoken around them are much the same in all children.

The crucial step in this first version of the poverty of the stimulus argument is the observation that if the child's innate learning mechanism is to accomplish its task, it must have a strong bias in favor of acquiring certain grammars and against acquiring others. This is because the data that the mechanism has been exposed to by the time grammar acquisition is complete is equally compatible with an indefinitely large class of grammars, many of which will depart in significant ways from the grammar that the child actually attains. The acquisition mechanism must project from the limited data it has available to a correct grammar – one that classifies sentences the way others in the linguistic community classify them. Thus it must somehow reject the indefinitely large class of *incorrect* grammars that are equally compatible with the data. The thesis that we will call *minimal nativism* is simply the claim that the child approaches the task of language acquisition with an innate learning mechanism that is strongly biased in favor of certain grammars and against others. But, of course, to say that the innate learning mechanism is biased in favor of certain grammars and against others does not commit us to any particular account of the mechanism underlying this bias. It is on just this point that the three levels of nativism differ.

Minimal nativism merely insists that the bias must be there. The higher levels of nativism make increasingly strong claims about the mechanism responsible for the bias.[9]

Before moving on to the next version of the argument, it is important to make clear exactly what does and does not follow from minimal nativism. One might think that by establishing the existence of a strongly biased innate learning mechanism, Chomsky has succeeded in undermining the empiricist conception of the mind. But this would be a mistake. For even the staunchest empiricist would readily agree that learning requires sophisticated innate mechanisms and biases. As Quine reminds us, the empiricist "is knowingly and cheerfully up to his neck in innate mechanisms of learning readiness".[10] If Chomsky's argument is supposed to undermine empiricism, then it must say something about the nature of these mechanisms and biases which calls into doubt the empiricist conception of the mind.

2.2. *The Argument Against Empiricism*

At first blush, it might be thought that it would be impossible to argue against *all* empiricist accounts of the mind. For while Chomsky might show that on one or another specific empiricist theory, the mind could not reliably produce the right grammar on the basis of the primary linguistic data, it would always be open to the resourceful empiricist to construct another theory, still adhering to empiricist principles, though diverging in one way or another from the particular empiricist theory that has been refuted. However, there is in Chomsky's writings an ingenious idea for circumventing this problem and refuting all empiricist theories in one fell swoop. We'll call this idea 'the Competent Scientist Gambit'. The basic idea is to portray a learning mechanism that is at least as powerful as anything dreamt of in the empiricist conception of the mind, and then argue that such a learning mechanism could not do what the child does. If this can be shown, then all empiricist theories will fall together. The 'learning mechanism' Chomsky suggests is a competent, rational scientist.

Suppose that we were to pose for such a scientist the task at which the child's mind is so adept. We will give the scientist a typical set of primary linguistic data drawn from some actual human language. Her job will be to discover the grammar of that language – the grammar that children exposed to those data will come to internally represent.

In going about the business of constructing and testing hypotheses about the grammar she is trying to discover, the scientist will be able to exploit any inferential strategy that would be permitted by any account of the mind compatible with empiricist strictures. She can record data, do sophisticated data analysis, think up imaginative hypotheses (or mundane ones) and test those hypotheses against the data available to her. Moreover, it is open to her to employ the sorts of methodological principles and intuitions typically employed in empirical theory construction and selection. In discussions of those methodological considerations, simplicity often looms large, and from time to time we will use the term 'simplicity' as a convenient label for the whole package of methodological principles and intuitions that a competent scientist has available.

There is, however, one thing that the competent scientist is not allowed to do. She is not allowed to learn the language from which the primary linguistic data are drawn. There is, of course, no reason to think that the scientist could not learn the language on the basis of that data. She is a normal human, and we are providing her with just the sort of data that generally suffices for normal humans to learn a language. The point of the prohibition is simply that if she were to learn the language, she would then have access to data that the child does not have. She would have her acquired linguistic intuitions about the grammaticality of sentences not presented in the data, as well as her intuitions about ambiguities, about paraphrases, and so on. But if her challenge is to try to do what the child does, then it is obviously unfair for her to use information not available to the child. Clearly it is absurd to suppose that in order to learn his language the child must first learn it, and then generate the data necessary for him to learn it.

We are supposing that after exposure to a decade or so of primary linguistic data from any natural language, the child succeeds in constructing a grammar that projects well beyond his data, and does so correctly, where the standard of correctness is set by the senior members of the child's linguistic community. If the scientist is to match the child's feat, she too must make a monumental projection from the data available to her, and come up with the grammar that has been internalized by those who are producing the data. Chomsky's contention is that given only the information embodied in the primary linguistic data, along with the methodological resources available to her, the competent scientist could not reliably do what the child does. That is, the scientist could not discover the grammar the child comes to internally represent when learning a language.

It is important to understand exactly what is being claimed when Chomsky makes this assertion. Chomsky does not deny that the competent scientist could *think up* the right grammar. Of course she could. *Ex hypothesis* she is intelligent, creative, and resourceful, so if she couldn't think up the right grammar, no one could. However, there is a sense in which this very intelligence and creativity is the scientist's undoing. For just as there is every reason to believe she can think up the *right* grammar – the one the child actually ends up with – so too there is every reason to believe she can think up an endless variety of *wrong* grammars that do not project from the data in the way the child's grammar does. The crucial contention for this version of the poverty of the stimulus argument is that *the methodological resources a scientist has available will not suffice to motivate the proper selection*. Even with the use of criteria such as simplicity, the scientist would still be plagued by an embarrassment of riches. In saying that the scientist would be incapable of 'coming up with' the right grammar, what is meant is that the scientist will have no reliable way of locating the right grammar in the space of possible grammars that are compatible with the limited data she has available.[11]

It now should be clear how the Competent Scientist Gambit is intended to undermine the empiricist conception of learning. It is plausible to view the competent scientist as a strong and generous characterization of the empiricist mind. (Indeed, there will be many things a competent scientist can do that the sort of mind conjured by the Classical Empiricists cannot.) Hence, if the competent scientist is not up to the task, then no learning mechanism compatible with empiricist principles will be adequate for the task of language acquisition. If it can be shown that something at least as resourceful as the empiricist mind would fail at language learning, Chomsky will have succeeded in showing that the empiricist conception of the mind must be mistaken.

Of course for all of this to work, some additional argument is going to be needed. What needs to be shown is that the set of methodological principles and biases available to a competent scientist will not be adequate for successful projection from the primary linguistic data to the grammar of the language from which the data are drawn. One way to show this would be to produce a pair of grammars with the following features:

(i)   on all intuitive measures of simplicity the grammars are comparable;

(ii)   the grammars make essentially the same judgments about linguistic phenomena that are likely to show up in the primary linguistic data; and

(iii)   the grammars make significantly different judgments about linguistic phenomena that are not likely to show up in the primary linguistic data.

If there are examples of this sort, our competent scientist will be unable to choose between the grammars. Since the grammars are both compatible with any plausible body of primary linguistic data, she cannot use the data to rule one out. And since they are both comparably simple, methodological considerations will be of no help. If, in these cases, language learners regularly project in the right way, it follows that the mechanisms responsible for language learning must be more powerful than the empiricist conception of the mind will allow.

In recent years, there has been a fair amount of work in linguistics aimed at compiling examples of just this sort. For example, Hornstein and Lightfoot[12] sketch a case in which the choice between two very different, though comparably simple grammars turns on the paraphrase relations among sentences like (1)–(3):

(1)   She told me three funny stories, but I didn't like the one about Max.

(2)   She told me three funny stories, but I didn't like the story about Max.

(3)   She told me three funny stories, but I didn't like the funny story about Max.

On one of the grammars under consideration, (2) would be considered a paraphrase of (1), though (3) would not. The other grammar correctly entails that both (2) and (3) might be paraphrases of (1). It is, Hornstein and Lightfoot maintain, very unlikely that every child who successfully learns English will have been exposed to primary linguistic data containing evidence about these sorts of relatively abstruse facts concerning paraphrase. If this is right, and if the only sorts of evidence that would suffice to distinguish between the two grammars are comparably abstruse, then our competent scientist is in trouble. Since she is intelligent and resourceful, she will be able to think up both grammars. Since neither grammar is simpler nor superior on other methodological grounds, such considerations will not assist her in making the correct choice. And, unlike the real linguists who actually did worry about the choice between these two grammars, she does not have, and cannot get, the kind of data that would enable her to make the right choice.

The argument just sketched is, of course, very much hostage to the linguistic facts. For the argument to be persuasive there must be a substantial number of examples in which the choice between two equally simple and natural grammars can be made only by appealing to the sort of abstruse evidence that is unlikely to be found in the primary linguistic data. There is by now a substantial collection of plausible cases in the literature.[13] If these cases survive critical scrutiny, Chomsky and his followers will have gone a long way toward making their case against empiricism.

This brings us to the conclusion of the second version of the poverty of the stimulus argument, a doctrine we shall call *anti-empiricism*. This doctrine maintains not only that the innate language learning mechanism must have strong biases, but also that these biases are not compatible with the account of mental mechanisms suggested by even a very generous characterization of the empiricist mind. Anti-empiricism makes a negative claim about the language learning mechanism – a claim about what its biases are not. The third version of the poverty of stimulus argument aims at establishing a positive claim about the way the language learning mechanism does its job.

2.3. *The Argument for Rationalism*

If the empiricist conception of the mind cannot account for the facts of language learning, what sorts of accounts of the mind can? One way of approaching this question is to focus on exactly why it was that our hypothetical scientist could not do what the child does. The problem was not that she could not think up the right grammar, but rather that she could also think up lots of wrong grammars that were equally simple and equally compatible with the data, and she had no way to decide among them. Confronted with this problem, one strategy that might enable the scientist to duplicate the child's accomplishment would be to narrow the range of grammars she must consider. Suppose it were the case that all the correct grammars of human languages – all the ones that speakers actually have represented in their heads – shared certain properties. If this were so, then the scientist's work would be greatly facilitated if she were informed about these properties at the outset. For then she would never have to consider any of the grammars that do not share the 'universal' features of all human grammars. The richer the collection of universal features, the stronger the constraints they will impose on the class of grammars that the scientist need consider; and the stronger the constraints, the easier her task will become.[14] What does all this suggest about the child's mind? The obvious hypothesis to extract from the analogy between the child's task and the scientist's is that the child's mind comes equipped with information about linguistic universals – biases that are applicable only in the area of language acquisition – that enable it to pick out the right grammar by narrowing the search space. On this hypothesis, the child begins with a rich body of innate information about language which serves to define the class of all human languages. The relatively impoverished environmental stimulus is "viewed as only a trigger; much of the ability eventually attained is determined by genetically encoded principles, which are triggered or activated by environmental stimulus rather than formed by it more or less directly".[15] Clearly this hypothesis goes well beyond the thesis that the biases built into the innate language learning mechanism are non-empiricist. As John Searle notes, "Chomsky is arguing not simply that the child must have 'learning readiness', 'biases', and 'dispositions', but that he must have a *specific* set of linguistic mechanisms at work."[16] Moreover, this domain specificity of innate mechanisms has been a traditional feature of rationalist conceptions of the mind. For Chomsky and his followers, the central argument for the claim that the child has domain specific language learning biases is, once again, an inference to the best explanation – it is "the only substantive proposal to deal with the problem of acquisition of knowledge of language".[17] And prior to the emergence of connectionism, Chomsky's argument was surely very plausible. Once we realize the difficulties facing the child, it is no easy matter to imagine how he could possibly solve the projection problem and end up with the right grammar, unless he approached the task with a rich set of constraints specifically tailored to the task at hand. The thesis that the innate language learning mechanism embodies such constraints is the conclusion to be drawn from the third version of the poverty of the stimulus argument. We'll call this view *rationalism.*

We've now completed our reconstruction of the three versions of the poverty of the stimulus argument and the conclusions that have been drawn from them. In Section 4 we will explore the ways in which connectionism might be thought to challenge these arguments. Before getting to that, however, we'll need to give a quick sketch of connectionism, and review some recent attempts to study linguistic phenomena in a connectionist framework.

3. AN OVERVIEW OF CONNECTIONIST RESEARCH ON LANGUAGE

Connectionism is a new style of cognitive modeling that has emerged during the last decade. Connectionist models consist of networks built from large numbers of extremely simple interacting units. Inspired by neuronal architecture, connectionist units are typically linked in such a way that they can excite or inhibit one another by sending activation signals down interconnecting pathways. Networks commonly involve a layer of input units, a layer of output units, and one or more intermediate (or 'hidden') layers, linked by weighted connections through which a wave of activation travels. When the processing proceeds in only one direction, as is the case with 'feed-forward' networks, units modify and transfer the activation signal only to subsequent units and layers. In other, more complicated networks, activation may involve feedback loops and bi-directional communication between nodes, comprising what are often referred to as 'recurrent' networks. The units themselves may have threshold values, which their total input must exceed for activation. Alternatively, they may act in analog fashion, taking an activation value anywhere between 0 and 100%. Connecting links have varying weights or strengths, and the exact nature of the activation signal transferred from one unit to another (that is, its strength and excitatory or inhibitory value) is typically a function of the connection weight and the activation level of the sending unit.

This architecture supports a style of computation quite unlike that exploited by earlier cognitive models. For the most part, pre-connectionist model builders have presupposed computational architectures that perform operations best described as 'symbol manipulations'. In such systems, information is generally stored in distinct locations separate from the structures performing computational operations. Information processing in such devices consists of the manipulation of discrete tokens or symbols, which are relocated, copied, and shuffled about, typically in accordance with rules or commands which are themselves encoded in a manner readily discernible by the system.

Connectionist information processing diverges from these earlier models in many ways. Perhaps the most striking aspect of connectionist information processing is that it typically does not involve anything like the manipulation of distinct symbolic tokens. While connectionist modelers sometimes invoke notions of representations to characterize elements of their networks, connectionist representations are generally not at all like the discrete symbolic entities found in classical architectures. This is especially true when the model employs 'distributed representations', where the same set of individual units and weights are used to encode divergent bits of information.[18] Another notable difference between connectionist models and earlier cognitive models is that in connectionist models the distinction between structures that store information and structures that process information is virtually non-existent. Information is 'stored' in the connection weights between individual units, which serve as central elements in the processing as well. Hence, familiar notions of stored programs or autonomous command structures which govern computational processing seem to have no place in connectionist architecture.

These differences loom large in the debate over the psychological reality of linguistic rules. As we saw in Section 2.1, Chomsky's formulations of the poverty of the stimulus arguments presupposes that when a child has learned a language he or she ends up with an internally represented generative grammar – typically a set of re-write or production rules each of which consists of a sequence of distinct symbols. Pre-connectionist cognitive models, which view cognition as symbol manipulation, are entirely comfortable with this view. But connectionist models, particularly those exploiting highly distributed representations and non-modular computational strategies, cannot readily accommodate the sorts of symbolic rules posited by generative grammarians. In defense of the claim that linguistic abilities are subserved by an internally represented grammar, Chomsky offered an inference to the best explanation argument. Appeal to internalized grammatical rules was not only the best way to explain linguistic judgments and behavior,

Chomsky maintained, it was the *only* explicit, well-developed hypothesis that had ever been suggested. Prior to the emergence of connectionism, that argument had considerable plausibility.[19] If, however, it turns out that connectionist models can account for much the same range of data about linguistic intuitions and linguistic behavior, it will no longer be possible for Chomsky and his followers to claim that their internalized rule explanations are the "only game in town".

Since connectionist information processing is governed by connection weights between units, the computations can be altered simply by changing the value of these weights. Connectionist researchers realized early on that if weight changes could be executed in a purposeful manner, then these models would manifest a form of learning that seems biologically plausible, and quite revolutionary from a computational perspective. Recent developments have overcome past difficulties in multi-layer weight adjustment, and there are now very powerful learning strategies that enable connectionist networks to, in a sense, program themselves. Perhaps the most widely used learning algorithm is the 'generalized delta rule' or 'back propagation', developed by Rumelhart, Hinton, and Williams.[20] On this learning strategy, a network undergoes a training period during which it is presented with a series of inputs and allowed to produce an output for each presentation. A comparison is made between the actual output and a target output for each presentation, resulting in an error signal. This signal is subsequently propagated back through the network, adjusting weights in accordance with the learning algorithm. Because the weights are fixed after training, the system is subsequently able to make 'educated' responses to new inputs that were not presented during the learning period. The success of most models is determined by how well they perform such generalizations within a particular task domain.[21]

So much for our general overview. There are many other styles of connectionist processing and learning, but this should suffice to give a sense of the basic elements of the new paradigm. Let's turn now to the growing body of connectionist research devoted to developing models of language processing and language acquisition. Much of this research has been motivated by increasing skepticism about Chomsky's account of language acquisition, and by the suspicion that language processing and acquisition might be more naturally explained by models with connectionist architectures. Prior to the emergence of connectionism,

Chomsky often stressed that "it is difficult to imagine how the vague suggestions about conditioning and associative nets that one finds in philosophical and psychological speculations of an empiricist cast might be refined or elaborated so as to provide for attested competence . . . ."[22] Many connectionists believe that their new computational tools overcome such failures of the imagination, and have developed impressive models aimed at making the point.

A typical model of this sort is PARSNIP, developed by Hanson and Kegl. [23] This is an auto-associator network[24] that was trained on three sets of syntactically tagged natural language sentences. Beginning with the assumption "that natural language reveals to the hearer a rich set of linguistic constraints . . . that serve to delimit the possible grammars that can be learned" (p. 108), the modelers found that a network trained to produce veridical copies of input could also "induce grammar-like behavior" while performing various linguistic tasks.[25]

The network learned to produce correct syntactic category labels corresponding to each position of the sentence originally presented to it, and it was able to generalize to another 1000 sentences which were distinct from all three training samples. PARSNIP does sentence completion on sentences, and also recognizes novel sentence patterns absent from the presented corpus. One interesting parallel between PARSNIP and human language users is the fact that PARSNIP correctly reproduces test sentences reflecting deep center-embedded patterns which it has never seen before while failing to reproduce multiply center-embedded patterns.[26]

While Hanson and Kegl concede that their model has certain psychologically implausible features (such as insensitivity to temporal factors), they maintain that

there are important parallels between the task given to PARSNIP and the task that arises for children as they learn a natural language. Both PARSNIP and the child are only exposed to sentences from natural language, they both must induce general rules and larger constituents from just the regularities to which they are exposed, both on the basis of only positive evidence. PARSNIP's ability to generalize knowledge of constituent structure has been extracted from its experience with natural language sentences.[27]

A number of connectionist models attempt to account for aspects of language that have been difficult to capture in more conventional rule-based systems. It appears that sensitivity to several different sources of information (such as cues from phonetic, semantic, and contextual factors) is much easier to implement in connectionist networks with distributed encodings and parallel processing. One system exploiting this type of architecture was designed by McClelland and Kawamoto (1986) to assign correct case roles to constituents of sentences. The model invokes word order and semantic constraints to determine case assignments and to select contextually appropriate readings of ambiguous words. A similar but more complex model of semantic processing developed by St. John and McClelland (1988) learns mappings between words in particular contexts and concepts, and predicts additional meanings implicit in the sentence.

While these systems focus primarily on semantic aspects of language comprehension, a number of connectionist models have been developed to account for syntactic, phonological, and other non-semantic components of language processing. For example, Fanty (1985) has developed a connectionist parser that incorporates all levels of the parse tree at the same time, producing the surface structure of the sentence as its output. Other efforts at connectionist parsing include models by Cottrell (1985), Waltz and Pollack (1985), Selman and Hirst (1985), and Charniak and Santos (1986). Rumelhart and McClelland (1986b) have produced a network designed to model the acquisition of English past-tense verbs. The most intriguing feature of this model is its ability to replicate putative aspects of human past tense learning such as overgeneralization of regular past-tense forms to irregular forms without incorporating the sort of discrete symbolic rules commonly assumed to account for such phenomena.[28] Elman (1988) has produced a model that learns to divide an unbroken stream of input into phonemes, morphemes, and words, a capacity often claimed to be largely innate. The model also produced representations of lexical classes through exposure to word order alone, distinguishing nouns and verbs, for example, and arranging their representations into various semantic hierarchies.

It should be clear from this (by no means exhaustive) survey that connectionist language modeling is a robust and thriving area of research. As we noted at the outset, it is too soon to tell just how successful such work will ultimately be. However, our concern here is not to debate the superiority of connectionist models but to explore how the arguments for nativism will fare if connectionist models prove to be empirically accurate accounts of the mechanisms underlying language acquisition and linguistic competence. That is the issue we'll tackle in the section to follow.

4. CONNECTIONISM AND NATIVISM

In Section 2 we detailed three versions of the poverty of the stimulus argument that yield three distinct conclusions making progressively stronger nativist claims. There are two ways in which it might be thought that advances in connectionist language modeling could threaten those arguments. The first focuses on the output of the language acquisition process, the second on the nature of the process itself. We'll begin by sketching both of these challenges, and then go on to ask how much damage they do to each version of the argument from the poverty of the stimulus.

4.1. The First Connectionist Challenge: Adult Competence Is Not Subserved by a Grammar

As set out in Section 2, all three versions of the argument from the poverty of the stimulus begin with the assumption that when a person learns a language he or she ends up with an internally represented grammar of that language, where a grammar is taken to be a system of generative rules built out of an appropriate symbolic vocabulary. The Chomskian defense of this assumption is that "it's the only game in town" for explaining language competence. But, as we saw in Section 3, connectionist models don't readily accommodate the sorts of symbolic rules exploited by generative grammarians. Thus, if it turns out that connectionist models of adult linguistic competence can account for a wide range of linguistic judgments and abilities, Chomskians will no longer be able to claim that a theory positing an internalized grammar is the only option available. And if connectionist models of linguistic competence prove to be empirically *superior* to models invoking internalized grammars, the poverty of the stimulus arguments will have to do without the assumption that the output of the acquisition process includes an internally represented grammar.

4.2. The Second Connectionist Challenge: Connectionist Learning Algorithms Can Model Language Acquisition

All three versions of the poverty of the stimulus argument conclude that the mechanism responsible for language acquisition must be biased in favor of certain outcomes and against others. On the anti-empiricist version of the argument, the biases are claimed to be incompatible with the account of the mind envisioned in the empiricist tradition. On the rationalist version, the biases are further claimed to be specific to language and applicable only in the domain of language acquisition. But suppose it could be shown that a system using back propagation or another connectionist learning algorithm can do a good job at modeling some impressive part of the child's accomplishment in learning a language. Suppose, for example, that a connectionist acquisition model could mimic the language learner's projection from primary linguistic data to judgments about sentences that he or she has never heard. We might imagine the hypothetical connectionist acquisition model behaving as follows: When provided with a sample of primary linguistic data from any natural language (i.e., a large set of utterances of the sort that a child learning the language might be exposed to, perhaps accompanied by some information about the setting in which the utterance occurs) the model learns to distinguish grammatical sentences in that language from ungrammatical ones with much the same accuracy that a human learner does.

It might well be thought that the existence of such a model would refute all three versions of nativism. For, it might be argued, back propagation and other connectionist learning algorithms, far from being restricted to language, appear to be enormously general in their domain of application. Back propagation has been used successfully in training networks to perform very diverse tasks – from transforming written text into phonemes to distinguishing sonar echoes of rocks from those of undersea mines.[29] Thus the learning model we have imagined appears to pose a direct challenge to the doctrine we have been calling 'rationalism'. Moreover, connectionist learning algorithms like back propagation seem to be very much in the spirit of the simple, general-purpose learning mechanisms envisioned in the empiricist tradition. Historically, back propagation can be viewed as a variant on a simple learning rule suggested by Hebb.[30] And the (unmodified) 'delta rule' was first proposed by Sutton and Barto as part of their theory of classical conditioning.[31] So if the sort of connectionist acquisition model we have been imagining could actually be built, it would appear to pose a challenge to the doctrine we have been calling 'anti-empiricism'. It might even be urged that the existence of such a model would threaten minimal nativism, since back propagation and other connectionist learning algorithms seem remarkably free from biases of any sort. This may be what Sampson has in mind when he writes: "[T]he knowledge eventually stored in the system, in the pattern of weights, is derived entirely from the input". "The system's only contribution is to react in a passive, mechanical way to individual data items".[32]

These challenges make it sound like connectionism is on a collision course with Chomsky's nativism. On the one hand, if empirically successful connectionist models of adult linguistic competence can be built, a central assumption of the arguments from the poverty of the stimulus will be undermined. On the other hand, if connectionist learning algorithms can project from the primary linguistic data in the way the child does, the conclusions of all three arguments are threatened. However, on our view, even if things turn out well for connectionism, the challenge it will pose to Chomskian nativism will be far from devastating. It is true that in the wake of the connectionist achievements we have been imagining all three versions of the argument from the poverty of the stimulus would come unglued. But this alone would not refute any of Chomsky's nativist conclusions. As we'll see in the section to follow, we can readily formulate a new version of the argument for minimal nativism that sidesteps both connectionist challenges. The argument for anti-empiricism can also be reconstructed, as we'll see in Section 4.4, though it will require a sort of empirical evidence rather different from that exploited in Section 2.2. And, as we shall argue in Section 4.5, even Chomskian rationalism may turn out to be compatible with our hypothesized connectionist achievements.

4.3. *Connectionism and Minimal Nativism*

For argument's sake, let's grant that, despite Chomsky's argument to the contrary, the mechanisms subserving the linguistic skills of a competent speaker do not exploit an internally represented grammar. Rather, we'll suppose that a trained up connectionist network underlies a speaker's ability to judge sentences as grammatical or ungrammatical, etc. On this assumption, the job of the language acquisition mechanism will be to produce an appropriate network, one which judges sentences the way other speakers of the language do. The input available to the acquisition mechanism will be a typically untidy body of primary linguistic data drawn (mostly) from the language being acquired. And, of course, the network that is the output of the acquisition mechanism will have to respond appropriately to a vast class of sentences that the acquisition mechanism was never exposed to.

But now just as there are indefinitely many grammars which are comparably compatible with any given body of primarily linguistic data, though they diverge in the judgments they make about sentences not in that body of data, so too there are indefinitely many connectionist networks that agree, near enough, in their judgments about a given body of primary linguistic data, while diverging in their judgments about sentences not included in the data. Thus the language acquisition mechanism must somehow reject an indefinitely large class of networks all of which are comparably compatible with the data. To do this, obviously the mechanism will have to be strongly biased in favor of acquiring certain networks and against acquiring others. And that is just what minimal nativism maintains. All of this is quite independent of any assumption we might make about the algorithm used by the acquisition mechanism. If a connectionist acquisition mechanism using back propagation can in fact produce a trained up network that makes the right judgments about vast numbers of sentences not included in the primary linguistic data, then the conclusion to be drawn is not that minimal nativism is false, but rather that the learning algorithm being used is strongly biased in favor of certain projections and against others. This should be no surprise. The task of the language acquisition mechanism is an inductive learning task. And as Goodman and others demonstrated long ago, any successful inductive learning strategy must be strongly biased.[33]

4.4. Connectionism and Anti-empiricism

While minimal nativism claims merely that the language learning mechanism must be biased, the Chomskian argument for anti-empiricism maintains that simplicity and other methodological principles of the sort that a scientist might use in deciding among theories will not suffice in explaining the child's success in learning language. Recall that to make this point, the anti-empiricist argument outlined in Section 2.2 needed some sophisticated linguistic evidence. It required us to find cases in which a pair of grammars that are near enough equal with respect to simplicity and other methodological virtues also agree in their judgments about typical bodies of primary linguistic data. If these grammars disagree in their judgments about cases not likely to be found in the primary linguistic data, then the competent scientist trying to duplicate the child's accomplishment would have no way of deciding among them.

This argument for anti-empiricism clearly requires that the mechanism underlying linguistic competence be a grammar, since it rests upon very specific claims about the formal properties of grammars. But as we saw in Section 4.1, the success of connectionism would challenge this assumption. Since connectionist models of competence do not use anything like a grammar, the fact that different *grammars* are compatible with the data and equally simple would not suffice to establish anti-empiricism, if those connectionist models turn out to be right. Hence, the sort of connectionist models of linguistic competence that we have been imagining undermine the standard Chomskian formulation of the argument for anti-empiricism. This hardly constitutes a refutation of anti-empiricism, however, since it is possible to reconstruct an anti-empiricist argument parallel to Chomsky's which assumes that linguistic competence is subserved by a connectionist network.

Since we are assuming that adult linguistic competence is subserved by a connectionist network rather than a grammar, we will have to assemble cases in which a pair of connectionist networks have the following properties:

(i)   the networks make much the same judgments about sentences likely to show up in the primary linguistic data;

(ii)   the networks make significantly different judgments about sentences that are not likely to show up in the primary linguistic data; and

(iii)   on intuitive measures of simplicity (and on other methodological grounds) the networks are much the same.

Since connectionist studies of language are of very recent vintage, and since many researchers in the area are skeptical about nativism, there has been no systematic effort to find such examples. Thus the data needed to secure our reconstructed anti-nativist argument are not available. But there is certainly no *a priori* reason to suppose that the evidence required cannot be found. And in assessing the threat connectionism poses for anti-empiricism, this last point is the crucial one. What it shows is that even if the suppositions in Sections 4.1 and 4.2 are correct, the truth of anti-empiricism will remain an open issue, to be decided by further empirical work. If the appropriate linguistic evidence *can* be found, and if the language acquisition mechanism is indeed a connectionist device exploiting back propagation, then the conclusion to be drawn is not that anti-empiricism is mistaken, but that the connectionist acquisition mechanism embodies biases different from those invoked in the empiricist tradition. More specifically, if the data turn out right, then the connectionist acquisition mechanism must be using something different from simplicity and other intuitive methodological principles. For *ex hypothesis* the acquisition mechanism is preferring one network to another, even though they are comparably simple and equally compatible with the data. Of course, if the data turn out the other way – if the appropriate linguistic examples are not to be found – then we will have no reason to regard anti-empiricism as true.

Before leaving the topic of anti-empiricism, there is one final point that needs attention. As we noted in Section 4.2, back propagation, the most widely used connectionist learning algorithm, was inspired by Hebbian learning rules and by work on classical conditioning. And while back propagation is significantly more sophisticated than Hebb's rule, or the (unmodified) delta rule invoked in the explanation of classical conditioning, it clearly shares a strong family resemblance with them. But, it might be argued, Hebb's rule, and the processes of classical conditioning are surely of a piece with the sort of mental processes that have been posited in the empiricist tradition. So if, as we have been assuming, a connectionist language acquisition device using back propagation could project from the data the way a child does, why should we not conclude that an empiricist acquisition device could succeed in learning language?

As we see it, the issue that is being raised here is how the notion of an 'empiricist' learning mechanism is best understood. Chomsky and his followers have adopted the competent scientist gambit as the acid test for empiricism. Any acquisition mechanism that can reliably do things a competent scientist cannot do does not count as an empiricist mechanism. And on this test it may well turn out that connectionist devices exploiting back propagation are not empiricist mechanisms. The alternative account of the notion of an 'empiricist' learning mechanism rejects the competent scientist standard, with its appeal to intuitive simplicity and other intuitive methodological considerations, and opts instead for the family resemblance criterion. On this account connectionist devices exploiting back propagation probably are empiricist mechanisms. As we see it, the dispute here is largely a verbal one. It will be an interesting and important fact if the competent scientist account of empiricism and the family resemblance account turn out not to coincide. But if this happens, who gets to keep the word 'empiricist' is a matter of very little moment.

4.5. *Connectionism and Rationalism*

Rationalism, as we have been using the term, is the thesis that the innate language learning mechanism embodies biases or constraints that are specific to the task of language learning, and of no use in other domains. The Chomskian justification for this thesis relies on the claim that there are no plausible alternatives. Thus in 1980, before the flourishing of connectionism, Wexler and Culicover wrote:

> At the present the constraints we need are quite specifically linguistic. More general theories would be intriguing, as insightful generalization always is, but until we have reason to believe the generalizations (or to formulate them coherently), we must remain skeptical.[34]

Here again, the connectionist achievements we've posited undermine the Chomskian argument. For, as we have noted, connectionist learning algorithms are anything but specifically linguistic. They have been used successfully in a wide variety of domains. So if a connectionist acquisition device could project from the primary linguistic data in the way the child does, Chomskians can no longer claim that rationalist acquisition models are the only game in town.

Undermining Chomsky's version of the argument for rationalism does not, however, show that rationalism is false; nor does it show that connectionism is incompatible with rationalism. For there are a great variety of connectionist learning devices that exploit back propagation. Some of them require idiosyncratic architectures or a great deal of pre-wiring and pre-tuning before they will do an acceptable job of learning in the task domain for which they are designed.[35] And as McClelland and Rumelhart note, such models are "clearly consistent with a rabidly nativist world view".[36] While connectionist research has produced learning strategies that are not domain specific, the extent to which these strategies can succeed in language acquisition without exploiting special architectures is currently unknown. If the only successful connectionist language acquisition devices are of a sort that require language specific architectures and/or language specific pre-tuning, then even the rationalist version of nativism will have nothing to fear from connectionism. Recently Rumelhart and others have been exploring ways in which connectionist learning algorithms themselves can be modified so as to bias learning in one direction or another.[37] If the best connectionist models of language acquisition exploit a learning algorithm that is particularly adept at language learning and largely useless in other domains, then again rationalism and connectionism will turn out to be comfortably compatible.

Of course, it is also conceivable that connectionist learning models will be able to duplicate significant aspects of the language learner's accomplishment without invoking idiosyncratic architectures, specialized pre-tuning or domain specific learning algorithms, and that much the same models will be able to master significant cognitive tasks in domains far removed from language. If such non-domain-specific models were to be developed, they would pose a genuine challenge for Chomskian rationalism.

5. CONCLUSION

The central claim of this last section has been that the putative incompatibility between connectionism and nativism has been much exaggerated. If adult linguistic competence is subserved by a connectionist network, and connectionist learning devices can duplicate the child's projection from primary linguistic data, all three versions of Chomsky's argument from the poverty of the stimulus will be undermined. However, parallel arguments for minimal nativism and anti-empiricism are easy to reconstruct. On our view, the argument for minimal nativism is entirely conclusive. The argument for anti-empiricism depends on empirical premises whose plausibility requires further investigation. There is no comparable reconstruction of the Chomskian argument for rationalism. However, if the only connectionist language acquisition models capable of projecting the way the child projects invoke language specific algorithms or architectures, then even rationalism will be sustained.

One final point is worth stressing. If it should turn out that non-domain specific models, like those envisioned at the end of Section 4.5, are capable of duplicating significant aspects of the child's accomplishment, and if the argument against empiricism can be successfully reconstructed, then our account of language acquisition would be located in the seldom explored terrain between rationalism and empiricism. It is here, perhaps, that connectionism may hold the most exciting potential for contributing to the nativism debate.

NOTES

[1] Fodor (1981), p. 258

[2] Hornstein and Lightfoot (1981b).

[3] Chomsky (1972), p. 88.

[4] Papert (1987), p. 8.

[5] Parts of this section are borrowed from Stich (forthcoming).

[6] Chomsky (1969), pp. 155–56.

[7] Chomsky (1980a), p. 48.

[8] Chomsky (1980b), p. 12.

[9] It is important to note that the relation between the primary linguistic data and a set of possible grammars is, in many ways, analogous to the abductive relation between evidential data and a set of different explanatory hypotheses. It is a truism in the philosophy of science that abductive inference – the projection from a body of data to an hypothesis that goes beyond the data – cannot be based upon the evidence alone. It requires an appeal to inferential principles or methodological criteria not included in the data. Similarly, since a child's primary linguistic data is compatible with a number of different grammars, his projection must be guided by some antecedent bias or set of constraints. For more on projection and language acquisition, see Gold (1967), Peters (1972), Wexler and Culicover (1980), and Morgan (1986).

[10] (1969, p. 95).

[11] Actually, this understates the difficulty that the scientist confronts since, as noted earlier, the primary linguistic data will typically be messy data, containing all sorts of sentences and sentence fragments that the correct grammar will not generate. So the task the scientist confronts is to locate the correct grammar from the enormous class of grammars that are largely (though not necessarily entirely) compatible with the primary linguistic data.

[12] Hornstein and Lightfoot (1981b). See also Hornstein, 1984, Chapter 1.

[13] See, for example, Lightfoot (1982) pp. 51–57, and the essays in Hornstein and Lightfoot (1981a).

[14] Actually, what is important here is not that all the correct grammars share certain properties, but only that they are all members of some quite restricted class. Since the distinction makes little difference to our current concerns, we shall ignore it in what follows.

[15] Lightfoot (1982), p. 21.

[16] Searle (1974), p. 22.

[17] Chomsky (1972), p. 88.

[18] For more on the contrast between discrete and distributed representations, see Ramsey, Stich and Garon (forthcoming).

[19] Prior to connectionism there were some dissenting voices. See, for example, Stich (1971), Cummins (1977) and Stabler (1983). However, a common response to the critics

was the question: 'What else could it be?' Thus, for example, Berwick writes, "I don't share Stabler's fear that 'we ought to worry about whether we can justify the current emphasis on program-using systems in theories about how people process language'. It's the only game in town" (1983, p. 403).

[20] Rumelhart, Hinton, and Williams (1986).

[21] For more on connectionist learning techniques, see Rumelhart and McClelland (1986a), Chapters 5, 7, 8, and 11. See also Hinton (1987).

[22] Chomsky (1980c), p. 238.

[23] Hanson and Kegl (1987).

[24] An auto-associator network is one that attempts to reproduce on the output nodes whatever input it receives on the input nodes. Hence, its input also serves as its teacher and source of the error signal during the training period.

[25] It should be noted here that Hanson and Kegl do not feel their model supports anti-nativist conclusions; rather, they believe it helps to delineate those aspects of grammatical structure which can be extracted from the data.

[26] Hanson and Kegl (1987), p. 106.

[27] Ibid., p. 117.

[28] For a critical analysis of this network, see Pinker and Prince (1988).

[29] Sejnowski and Rosenberg (1987); Gorman and Sejnowski (forthcoming).

[30] See Rumelhart, Hinton and McClelland (1986), p. 53

[31] See McClelland, Rumelhart and Hinton (1986), p. 43.

[32] Sampson (1987a), p. 877. Sampson (1987b), p. 643.

[33] See Goodman (1965). Compare Morgan (1986), p. 15: "It is fairly trivial to demonstrate that no unbiased inductive mechanism can reliably succeed in solving this sort of projection problem."

[34] Wexler and Culicover (1980), p. 10.

[35] We are indebted to Jeffrey Elman for convincing us of the importance of this point.

[36] Rumelhart and McClelland (1986c), p. 140.

[37] Rumelhart (personal communication).

REFERENCES

Berwick, R.: 1983, 'Using What You Know: A Computer–Science Perspective', *Behavioral and Brain Sciences* **6**, 402–403.

Charniak, E. and E. Santos: 1986, 'A Connectionist Context-free Parser which is not Context-free, but then it is not Really Connectionist Either', Department of Computer Science, Brown University.

Chomsky, N.: 1965, *Aspects of the Theory of Syntax*, MIT Press, Cambridge, Massachusetts.

Chomsky, N.: 1966, *Cartesian Linguistics: A Chapter in the History of Rationalistic Thought*, Harper and Row, New York.

Chomsky, N.: 1969, 'Comments on Harman's Reply', in S. Hook (ed.), *Language and Philosophy*, New York University Press, New York, pp. 152–159.

Chomsky, N.: 1972, *Language and Mind*, Harcourt Brace Jovanovich, New York.

Chomsky, N.: 1975, *Reflections on Language*, Pantheon Books, New York.

Chomsky, N.: 1980a, *Rules and Representations*, Columbia University Press, New York.
Chomsky, N.: 1980b, 'Rules and Representations', *Behavioral and Brain Sciences* **3**, 1–61.
Chomsky, N.: 1980c, 'Recent Contributions to the Theory of Innate Ideas: Summary of Oral Presentation', in H. Morick (ed.), *Challenges to Empiricism*, Hackett, Indianapolis, pp. 230–40.
Chomsky, N.: 1986, *Knowledge of Language*, Praeger, New York.
Chomsky, N.: 1988, *Language and Problems of Knowledge*, MIT Press, Cambridge, Massachusetts.
Cottrell, G.: 1985, 'Connectionist Parsing', in *Proceedings of the Seventh Annual Cognitive Science Society*, pp. 201–11.
Cummins, R.: 1977, 'Programs in the Explanation of Behavior', *Philosophy of Science* **44**, 269–87.
Elman, J.: 1988, 'Finding Structure in Time', CRL Technical Report 8801.
Fanty, M.: 1985, 'Context-Free Parsing in Connectionist Networks', Technical Report No. 174, Department of Computer Science, University of Rochester.
Fodor, J.: 1981, *Representations*, MIT Press, Cambridge, Massachusetts.
Gold, E. M.: 1967, 'Language Identification in the Limit', *Information and Control* **10**, 447–74.
Goodman, N.: 1965, *Fact, Fiction and Forecast*, 2nd ed., Bobbs Merrill, Indianapolis.
Gorman, R. and T. Sejnowski: forthcoming, 'Learned Classification of Sonar Targets Using a Massively Parallel Network', to appear in *IEEE Transactions: Acoustics, Speech, and Signal Processing*.
Hanson, S. and J. Kegl: 1987, 'PARSNIP: A Connectionist Network that Learns Natural Language Grammar from Exposure to Natural Language Sentences', in *Proceedings of the Ninth Annual Conference of the Cognitive Science Society*, pp. 106–19.
Hinton, G.: 1987, 'Connectionist Learning Procedures', Tech Report No. CMUCS-87-115.
Hornstein, N.: 1984, *Logic as Grammar*, MIT Press, Cambridge, Massachusetts.
Hornstein, N. and D. Lightfoot: 1981, *Explanations in Linguistics*, Longman, London.
Hornstein, N. and D. Lightfoot: 1981b, 'Introduction', in Hornstein and Lightfoot (1981a), pp. 9–31.
Lightfoot, D.: 1982, *The Language Lottery*, MIT/Bradford Press, Cambridge, Masssachusetts.
McClelland, J., D. Rumelhart, and D. Hinton: 1986, 'The Appeal of Parallel Distributed Processing', in Rumelhart and McClelland (1986a), Vol. I.
McClelland, J. L., and A. Kawamoto: 1986, 'Mechanisms of Sentence Processing: Assigning Roles to Constituents', in Rumelhart and McClelland (1986a), Vol. II.
Morgan, J.: 1986, *From Simple Input to Complex Grammar*, MIT Press, Cambridge, Massachusetts.
Papert, S.: 1988, 'One AI or Many?', *Daedalus* **117**, 1–14.
Peters, S.: 1972, 'The Projection Problem: How is a Grammar to be Selected?', in *Goals of Linguistic Theory*, Prentice-Hall, Englewood Cliffs, New Jersey.
Pinker, S., and A. Prince: forthcoming, 'On Language and Connectionism: Analysis of a Parallel Distributed Processing Model of Language Acquisition', to appear in *Cognition*.
Quine, W. V.: 1969, 'Linguistics and Philosophy', in S. Hook (ed.), *Language and Philosophy*, New York University Press, pp. 95–98.

Ramsey, W., D. Rumelhart, and S. Stich: forthcoming, *Philosophy and Connectionist Theory*, Lawrence Erlbaum Associates, Hillsdale, New Jersey.

Ramsey, W., S. Stich and J. Garon: forthcoming, 'Connectionism, Eliminativism and the Future of Folk Psychology', to appear in Ramsey, Rumelhart, and Stich.

Rumelhart, D., G. Hinton and J. McClelland: 1986, A General Framework for Parallel Distributed Processing', in Rumelhart and McClelland (1986a), Vol. I.

Rumelhart, D., G. Hinton and R. Williams: 1986, 'Learning Internal Representations by Error Propagation', in Rumelhart and McClelland (1986a), Vol. I.

Rumelhart, D. and J. McClelland: 1986a, *Parallel Distributed Processing: Explorations in the Microstructure of Cognition*, Vols. I & II, MIT/Bradford Press, Cambridge, Massachusetts.

Rumelhart, D. and J. McClelland: 1986b, 'On Learning the Past Tense of English Verbs', in Rumelhart and McClelland (1986a), Vol. II.

Rumelhart, D. and J. McClelland: 1986c, 'PDP Models and General Issues in Cognitive Science', in Rumelhart and McClelland (1986a), Vol. I.

Sampson, G.: 1987a, 'Review Article. Parallel Distributed Processing', *Language* **63**, 871–86.

Sampson, G.: 1987b, 'A Turning Point in Linguistics', *Times Literary Supplement*, June 12, p. 643.

Searle, J.: 1974, 'Chomsky's Revolution in Linguistics', in Gilbert Harman (ed.), *On Noam Chomsky: Critical Essays*, Doubleday, New York, pp. 2–33.

Sejnowski, T. C. Rosenberg 1987, 'Parallel Networks that Learn to Pronounce English Text', *Complex Systems* **1**, 145–68.

Selman, B. and G. Hirst: 1985, 'A Rule-Based Connectionist Parsing System', *Proceedings of the Seventh Annual Conference of the Cognitive Science Society*.

St. John, M. F. and J. L. McClelland: 1988, 'Learning and Applying Contextual Constraints in Sentence Comprehension', in *Proceedings of the 10th Annual Cognitive Science Society Conference*, Lawrence Erlbaum Associates, Hillsdale, New Jersey.

Stabler, E.: 1983, 'How Are Grammars Represented?', *Behavioral and Brain Sciences* **6**, 391–421.

Stich, S.: 1971, 'What Every Speaker Knows', *Philosophical Review* **80**, 476–96.

Stich, S.: forthcoming, 'The Dispute Over Innate Ideas', to appear in M. Dascal et al. (eds.), *Sprachphilosophie: Ein Internationales Handbuch Zeitgenossischer Forschung*.

Waltz, D. L. and J. B. Pollack: 1985, 'Massively Parallel Parsing: A Strongly Interactive Model of Natural Interpretation', *Cognitive Science* **9**, 51-74.

Wexler, K. and P. W. Culicover: 1980, *Formal Principles of Language Acquisition*, MIT Press, Cambridge, MA.

Dept. of Philosophy
University of Notre Dame
Notre Dame, 46556
U.S.A.

and

Dept. of Philosophy
Rutgers, The State University of New Jersey
New Brunswick, NJ 08903
U.S.A.

PART I
CONCEPTS AND CONTENT

DAVID BRADDON-MITCHELL AND JOHN FITZPATRICK

EXPLANATION AND THE LANGUAGE OF THOUGHT*

ABSTRACT. In this paper we argue that the insistence by Fodor et. al. that the Language of Thought hypothesis must be true rests on mistakes about the kinds of explanations that must be provided of cognitive phenomena. After examining the canonical arguments for the LOT, we identify a weak version of the LOT hypothesis which we think accounts for some of the intuitions that there must be a LOT.

We then consider what kinds of explanation cognitive phenomena require, and conclude that three main confusions lead to the invalid inference of the truth of a stronger LOT hypothesis from the weak and trivial version. These confusions concern the relationship between syntax and semantics, the nature of higher-level causation in cognitive science, and differing roles of explanations invoking intrinsic structures of minds on the one hand, and aetiological or evolutionary accounts of their properties on the other.

A potential problem in philosophy is that metatheorists and theorists rarely talk to each other. Sometimes this is no problem; plausibly, in the case of ethics, a metaethical theory is tested against its success in accounting for ethical practice or at least substantive ethical theory. In the philosophy of psychology, though, it may well be a problem. Views in the philosophy of explanation should, we think, have considerable bearing on substantive explanations in the philosophy of psychology.

In this paper we examine Jerry Fodor's famous Language of Thought (hereafter sometimes LOT) hypothesis in the light of some of our views about explanation. Roughly, we will argue that if you have the right views about psychological explanation, then you don't need the Language of Thought to explain any of the available data. This is not to say that the Language of Thought hypothesis is wrong – we take that to be an empirical matter for sorting out by psychologists not of the armchair persuasion. Rather, we argue that there is no prima facie case for it to be made out by philosophers or psychologists of a philosophical bent.

The plan is as follows: in section one we will outline what the substantial Language of Thought hypothesis is, and we will run through the currently canonical list of Fodorian arguments for it. We also take passing swipes at some of these, so as to leave the substantial arguments for the rest of the paper.

J. H. Fetzer (ed.), Epistemology and Cognition, 35–61.

In section two we run through a weak version of the Language of Thought hypothesis, and explain why it might be the plausibility of this which has led to such acceptance as the substantial Language of Thought hypothesis has had.

Sections three and four deal with questions in the theory of explanation and how they bear on the strong version of the hypothesis. In section three we argue that there may be no call for *synchronic* structural explanations of the behaviour of complex organisms at all. This, we argue, is because of the possibility that here may be *diachronic* explanations of the behaviour, which do not support the hypothesis that there are elegant synchronic structures. Section four is crucial: here we argue that if supervening state ascriptions (such as mental states) are not required to causally interact with one another, then while they may in some way explain behaviour they do not cause it. If they do not cause it, then there is no need to take them to be intrinsic states. Thus the argument for the strong LOT is blocked, though not the weak one. We conclude that it is Fodor's insistence that high level structural states must not only explain but also cause behaviour, which generates the strong Language of Thought from the weak one.

1.   THE LANGUAGE OF THOUGHT

The Language of Thought hypothesis, as it was first introduced, made two claims: that we needed to postulate an internal representational system (probably innate) which was rich enough to support complex linguistic and cognitive skills, and that this system of representation had a particular structure much like that of a language. The gist of the former claim goes for the most part unargued these days; just about all of us are representationalists of some sort. It's the latter claim that remains a point of in-house debate among representationalists. In this section we detail this latter claim and summarize the arguments for it.

1.1. *What is the Lot Hypothesis?*

The LOT is made up of three subclaims. First the claim that mental representations:[1]

... have a *combinatorial syntax and semantics*, in which (a) there is a distinction between structurally atomic and structurally molecular representations; (b) structurally molecular representations have syntactic constituents that are themselves either structurally molecular or atomic; and (c) the semantic content of a (molecular) representation is a function of the semantic contents of its parts together with its constituent structure. (Fodor and Pylyshyn 1988, p. 12)

When Fodor says that mental representations have 'constituent structure' he is talking about (a) to (c). Because mental states are constituted in part by structured representations, cognitive processes may be defined in terms of those representations. A cognitive process is the transformation of "any mental representation that satisfies a given structural description...into a mental representation that satisfies another structural description" (Fodor and Pylyshyn 1988, p. 13). An obvious example of this structure sensitivity of a mental process is that of inference. It is a process of inference, for example, that will transform a representation of the form 'P & Q' into a representation of the form 'P'.

The LOT also makes a substantive commitment to the physical instantiation of structured representations. Mental representations:

. . . are assumed to correspond to real physical structures in the brain and the *combinatorial structure* of a representation is supposed to have a counterpart in structural relations among physical properties of the brain. For example, the relation 'part of', which holds between a relatively simple symbol and a more complex one, is assumed to correspond to some physical relation among brain states. (Fodor and Pylyshyn 1988, p. 13)

The requirement that the properties of mental representations proposed by the LOT are instantiated in the brain makes the LOT a considerably strong thesis. In order for a cognitive system to qualify as instantiating the LOT, it must possess more than mere input-output properties. In fact, the LOT is an even stronger thesis since it is also committed to the claim that:

. . . the physical properties onto which the structure of the symbols is mapped *are the very properties that cause the system to behave* as it does. In other words the physical counterparts of the symbols, and their structural properties, cause the system's behaviour. (Fodor and Pylyshyn 1988, p. 16)

As we shall soon see, this final claim regarding the causally efficacious structure of mental representations is crucial for the current work.

1.2. *Arguments for the LOT*

We should accept the LOT if there are good arguments in its support. The arguments currently on offer, found in 'Fodor's Guide to Mental Representation' and *Psychosemantics* (Fodor 1985 and 1987) and Fodor and Pylyshyn's 'Connectionism and Cognitive Architecture: A Critical Analysis' (1988), come in two basic kinds: arguments from the explanation of cognitive capacities and a methodological argument. In the remainder of this section we review these arguments with the aim of assessing their support for the LOT in the next section.

1.2.1. *Explaining Cognitive Capacities.* There are four arguments from the explanation of cognitive capacities.[2] As Fodor himself admits, all these arguments are really very much the same (Fodor and Pylyshyn 1988, p. 48). So, a description of two of them will suffice in order to give a flavour of the style of argument. Cognitive capacities exhibit two properties – productivity and systematicity.[3] Cognitive capacities are productive because we are constantly thinking new and novel thoughts and believing and desiring new and novel things. Cognitive capacities are systematic because our ability to think some thought or believe some proposition is intrinsically connected to the ability to think or believe certain other thoughts and propositions. It is in virtue of this property that you don't come across cognitive systems with the ability to think that Jill loves Mary without the ability to think that Mary loves Jill.

The strategy Fodor uses to explain these capacities derives from the work of Chomsky (1968). Chomsky thought that linguistic capacities are also productive and systematic. To account for this, he claimed that the structures underlying linguistic competence are generative. That is, one's (tacit) knowledge or cognizing of a language consists in the mastering of a combinatorial syntax and semantics. It is out of this syntax and semantics that the entities over which linguistic capacities range (sentences and utterances) are constructed. Fodor's argument for the constituency of the representations over which cognitive processes range immediately follows. Since we explain the productivity and systematicity of linguistic capacities by postulating the constituency of sentences, and assuming the psycholinguistic premise that we use language to express our thoughts, then we make the same inference in the cognitive case as we do in the linguistic case: viz., that the productivity and systematicity of cognitive capacities is explained by the constituency of mental representations. Mental representations have constituent structure because there is a combinatorial syntax and semantics for cognition. In short, productivity and systematicity are explained by there being a Language of Thought.

This argument style rests heavily on the assumption that the Chomskian enterprise will be vindicated. By citing Chomsky in the premise of his arguments, Fodor uses it as evidence for accepting the LOT. But why should we let Fodor use Chomsky to lend credibility to the LOT story? There are two reasons why we shouldn't. First, it is surely still an open question as to whether or not grammars are psychologically real entities in the way Chomsky maintains. We shouldn't let the plausibility of one contentious empirical hypothesis depend upon the truth of another contentious empirical hypothesis.

The second reason why one shouldn't take the linguistic case as evidence for the cognitive case is that both the linguistic and cognitive cases would seem to be two sides of the same coin. In both cases we are trying to explain a particular capacity of a subject by postulating some intrinsic psychological fact about that subject. The fact that we do seem to use language to express our thoughts, and that both thoughts and sentences are representational, semantically evaluable, etc., would suggest that these hypotheses are closely related. Indeed, they are probably closely enough related so that they both either stand or fall together. Of course, by taking one as a datum and using it in an argument for the other, the latter follows and vice versa. But that's because they are essentially the same style of answer to similar problems.

We can assume that in some sense the LOT can explain productivity and systematicity. But Fodor's claim in the argument from the explanation of cognitive capacities is stronger than this implies. He claims that *only* LOT can explain these properties of cognitive capacities, since you have to have structured representations in order to get these two properties. To see why Fodor and Pylyshyn think this, let's take a look at an alternative to the LOT which postulates unstructured representations to see how it tries to account for systematicity and productivity.

The alternative view is that of Connectionism or Parallel Distributed Processing (PDP).[4] Connectionism is described as the 'new wave' of cognitive science. It proposes models of cognitive architecture which are highly parallel instead of serial and are 'brain-styled' to the extent that they build models based in part upon the properties of neurons and neuronal organizations. With Connectionism one doesn't get structured representations that have a combinatorial syntax and semantics. Instead, one gets a network of atomic nodes with each connexion having its own excitatory and/or inhibitory thresholds, according to which the spread of activation within the network occurs. Some Connectionists[5] want to interpret the nodes featuring in a network semantically. They might interpret nodes to be representations such as 'A & B', 'A', 'B', etc. Although the nodes are labeled in this way as being structured, this labeling is in fact irrelevant to the properties of the nodes; they're unitary. All they have are causal powers defined relationally with respect to other nodes via the internodal connexions. They have no intrinsic structure relevant to their semantic interpretation. In order for 'A' to be represented in addition to 'A & B', the Connectionist cognitive architect must separately build 'A' into the architecture, unlike a LOT architecture where once one has 'A & B' represented one automatically has 'A' represented.

From this description Fodor and Pylyshyn draw some implications for productivity and systematicity. While the Connectionist can model a finite performance mental history, that very model is not going to generate an infinite capacity. In such a model, the architect also has the option of constructing a model in which you get, say, the thought that Mary loves Jill without the thought that Jill loves Mary. Of course, the Connectionist architect can build her network so as to be consistent with a finite and systematic mental life; you can build Connectionist and LOT architectures which are input-output equivalent. Fodor claims, however, that it is just as likely that there are mental lives which do not satisfy systematicity, say, at this input-output level. If Connectionist models are accurate, then we should expect there to be gaps in cognitive competence since the systems don't have representations with syntactic structure; the systematicity of the system doesn't follow from the architecture. Connectionist architecture treats mental representations as a list instead of a generated set. Where the list happens to differ, then cognitive gaps may appear. Cognitive gaps, however, don't seem to appear. For these reasons Fodor and Pylyshyn believe that only a LOT architecture can truly explain the properties of our cognitive capacities. Sections three and four address this argument directly.

1.2.2. *The Methodological Argument.* The second argument which Fodor cites in support of the LOT is the methodological argument. This argument provides a methodological basis for the inference to the types of structures required by a LOT architecture from the capacities of the system evident in the argument from cognitive capacities. The argument goes like this. Fodor comes up with what he takes to be a plausible (not surprisingly, given his interests) principle of nondemonstrative inference:

Principle P: Suppose there is a kind of event c_1 of which the normal effect is a kind of event e_1; and a kind of event c_2 of the which the normal effect is a kind of event e_2; and a kind of event c_3 of which the normal effect is a complex event e_1 & e_2. Viz.:

$c_1 \rightarrow e_1$
$c_2 \rightarrow e_2$
$c_3 \rightarrow e_1$ & e_2

Then, *ceteris paribus*, it is reasonable to infer that c_3 is a complex event whose constituents include c_1 and c_2. (Fodor 1987, p. 141)

For example, if e_1 is the raising of my hand and e_2 is the hopping on my right foot, then we infer that the cause of my simultaneously doing e_1 and e_2 is the conjunction of c_1 and c_2, i.e., c_3, and not some other cause c_4. Fodor's claim is that unless we accept the LOT we are going to flout this principle. If mental representations are not structured (as in the case with Connectionism) then whenever we think the thought that 'A & B', that thought has a different etiology from the thought that 'A'.

Just when principle P ought be invoked is crucial. One is required to ascertain that the event being explained is in fact complex. If the event in question is not complex, then the principle should not be invoked. In the case of my raising my arm and hopping on my right foot, it seems unquestionable that this seemingly joint action is a conjunction of two other physical events. So, the adherence to principle P would be recommended. However, in the case of the outputs of our cognitive system, although it seems that our thoughts and beliefs have constituent structure, we had better be careful in adopting principle P, since automatically concluding that they have constituent structure might be to beg the questions at issue in favour of the LOT.

This can be seen in Fodor's own example of synergism (1987, p. 143). Synergisms are behaviours which, although appearing to be complex, are in fact behavioural wholes; the elements are in effect fused to one another. One way in which synergisms develop is through learning.

Perhaps an organism's raising its arm and hopping on one foot is a synergism because it was learned as part of a rudimentary system of communication, the behavioural elements of the language having a different etiology from that of the individual pieces of behaviour 'fused' to form the linguistic behaviour. Invoking principle P in this case would lead us astray since we need some independent account of whether or not some behaviour is to count as a synergism.

The same applies in the case of cognitive capacities. We need some story as to which behaviours are synergisms and which are not. Only then can we apply principle P in support of the LOT. What about the case of beliefs? Does the etiology of the belief that P & Q have as a component that of the belief that P? Suppose we want to know whether an agent's uttering 'P & Q' is just a composite of the separate etiologies of an agent's uttering 'P' and 'Q' separately. According to Fodor, principle P would suggest that the proximal causes are the same, viz., $\{P, Q\} \rightarrow$ 'P' and 'Q' and $\{P, Q\} \rightarrow$ 'P & Q'. There is at least one important sense, though, in which this may not be true.

Contrary to the Fodorian principle that systematic behaviour should just "follow from" the architecture, we do not think that all consequences of an agent's belief set are automatically believed by the agent. Consider the case of closure under adjunction. Someone may believe that P, Q, R, and S, but if asked in a quiz whether a sufficiently long conjunction is true, she may have to form a belief token that P & Q & R & S. And she does this by considering the evidence in the same way as she would for any other belief, even if the evidence on which she bases her judgement is her own several epistemic states. This is a special case of the realization in AI that allowing beliefs to be closed under deduction in general will lead to the inability to distinguish between the deductive consequences of a given belief set which have actually been generated, where they are likely to be useful in future proofs, and those which have not been explicitly generated.[6] This suggests the following alternative model of the proximate etiology of our agent's uttering 'P & Q', viz., $\{P, Q\} \rightarrow$ 'P' and 'Q' whereas $\{P \& Q\} \rightarrow$ 'P & Q'. In this case the proximate etiology varies across the utterances, despite Fodor's principle.

Fodor might reply that the belief that P & Q has as its proximate cause P and Q in which case the model looks like this: $\{P, Q\} \rightarrow \{P \& Q\} \rightarrow$ 'P & Q'. In this way, one's citing of the proximate causes will conform to principle P. There would, however, seem to be no necessity to go back that extra causal step in explaining the utterance of 'P & Q', since the reason why that utterance is made is because the agent believes that P & Q. The only reason to cite the extra step would be to ensure that principle is adhered to, and hence get a LOT. But opting for the extra causal step needs to be argued for independently, not from the assumption that we want to secure the LOT.

Whatever one thinks of this argument, though, it makes Fodor's Principle P less convincing as an argument for the LOT; since if the LOT is true and there is constituent structure, then the methodological argument is applicable. If, however, it is not true, and the argument for distinct etiologies of apparently constituent behaviours goes through, then the methodological argument is inapplicable. In sum, if perhaps a little too strongly, the methodological argument is good in the case of psychology if and only if the LOT is true – and there is no independent way to establish the validity of the methodological argument.

2. HOW NOT TO GET A **LOT** FOR FREE

The LOT hypothesis as described in the previous section is essentially the claim that there is a combinatorial syntax and semantics for mental representations with the ensuing constituent structure being mapped onto the physical properties of the brain. This raises the following question: in virtue of what does such a mapping exist?

One way of getting such a mapping is to construe the LOT hypothesis as postulating an algorithm for generating our productive and systematic capacities. Such an algorithm might be the neatest and simplest way of describing those capacities. Of course, constituent representational structure might feature in that algorithm. If you think that no matter how the brain actually operates it is that algorithm which is realized, no matter how irregularly it maps on to the actual structure of the brain, then you can have, trivially, a Language of Thought. On such a view it is an input-output specification which is constitutive of some algorithm's being realised.

There are, however, any number of algorithms which could account for our behaviour. There are as many algorithms as you like for performing the functions of a pocket calculator, let alone a human mind. If you cull these by saying that any algorithm that does the same thing – i.e., is an algorithm for a human brain or a pocket calculator – is the same algorithm, then you have returned to the mere top level of input and output.

Fodor wants more than this; he thinks that it is internal functional role which will identify internal states (1987, Chap. 2). This at least sounds like he does not want it to be a mere mapping of the top (input-output) level. So we need some extra, independent, motivation for supposing that some algorithm or architectural description which is compatible with the description at the level of input and output is the real one. If a taxonomy of the system motivated in some other way reveals similar structures which could be said to realize the algorithm, then perhaps that would do.

Fodor makes of lot of the fact that token states are syntactic states. In the next section we consider whether a syntactic analysis could provide such a motivation.

2.1. *Syntax and Semantics*

Fodor takes constituent structure to be syntactic structure. But on this construal of structure, a LOT can be had, if not for free, then very cheaply. We can see this by examining the relation between syntax and semantics. We have two related claims to make: first, that if you have a semantic interpretation and something to map it on to, then you can generate a trivial syntax; and second, that you can't have a syntax properly so described without a prior semantics of which it is the syntax.

The LOT requires that mental representations have syntactic structures realized in the brain. The problem here is what is going to count as syntactic structure. Syntax and semantics are intimately related. The practice of logicians to behave as though the syntax comes first and then an interpretation is applied puts the cart before the horse. A syntax is a simple, if not the simplest, description of a supposedly meaning-bearing system, given its intended meaning. A syntactic constituent of such a system is that which makes some uniform semantic contribution to that system. What this means is that a syntactic item is taken to be a syntactic item because it stands in a signifying relation to some semantic interpretation.

Now suppose that the One True Cognitive Science is completed, and we have state descriptions of the brain which we can pair off with attributions of mental state content given the standard semantics. The important question, then, is what kind of similarity between these descriptions is required to get an account of what the syntactic tokens which represent the same content are. One possible syntax – perhaps the crudest and hence useless, but a syntax nevertheless – would be a disjunctive one. Simply disjoin all the state descriptions which are true whenever a given content attribution is made, and count the disjunction as a syntactic token. This disjunctive state would then be the syntactic token of the mental state. In such a case you can get a syntax just by virtue of applying a semantics to something which you stipulate is representational, just in the same way as you can, if you must, map *Principia Mathematica* onto the Canberra Telephone Directory. What is more, you can come up with a syntax in which various addresses and numbers represent thrilling theorems of meta-arithmetic, and, with a massively gerrymandered account of similarity relations among syntactic tokens, you can get constituent structure off the ground. So it seems that the first claim – that whenever you have a semantic interpretation and something to map it on to you can get a trivial syntax – looks fairly plausible.

In fact, we are neutral about whether such a syntax is a trivial syntax or no syntax at all; what is worth insisting on is that an account has to be given of what makes something a 'real' syntax or a nontrivial one. If trivial syntax is what you appeal to, then syntax will not do the job of getting the strong LOT hypothesis from the weak one. It will not provide the independent motivation that we mentioned in our last section: the kind of motivation which will make the syntax a bona fide structural realizer. Some kind of independent taxonomy will be required on to which it could turn out as a matter of empirical fact that the ascribed syntax maps.

In their more a prioristic moods (especially toward the end of Fodor and Pylyshyn 1988), Pylyshyn and Fodor seem to think that they can provide an independent and intrinsic structural account of the mind by simply taking the trivial syntactic story and forgetting about the semantics whence it came. The assumption seems to be that if you have mapped the semantics on to the brain, and you are left with a taxonomy which gives you syntactic tokens, that there is no problem in then determining whether the syntactic tokens have constituent structure.

Having got these tokens, however, how do we go about deciding whether the tokens whose content is constituent are a constituent part, qua syntactic token, of other syntactic tokens? What is crucial here is that there is one way which is too easy. If the taxonomy of syntactic tokens comes from their being the token states that are realized when certain content attributions are made, then they can be described as having constitutive structure in virtue of their relationships to the ascribed content.

This allows you to stubbornly insist that it is syntactic tokens that you are talking about, while there is nothing intrinsic about the brain which determines which token is a constituent part of another token in any given situation. What has happened at this point is that the move decomposes the syntactic tokens from a story about the semantic content of the tokens, and then posits relations among the tokens which come only from the interpretation provided by the semantic content. The temptation then is to think that you have structure even if you jettison the semantic story which led to the taxonomy of those syntactic tokens. But in effect, we don't have any syntactic tokens in the absence of the semantic content.[7] For a substantial syntactic account to be given, two factors are required: a semantics, to ensure that it really is a syntax that is being given rather than any other kind of description, and an independent motivation for the taxonomy of syntactic tokens, so as to avoid the merely trivial kind of syntax described above.

The upshot of this is that we can get mental representations with some form of syntactic structure which in some way gets realized in the brain but which does not satisfy the demands of Fodor's strong version of the LOT.

If this is the version of the LOT that one finds convincing, then it's easy to see how the arguments from cognitive capacities and methodology support the LOT. The cognitive inquirer chooses a syntax, or more accurately imposes a syntax, upon a cognitive system in order to account as neatly as possible for the capacities of the system such as productivity and systematicity. The methodological argument's principle P provides a general strategy for imposing neatness onto our explanations in much the same way as the weak LOT does. Again, though, we have not generated the strong LOT hypothesis.

3. EXPLANATION I: SYNCHRONIC AND DIACHRONIC EXPLANATIONS

We do not think that the traditional arguments which have been outlined bear on the strong version of the Language of Thought hypothesis, partly because it is not at all clear what kind of explanation the LOT is supposed to be. In this section we attempt to determine what type of explanation the LOT is providing. Fodor thinks that we need the LOT because in order to explain putative capacities such as productivity and systematicity, a mechanism or a particular state of an organism must be postulated in order to guarantee the presence of those capacities. If there is a LOT then we get these capacities automatically. If there is not, claims Fodor, then it is unlikely that these capacities would be evident. While other architectures may allow systematicity and productivity, none guarantee it. Our claim is that the presence of these capacities can be adequately explained without the postulation of some specific mechanism or state of the organism which neatly and elegantly captures features of the organism which are visible at the behavioural level. Such an explanation is to be had from, roughly, the pressure of evolutionary forces. An evolutionary style of explanation raises the probability that a cognitive system generates systematicity and productivity without making the commitment to a specific mechanism such as the LOT. We then go on to claim that such evolutionary explanations can place constraints on what remains to be explained by other kinds of explanation.

We start by distinguishing *diachronic* explanations from instantiation theory or *synchronic* explanations.[8] The diachronic explanations, including evolutionary explanations, are concerned to give a causal account of how a system came to be in its present state. The most usual explananda are states of a system or states of affairs, and the usual explanantia are earlier states of the system or states of affairs together with transition laws which describe the generation of the later state from the earlier.

The second kind of explanation which might be asked for – which we contend the LOT hypothesis is providing – is of the synchronic or instantiation theory kind. In this kind of explanation we are concerned to give an account of what it (actually) is for a system to have a certain property in terms of the structural states of that system. An explanation of the ductility, colour, and conductivity of gold by appeal to its atomic structure and the interaction of its outer electron shells with other gold atoms would, for example, be an explanation of the observable properties of gold by appeal to the structural properties of the system which instantiates gold. It is no part of such an explanation to claim that anything which has the phenomenal properties of gold must have the underlying properties that gold does have, but rather that in fact the phenomenal properties of gold are explained by the structure it actually has.

Are the facts that the friends of a LOT are trying to explain explicable by a diachronic explanation? A diachronic explanation requires only that some previous state of the system together with some transition laws entail the explanandum state. This will be trivially possible if physicalism is true; some complete neurological description coupled with a list of inputs and the right neurological laws will provide an account of why some new state is the way it is. Can we get an explanation of productivity and systematicity of thought out of all this?

We can certainly get something which looks like an explanation of productive and systematic behaviour in each instance, which is why the question of exactly what is being explained is so crucial. But the friends of the LOT want more; they want an account of why, in general, the behaviour is (almost) always systematic or productive. In short, they want an explanation of the systematicity and productivity of the system as a whole. This is why we should see what the friends of the LOT are engaged in as a kind of synchronic explanation. They want an account of what property of the system it is which realizes these capacities.

Must we provide a synchronic explanation of these capacities as the friends of the LOT seem to imply? We think not.

First it is far from the case that the bare story about neurophysiological states and laws exhausts what diachronic theories can say about the mind. You can jump up a level, and ask of the system as a whole how it came to have the behavioural properties – or the functional properties at the highest level – that it does. And the best kind of candidate for that, it seems to us, is some kind of evolutionary account.

We do not have such an account on offer here; we do, however, think that there must be some such account of how the mind has been tailored to be what it is now. Nor do we need such an account in detail; that one is required is common ground between us and the LOTers (if the LOT hypothesis is true then a diachronic story will tell us why there is a LOT which can be used to synchronically explain why cognitive capacities are the way they are). Our claim is rather that this sort of story removes the surprise with which both Fodor and Pylyshyn think we should greet the news that minds are, more or less, productive and systematic. So we think that the objection – that diachronic stories (or neurophysiological or connectionist ones supplemented with an etiological account) do not explain because it is a mere accident that the system is productive and systematic – is misjudged. It is no accident: it was selected to be that way, and this selection plays an important part in diachronic explanation of minds if the time dimension is long enough.

So the Language of Thought hypothesis rests on an explanatory imperative to provide a simple, elegant synchronic explanation of the structural properties of the brain in virtue of which it displays its productivity and systematicity of output. If there is an empirically adequate low-level account of the operations of the brain forthcoming, and if any surprise at high level regularities which it displays can be removed by some evolutionary account, then there is no requirement to produce the neat synchronic account.

The imperative to produce a neat synchronic architecture of the mind in which, in Fodor's and Pylyshyn's words, systematicity simply "follows from" the architecture, rests on a confusion between the roles of diachronic and instantiation explanations, this being caused by a neglect of other routes to eliminating the surprise which the Language of Thought hypothesis attempts to reduce. Synchronic instantiation explanations are not required to be neat. With complex systems it is often the case that the details of their operation, even at a functional level, are messy. When we explain the properties of a chemical by its physical structure, we do not look for analogues in this structure of the phenomenal properties that we seek to explain. It is enough that these structures account for, more or less regularly, the explanandum properties. In the thought case it may indeed be surprising that the complex physical system displays these properties, but having given this instantiation account, why are we obliged to try to remove the surprise at the instantiation theory level? This seems to be the hidden requirement that lurks in some versions of the LOT argument. Instantiation theories explain simply by describing the actual mechanism; in some sense it is a fairly weak explanation, but that is all they do. Surprise at what they do is often best removed by a diachronic account. In the case of the mind and the productivity of thought, we have a candidate in the form of evolutionary pressure; the need to remove this surprise by appeal to some structural feature of the mind mistakes the purpose of instantiation theories of the mind.

3.1. *A Slightly Stronger Claim*

Our slightly stronger claim is that an etiological or evolutionary explanation can not only remove the requirement that a synchronic explanation of a certain kind be provided; it can also actually constrain the sort of account we should give.

We propose two constraints on an evolutionary explanation of how our cognitive capacities got to be the way they are:

(1)   That whatever the explanation, it must account for the continuity or discontinuity between the apparent systematic and productive capacities of human minds, and whatever capacities are exhibited by infraverbal mentation

and

(2)   that the minds which have evolved must have done so in incremental stages; however the mind works it got that way by additions and changes of an ad hoc nature, much the way a tree which is pruned to look like a giraffe gets that way. Each change does not proceed according to a plan; it is only the overall direction of change which is determined.[9]

Something in the spirit of these constraints has been used by, for example, Dennett (1984) to argue against (or at least motivate the arguments of others against) computationalism as a doctrine of the mind. Regardless of whether they bear on computationalism (whatever that really is) we think they do put constraints of some kind on a synchronic theory of the mind. Consider the following passage from Fodor and Pylyshyn:

It's possible to imagine a Connectionist being prepared to admit that while systematicity doesn't *follow from* – and hence is not explained by – Connectionist architecture, it is nevertheless *compatible* with that architecture....The only mechanism that is known to be able to produce pervasive systematicity is Classical architecture (Fodor and Pylyshyn 1988, p. 49).

The thing to notice about this claim is that it is supposed to be an advantage of classical theories that they and their attendant LOT simply guarantee systematicity: thus the classical picture removes all possible surprise at systematic behaviour. The constraints on an evolutionary account which we give above, however, suggest that it might even be a disadvantage that systematicity and productivity are guaranteed.

A theory of the functioning of minds which allowed, more or less, systematicity to appear according to how they evolve, without that property being guaranteed by the basic architecture, would make the mind's etiology more credible. In much the same way, a theory of the structure of trees which shows how it is possible to trim them to look like giraffes is going to be more illuminating than an account of the structure of a giraffe-tree on which its giraffe shape is guaranteed, even though a trivial theory of that kind is to be had for the asking – or at least the measuring.

4. EXPLANATION II: IMPLEMENTATION AND LEVELS OF EXPLANATION

It seems that Fodor believes that taking a Connectionist approach to the explanation of our apparently productive and systematic capacities is to make a kind of mistake about explanatory levels. We take it that this kind of objection might also be leveled at our claim that an etiological explanation will go a fair way toward being sufficient for the explanation of these properties.

The idea is that there are lots of different levels of explanation. Of course, the changing states of the brain can be explained by some neurophysiological story, and perhaps some etiological account can be given of why certain high level regularities appear in these state changes when viewed from some high level. But neither of these is a psychological explanation of the supposed productivity and systematicity of thought, for that would have to be at the psychological level; and the only explanation going at that level is the Language of Thought. As Fodor and Pylyshyn write:

It seems certain that the world has causal structure at very many different levels of analysis, with the individuals recognized at the lowest levels being, in general, very small and the individuals recognized at the highest levels being, in general, very large. Thus there is a scientific story to be told about quarks; and a scientific story to be told about atoms; and a scientific story to be told about molecules... ditto rocks and stones and rivers... ditto galaxies. And the story that scientists tell about the causal structure that the world has at any one of these levels may be quite different from the story that they tell at the next level up or down. The methodological implication for psychology is this: if you want to have an argument about *cognitive* architecture, you had better specify the level of analysis that's supposed to be at issue. (Fodor and Pylyshyn 1988, p. 9)

This, then, is the Fodor and Pylyshyn doctrine about levels of explanation. We can agree that the world is organized at many levels, many of which are scientifically (or otherwise) interesting. But notice that for Fodor and Pylyshyn there must be causal structure at many levels. The Big things at the high levels cause things to happen to other Big things, just as the little 'uns cause things to happen to other little 'uns, while the Big things are composed of the little things to tie the whole story down respectably. We think that it is this requirement that causation proceeds at every level which, in a very subtle way, commits Fodor and Pylyshyn to the Language of Thought before all the evidence is in.

It is perhaps timely to consider a diagram made famous in Chapter 1 of Fodor's *The Language of Thought* (1975, ch. 1) which describes the relationship of the special sciences to physics.

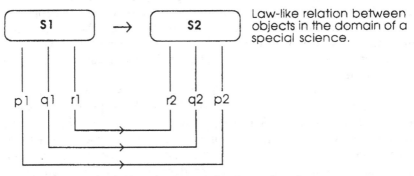

Law-like relation between objects in the domain of a special science.

Law-Like causal relations between the lower level realizers of S1, and the lower level realizers of S2

There are two ways of reading a diagram like this. The lawlike relations which hold between S1 and S2 can be taken to be causal laws that justify the claim that S1 caused S2 or else in a less orthodox way that S1 may in some circumstances explain S2. In this case, S1 would explain S2 by virtue of its being a good description of genuine regularities in the world and by virtue of the fact that in general one of its realizations will cause one of the realizations of S2.

We think that there are good reasons for preferring an account in which the high level properties do not do the causing. First, if there is some lower level causal interaction going on which is sufficient for the state changes of the system, then the high level causal interactions are idle. What purpose would overdetermination of the causal history have? The second, and related reason is that the higher level properties are related to the lower level ones by relations of supervenience and multiple instantiability. But in each particular case only the actual instantiation of the higher level property is present, so to claim that the higher level property is causally efficacious seems to rely on the other possible but nonactual realizations doing some causal work. But in fact, it does not matter to the particular case what is nonactual.

The motivation for Fodor's claims about causation proceeding at the high level is, of course, to avoid reductionism. He wants to preserve the special sciences as genuine fields of inquiry, not reducible to physics. This can be achieved, though, by noting that regularities can be observed at high levels which may not be observable at lower levels. And if high-level entities can explain, partly in virtue of the fact that they token the existence of a causal process at a lower level, that may be enough.

4.1. *Why High-Level Causation Brings on the Language of Thought*

Fodor and Pylyshyn believe that the scientifically explanatory higher level properties are causally efficacious ones. Psychological properties are certainly high-level, and they take it as uncontroversial that they are causally efficacious. The methodology is this. Look for high-level generalizations, and if one is found which looks like it has the desirable properties of simplicity and power, then find the causally efficacious items in that domain which explain phenomena at that level. In the psychological case, you start with content (which even Fodor admits, is an extrinsic property, and is causally neutral with respect to behaviour) and then look for the things at a high level which have the content – the semantic tokens which are realized in the brain. Now there are various behavioural regularities which need to be explained, and they are regularities when seen from the perspective of content. Content is not causally effective, so it must be whatever has that content which is causally significant. So a taxonomy of the mind is given in which it is mapped, at some high level, in a way which mirrors the content (see Fodor 1987, pp. 12–17 and 1985, 93–94).

So far so good. In fact at this point we could have our Language of Thought, although it would be the too easy one described in section 2. It would be an extrinsic property of the brain; it would be the mere mapping of our semantics on to the brain to create a stipulatory syntax. The crucial move comes when it is assumed that high-level true powerful generalizations must have causal structure. As soon as this is required, Fodor must insist that his too easy Language of Thought is pretty close to the Real Thing. If our stipulatory syntax is to have causal structure, then it had better not be an extrinsic property of the brain; no constitutively extrinsic properties are going to have causal powers over narrow behaviour. If one of our syntactic states is required to cause another, then it just has to have intrinsic causal powers.

This may be what underlies Fodor and Pylyshyn's insistence that etiological explanations or connectionist explanations are making a level mistake. If causation proceeds at every level, then a causal explanation at one level will not nearly exhaust our requirement to explain causally. And if explanations at the psychological level are bound to be causal, and if the psychological level mirrors our semantics in the way Fodor thinks it does, then intrinsic entities which can enter into the right kind of causal relations specified by that schema are required.[10] If we had to have those, maybe a strong Language of Thought would indeed be required.

This requirement can be sidestepped if, as above, we do not require that all the high-level properties be causally efficacious ones. Removing that requirement allows us to assess unblinkeredly whether or not the kinds of token syntactic states postulated by the Language of Thought are likely to feature as part of the intrinsic furniture of the mind.

4.2. *The Fallacy of the Implementation Fallacy*

It is the concern about levels of explanation that we believe underlies Fodor and Pylyshyn's argument that connectionism could only be a theory of cognitive implementation, not of cognitive architecture. They take it that even if it turns out that the kinds of networks that connectionists hypothesize actually exist, this would be no argument for connectionism as a cognitive architecture. Rather, they take it that this would merely show that the classical architecture (complete with Language of Thought) was implemented in a connectionist network.

Fodor and Pylyshyn make much of the fact that different computer programs are able to be emulated by others, or that machines of one kind can be emulated by machines of another kind. The actual physical instruction set of one machine can be emulated by operations which consist of a series of operations in the instruction set of the other machine. The emulated machine is said to be a virtual machine.

Just as in the language and grammar case, Fodor and Pylyshyn take views from an area where the philosophical problems abound as a given. After all, under what conditions are assertions about the real logical architecture of a machine assertable? If the architecture of one machine is emulated on another, then in virtue of what is the logical architecture of the emulated machine the 'true' architecture of the machine? There are certainly pragmatic considerations that make the notion of the true architecture useful and perhaps explanatory. A number of considerations might be brought to bear.

(1)   It is when the machine's output is described as the output of the logical architecture – not as the indescribably complex and apparently patternless output of the machine architecture – that the machine is intelligible to us.

(2)   The machine is designed to be input/output equivalent to the actual machine that the virtual machine is emulating.

(3)   Perhaps a little stronger: the algorithm which underlies the virtual machine's design, or even the design specification of the virtual machine's architecture, features causally in the creation of the machine emulation. The programmer looked at the design of the first machine, and the causal process which made the emulation was mediated by that design. Even here, though, this doesn't guarantee that anything is left intrinsically after the programs have been compiled and all trace of the original structure other than its input/output equivalence is lost. Perhaps the design's having featured causally is a good criterion for asserting that the virtual architecture is the true architecture, but that wouldn't guarantee the kind of intrinsic causally efficacious states that Fodor demands.

None of these provides very strong or robust criteria for being intrinsic causal realists about the states in computers which map onto high-level languages – the folk languages, if you like. Even if you think they are immensely powerful criteria, they don't seem to have plausible or sufficiently powerful analogues in the case of psychology. No one programmed us by following a Language of Thought implementation manual, so the Language of Thought wasn't instrumental in our being intrinsically structured the way we are. In case (2) it is not true that, even if we do act in a (more or less!) input/output equivalent way to a Language of Thought inspired architecture, it does not follow that it is the only architecture to which we act in an input/output equivalent way; and (1) is just too weak to give us the Fodorian goods.

More than any of these points, though, we want to stress that this talk of connectionism (or any other architecture) being just an implementation doesn't solve any problems about the Language of Thought, it merely sweeps them into another area. In fact we think that it remains almost exactly the same problem in its new cybernetic home. It just reemerges as the problem of the causal efficacy of representational syntactic states in complex and abstract computing environments. A definitive philosophical answer to the one problem will certainly help the other, but it does no good at all to just pretend that the problem is solved in one arena, and apply it in another.

The philosophical diagnosis of why it is that Fodor and Pylyshyn think it is so obvious that the problem is solved in the machine case – i.e., that virtual machine architecture is the true architecture at that level – is much the same as in the Language of Thought case proper. By insisting that high-level generalizations are true in virtue of causal connexions between high level entities, they become committed to a real, intrinsic causal structure at that level, even in the absence of any independent intrinsic structural motivation.

This does not mean that we think having features which are directly involved in causation is a necessary condition which true structural architectures must meet, but rather that in the absence of this condition we are owed an account of why we should favour one architecture over another in intrinsic terms.

6. CONCLUSION

We see the points made above as having a significant bearing not just on the Language of Thought hypothesis, but on traditional functionalism as a whole. Certainly you can have a functionalism at the highest level – that of inputs and outputs under a certain description – but, for better or for worse, that is rather like a kind of behaviourism. It is when the taxonomies created at this high level are turned back on the brain, and it is assumed that there are structural features which implement the high-level story in a way which mirrors that high level taxonomy, that

Fodor's strong Language of Thought is born. This is when our worries set in.

6.1. A Final Conjecture

We have said nothing about what counts as a sufficient motivation for something being a bona fide intrinsic structural property,[11] though we think that the following is, at least, a pretty good methodological heuristic. When investigations with very different interests end up taxonomizing things in similar ways, it is not a bad bet that there is some structural property at work. Physiology, for example, is often concerned with relatively abstract functions; but often physiologically significant taxonomies postulate entities which are realized by objects which appear in anatomical taxonomies with their quite different interests and guiding motivations. This is perhaps enough to say that, although 'heart' is a functional term, hearts are in fact structurally realized. There are functional hearts which are not anatomical hearts, and there could be anatomical hearts which are not functional hearts – imagine, for example, that some animal had two hearts, one of which played no part in the circulatory system. Despite the fact that anatomical hearts and functional hearts are independently identifiable in this way, nevertheless, some of their properties map on to each other neatly. And it is this mapability of the merely functional description on to the anatomical description which supports the view that the functional heart is in fact structurally realized.[12]

The same follows for psychology and the Language of Thought. With a proper conception of what needs explaining, and how it is to be explained, the fact that the Language of Thought is a neat functional specification of (some of the capacities of) minds is not enough. To give us the strong version of the hypothesis, we need an independently motivated taxonomy of the mind perhaps from the neurosciences – to come up with taxonomies the objects of which turn out, as a matter of fact, to realize the syntactic tokens beloved of Fodor. These partial isomorphisms between the objects postulated by different explanatory enterprises is just what will constitute the confirmation of the structural realization of the higher level's postulated entities. The strong Language of Thought hypothesis is, after all, an empirical hypothesis; its confirmation or disconfirmation must rely upon the discovery of such isomorphisms. Will they be forthcoming? We await with great interest the answer to that question.

NOTES

* We are indebted to Frank Jackson, Philip Pettit, Huw Price, and Kim Sterelny for their generous and useful comments on an earlier draft of this paper, and to discussions with Martin Davies on these and related issues.
[1] Fodor sometimes speaks as if he takes the LOT to be a doctrine about mental states rather than mental representations. He says:

> LOT claims that *mental states* – and not just their propositional objects – *typically have constituent structure*. So far as I can see, this is the only real difference between LOT and the sorts of Intentional Realism that even Aunty admits to be respectable. So a defence of LOT has to be an argument that believing and desiring are typically structured states. (Fodor 1987, p. 136.)

The intuition that mental states have constituent structure (for example, the view that the belief that Becker is playing at Wimbledon and will win, somehow has the belief that he will win as a component, and the belief that he is playing at Wimbledon as a component) could be preserved without buying in to the strong LOT hypothesis, if you have an account of mental states in which they are not narrow states of the brain. On the other hand, if with Stalnaker (1984) you do not think that even content has structure, you may not want to preserve the intuition at all.
[2] They are the argument from productivity, the argument from systematicity, the argument from compositionality and the argument from inferential coherence.
[3] The argument from productivity gets played down by Fodor these days in favour of the argument from systematicity. The reason he gives is that because of our mortality only a finite proportion of our putative potentially infinite cognitive capacity in fact gets used. In order for a cognitive system to be truly productive we must idealize from the finite performances to infinite capacities. By refusing to idealize, one may claim that we are constantly thinking and believing new things while denying productivity; if we only lived long enough then we might well run out of novel things to think and believe. Fodor now favours the argument from systematicity because he claims we do not have to idealize:

> You can make these points about the systematicity of language without idealizing to astronomical computational capacities. *Productivity* is involved with our ability to understand sentences that are a billion trillion zillion words long. But *systematicity* involves facts that are much nearer to home: such facts as the one...that no native speaker comes to understand the form of words 'John loves Mary' except as he *also* comes to understand the form of words 'Mary loves John' (Fodor 1987, p. 150).

Contra Fodor, our claim is that systematicity is generated only when all cases of relevant word forms have the requisite properties. You might think that whenever we understand 'aRb' we also understand 'bRa' and yet deny systematicity by failing to idealize to all the other possible cases. So some idealization is also required in the case of systematicity. The facts associated with systematicity appear closer to home. That's because all the speakers we've come across can think both 'John loves Mary' and 'Mary loves John'. But at best this is systematicity on local scale since we are dealing only with finite performances. However, in order for capacities to be systematic we want systematicity on a global scale, and to get that we are required to idealize. If idealization detracts from the argument from productivity then it's also going to detract from the argument from systematicity. For the sake of argument, we will assume, along with Fodor and Pylyshyn, that cognitive capacities are systematic.

[4] A useful introduction to the cluster of views that goes under the name of Connectionism is Smolenskys 'On the Proper Treatment of Connectionism' (1988).

[5] The Connectionist label encompasses many different styles of cognitive models. Some models, such as those examined by Fodor and Pylyshyn, semantically interpret the nodes, whereas others do not. These latter models are ones in which information in the network is represented in a highly distributed manner. Following Fodor and Pylyshyn, we concern ourselves here with those models that interpret the nodes of the networks semantically.

[6] Recent automated theorem provers which attempt to model natural deduction, such as those by John Pollock (forthcoming) and Jeff Pelletier (1982) represent as separate entities those formulae which, at the semantic level, seem to be composed of constituent formulae. For a discussion of the problem of all deductive consequences being generated in the context of the Frame problem in AI, see (Dennett 1984).

[7] This obviously has repercussions for the Syntactic Theory of the Mind proposed by Stich (1983), since on the syntactic account of cognitive science, syntax might be derived from a semantics in just this way. Interestingly, the issue of how strong a claim the LOT hypothesis is making, and whether there is a LOT, applies to Stich's syntactic programme just as much as Fodor's; the only difference between them would be whether or not the syntactic states over which the LOT quantifies, if there were one, are representational.

[8] This is possibly a similar distinction to that between transition state and instantiation theory explanations in Chapter 1 of (Cummins 1984), except that we mean something a little more general than Cummins's notion of transition state explanation, since also included amongst diachronic explanations are long scale etiological explanations such as evolutionary ones.

[9] If it turns out that some kind of punctuated equilibrium account in which evolutionary change often or mostly does not proceed by incremental changes is right (see Eldredge and Gould 1972; Gould 1980), then this point will go by the wayside. This would still not, however, be evidence for the LOT architecture being selected.

[10] If you have a sufficiently weak view of supervenient causation, then high level properties might be able to be causally efficacious without having intrinsic structure, just so long as there is intrinsic structure picked out by the basic causal properties on which they supervene. Thus you might be able to buy into our account while believing with Jaegwon Kim (1979) in supervenient causation at high levels. You might also be able to have high level causation and yet do without the need for intrinsic structures at that level if you agree with Peter Menzies' more freewheeling account of high level causation in (Menzies 1988) in which he argues for the causal efficacy of relational properties, unhampered by the requirement that they be reducible to the causal properties of a base state. For arguments against these two positions, however, see chapter 5 of Braddon–Mitchell (1988).

[11] One of us offers the beginnings of an answer in chapter 4 of Braddon–Mitchell (1988).

[12] Our point is not one regarding how the expressions in the vocabulary of some explanatory enterprise – viz., different scientific theories – manage to refer to the same objects. Our point is, rather, that it is when two different theories, which seem to taxonomise the world differently, end up displaying some significant similarities that we should infer

that there is some bona fide intrinsic structural property at work. Perhaps, in the LOT case, the one theory mentions structural realizers of properties featuring in the second. This may be in some ways similar to the concerns of Philip Kitcher (1978) and Richard Burian (1986). (we are indebted to an anonymous referee for noticing this possibility). Kitcher and Burian are concerned with successive theories which seem intuitively to be about the same things at the same levels, and have replaced each other. We, on the other hand, are concerned with concurrent theories which are concerned with properties of things at different levels – such as cardiological and anatomical theories of the heart.

REFERENCES

Braddon-Mitchell, D.: 1988, *Explanation: A Causally Constrained Pragmatic Account*, unpublished Ph.D. Thesis, Australian National University.
Burian, R.: 1986, 'On Conceptual Change in Biology', in *Evolution at the Crossroads*, MIT Press, Cambridge, Massachusetts.
Chomsky, N.: 1965, *Aspects of the Theory of Syntax*, MIT Press, Cambridge, Massachusetts.
Chomsky, N.: 1980, *Rules and Representations*, Blackwell, Oxford.
Cummins, R.: 1984, *The Nature of Psychological Explanation*, MIT Press, Cambridge, Massachusetts.
Dennett, D.: 1978, 'Current Issues in the Philosophy of Mind', *American Philosophical Quarterly* **15**, 249–62.
Dennett, D.: 1984, 'Cognitive Wheels: The Frame Problem in AI', in C. Hookaway (ed.), *Minds, Machines and Evolution*, Cambridge University Press, Cambridge.
Devitt, M. and K. Sterelny: 1987, *Language and Reality*, MIT Press, Cambridge, Massachusetts.
Eldredge, N. and S. J. Gould: 1972, 'Punctuated Equilibria: An Alternative to Phyletic Gradualism', in T. Schopf (ed.), *Models in Paleobiology*, Freeman Cooper, San Francisco.
Fodor, J.: 1976, *The Language of Thought*, Harvester Press, Sussex.
Fodor, J.: 1985, 'Fodor's Guide to Mental Representation: The Intelligent Aunty's *Vade Mecum*', *Mind* **94**, 76–99.
Fodor, J.: 1987a, *Psychosemantics*, MIT Press, Cambridge, Massachusetts.
Fodor, J.: 1987b, 'Why There Still Has to Be a Language of Thought', in J. Fodor, *Psychosemantics*, MIT Press, Cambridge, Massachusetts, pp. 135–54.
Fodor, J. and Z. Pylyshyn: 1988, 'Connectionism and Cognitive Architecture: A Critical Analysis', *Cognition* **28**, 3–71.
Gould, S. J.: 1980, 'Is a New and General Theory of Evolution Emerging?', *Paleobiology* **6**, 119–30.
Hookaway, C. (ed.): 1984, *Minds, Machines and Evolution*, Cambridge University Press, Cambridge.
Jackson, F. and P. Pettit: 1988, 'Functionalism and Broad Content', *Mind* **97**, pp. 381–400.
Kitcher, P.: 1978, 'Theories, Theorists and Conceptual Change', *The Philosophical Review* **LXXXVII** No. 4, pp. 519–47.
Menzies, P.: 1988, 'Against Causal Reductionism', *Mind* **97**, 551–74.

Pelletier, J.: 1982, 'Completely Non-Clausal, Completely Heuristically Driven Automatic Theorem Proving', *Technical Report 82–7*, Department of Computing Science, University of Alberta.

Pollock, J.: (forthcoming), 'Interest Driven Reasoning', read to the Department of Philosophy, Research School of Social Sciences, Australian National University on May 31, 1988.

Ramsey, W., S. Stich and J. Garon: 'Connectionism, Eliminativism, and the Future of Folk Psychology', forthcoming in W. Ramsey, D. Rumelhart and S. Stich (eds.), *Philosophy and Connectionist Theory*, Erlbaum, New Jersey.

Schopf, T. (ed.): 1972, *Models in Paleobiology*, Freeman Cooper, San Francisco.

Smolensky, P.: 1988, 'On the Proper Treatment of Connectionism', forthcoming in *The Behavioral and Brain Sciences* 11 [references in the text are to a preprint from the University of Colorado, 1986].

Stalnaker, R.: 1984, *Inquiry*, MIT Press, Cambridge, Massachusetts.

Stich, S.: 1983, *From Folk Psychology to Cognitive Science*, MIT Press, Cambridge, Massachusetts.

The Research School of Social Sciences
The Australian National University
Canberra ACT 2601
Australia

CHARLES E. M. DUNLOP

CONCEPTUAL DEPENDENCY AS THE LANGUAGE
OF THOUGHT[1]

> The rule of the game, therefore, is not for the reader
> to say 'You can't do that', because what we describe
> can be and has been done, to varying degrees of suc-
> cess. Rather, you may say, 'That isn't quite right',
> or 'You've oversimplified a very deep philosophical
> problem'. . . .
>
> (Rieger 1975, p. 195)

> AI must come to terms with the fact it is concerned with
> many issues that are also of interest to philosophers. I
> hope that the cooperation here will be of more·use
> than was the head-butting that has gone on between
> AI people and linguists.
>
> (Schank 1980, p. 178)

ABSTRACT. Roger Schank's research in AI takes seriously the ideas that understanding
natural language involves mapping its expressions into an internal representation scheme
and that these internal representations have a syntax appropriate for computational
operations. It therefore falls within the computational approach to the study of mind.
This paper discusses certain aspects of Schank's approach in order to assess its potential
adequacy as a (partial) model of cognition. This version of the Language of Thought
hypothesis encounters some of the same difficulties that arise for Fodor's account.

Two influential and much-discussed themes in the philosophy of mind/
cognitive science literature are (1) that understanding natural language
involves mapping its expressions onto some kind of internal representation scheme, and (2) that the resulting representations exhibit a syntax
such that they are susceptible to computational operations. These ideas
have been taken seriously in Roger Schank's artificial intelligence
projects at Yale University, where a variety of computer programs
have been based upon them. Schank's ultimate research goal is not
only to build AI systems that exhibit human-like linguistic behavior,
but also to provide a psychologically accurate computer model of
various human mental processes involved in the understanding of
language. His work, therefore, falls squarely within the 'computational'
approach to the study of mind.

63

J. H. Fetzer (ed.), Epistemology and Cognition, 63–84.
© 1991 Kluwer Academic Publishers. Printed in the Netherlands.

Although computational theories of mental phenomena are committed to the apparatus of internal representations, they are often quite vague as to the *nature* of those representations. Schank's work has the merit of describing the hypothesized representation scheme in considerable detail. Since he regards it as providing a psychologically accurate necessary condition for the use of natural language, his theory may be viewed as one version of the Language of Thought hypothesis (which Schank calls 'Conceptual Dependency' theory, abbreviated as CD).

This paper discusses some aspects of Schank's representation scheme, with an eye toward assessing its adequacy as a (partial) model of cognition.[2] I shall begin by outlining various features of the theory, and at points later on I shall try to connect it with recent philosophical work by Jerry Fodor and others. Schank's own account, I shall argue, contains many of the same pitfalls that may be found in the philosophical discussions of the Language of Thought. Some of these pitfalls will be familiar to philosophers with an interest in the computational approach to mind; others, I believe, have received little if any treatment in the literature.

1. A PRELIMINARY ARGUMENT

Considerations of parsimony, Schank believes, argue for some sort of universal, internal representation scheme in the processing of sentences (Schank 1975, p. 28; Schank and Riesbeck 1981, pp. 14–16). To illustrate, suppose that the representation scheme was not universal, but rather language-specific. In that case, a speaker of English would map sentences onto English-specific representation structures, while a speaker of French would do the same vis-à-vis French-specific structures. Let E stand for some English sentence, and F for its French equivalent, while $R(E)$ stands for the internal representation of E, and $R(F)$ for its French counterpart. Then, a translation of E to F would require (i) mapping E onto $R(E)$; (ii) correlating $R(E)$ with $R(F)$; and (iii) mapping $R(F)$ onto F. Assuming that $R(E)$ is not identical to $R(F)$, an increasing number of representations along with language-specific correlation rules of type (ii) would be required as more languages entered the picture. Matters would be considerably simpler, however, if one universal representation scheme underlay a variety of languages.

In that case, translation of an English sentence into its French equivalent would require only mapping E onto R, and then R onto F.

This appeal of an interlingual representation scheme, incidentally, was recently noted in a *Time Magazine* account of Japanese language-translating machines. The Fujitsu Company has developed devices that provide at least rough translations between English, Japanese, French, and German (additional languages are planned as well). As a researcher from Fujitsu put it: 'If we did not use interlingua, then each pair of languages would require the development of a specific set of grammatical rules and a bilingual dictionary. Interlingua acts as the hub of a wheel'.[3]

Of course, the utility of an interlingua for machine translation does not prove that monolingual speakers employ a language of thought, although it does explain why Schank, whose projects include translation, might find it appealing. Further arguments will be considered later on. Note also that the argument just canvassed on behalf of an interlingual representation scheme is silent as to the *nature* of that scheme. But Schank goes on to say a good deal about that topic. His account is distinctive in its commitment to the primacy of meaning over syntax; Conceptual Dependency is essentially a meaning representation scheme. Thus, Schank's language-processing systems do not attempt to build separate syntactic representations of natural language sentences; in fact, syntactic considerations come into play only when required in order to help resolve ambiguities, find linguistic units that have been predicted by semantic features, etc.

2. CONCEPTUAL DEPENDENCY THEORY: VOCABULARY

Schank's work on natural language understanding has focused primarily on the representation of actions – broadly construed so as to include natural forces as 'agents'. Thus, 'John hit Mary' and 'Hurricane Gilbert hit Mexico' fall under the purview of actions, so conceived. With an eye toward obvious objections to this view, Schank emphasizes that his aim is to capture how ordinary speakers conceptualize the world, irrespective of whether such an account will withstand close ontological scrutiny (Schank 1973a, p. 206; Schank 1975, p. 41; cf. Rieger 1975, p. 187). It remains to be seen, of course, whether ordinary speakers do in fact view the world in the way that Schank's account dictates. If they do, and their view harbors some incoherence, then a computer model of their view will naturally exhibit the same incoherence.

The core of Schank's internal representation scheme, Conceptual Dependency, involves an ACT, which is an action performed on some OBJECT. The actor is known as a PICTURE PRODUCER (PP). ACTs are directed toward a LOCATION, which indicates their DIRECTION, and may result in an OBJECT's being in a particular STATE, or a RECIPIENT's coming to possess an OBJECT. From these ingredients, a conceptualization may be formed, i e., a representation structure which indicates what was done by whom, to what, etc.

These ingredients of CD theory sound suspiciously close to categories of natural language, but Schank takes pains to insist that the conceptual level is *extra*linguistic:

We have required that the meaning representation that we use be language-free . . . . [W]e began to believe that language and thought were separable structures (Schank 1975, p. 7).

What does this mean? In its most benign sense, the point would appear to be that internal representations are not identical to natural language sentences. But while this may be true under a narrow interpretation, Conceptual Dependency vocabulary bears a striking relationship to familiar terms in natural language. Consider, for instance, the eleven[4] primitive ACTs in CD theory (Schank 1975, pp. 40-44; Schank 1981, pp. 17-25):

Physical ACTS

PROPEL	Apply a force to
MOVE	Move a body part
INGEST	Take something to the inside of an animate object
EXPEL	Take something from inside an animate object, and force it out
GRASP	To physically grasp an object

ACTS That Cause State Changes

PTRANS	To change the location of something
ATRANS	To change an abstract relationship

ACTS Used Primarily as Instruments of other ACTS

SPEAK   To produce a sound
ATTEND   To direct a sense organ toward a particular
              stimulus

Mental ACTS

MTRANS   To transfer information
MBUILD   To create or combine thoughts

Schank's assumption is that the meaning of action-sentences can be captured by way of these eleven primitives. Consider, for example, the sentence 'John ate a frog'. Its CD analysis looks like this (Schank 1975, p. 24):

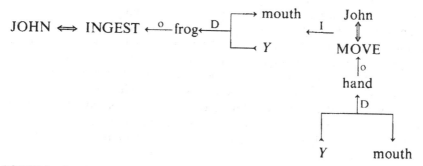

JOHN is the PP; INGEST is the ACT, and the symbol '⟺' marks a mutual dependency relation. The OBJECT of the ACT is designated by 'frog'; 'D' indicates the ACT's DIRECTION; and the INSTRUMENT of John's ACT is yet another ACT in which JOHN MOVEd his hand.

In what sense is this representation scheme 'extralinguistic'? To be sure MTRANS and MBUILD are not (so far as I know) terms of any natural language, and MOVE is defined more restrictively than its English language counterpart, although the meaning of INGEST offers no surprise. JOHN, according to Schank, is not the English name 'John', but rather a pointer to all the information that we have about John (apparently, a reduction of objects to bundles of properties is ultimately envisaged[5]). But if the categories just outlined actually represent the categories in which we think, there is little evidence that it is 'language-free'; indeed, it seems perverse to maintain that category terms that can be *defined* are extralinguistic. Moreover, Schank offers no argument for such a requirement. The success of his computational models does not derive from that assumption, and other considerations (philosophical, psychological, linguistic) may point in the opposite direction. Jerry Fodor once suggested that 'the language of thought may be very like a natural language' (Fodor 1975, p. 156).

The MTRANS primitive, denoting transfer of information, deserves special notice. Information conveyed in an MTRANS is always a complete conceptualization (corresponding to a proposition), with MTRANS taking the recipient case. Information transfer here is thought of in terms of a proximate source and a receiver. The eye, for example, may be regarded as the proximate information source. What is the 'receiver' here? Schank answers that information first goes to a Conceptual Processor, where all conscious thoughts occur. This CP, then, is viewed as the recipient. From the Conceptual Processor, information may go to an Intermediate Memory (as when we remember a telephone number just long enough to dial it), or to Long Term Memory (in cases where we need the telephone number on a later occasion). These sorts of mental categories have been argued for by various cognitive psychologists, and some interesting experiments have been cited in support of them. But I want to focus here for a moment on an odd restriction that Schank imposes on Long Term Memory, or LTM. He writes that it

contains all the information that is known by a person. We postulate that only true facts are stored in LTM and that false things are derived from them. (Schank 1975, p. 44)

Schank's 'postulate' (that only truths are stored in Long Term Memory), besides being unnecessary, has little to recommend it. After all, whether or not something is true often cannot be perceptually discriminated by an observer, and there is no reason to suppose that false beliefs arising in such circumstances cannot get into Long Term memory.[6] To clarify, suppose that I read in an encyclopedia that Abraham Lincoln was the sixteenth President of the United States, and suppose also that someone else (owing to a misprint) reads in a different encyclopedia that Lincoln was the fifteenth President. It is scarcely plausible to suppose that the information *I* got goes into my LTM, while the other person's information does not get represented in LTM; our relationships to our respective sources of information were virtually identical. Well, perhaps Schank means that what goes into each of our LTMs is not the encyclopedia's information *simpliciter*, but rather the information *that the encyclopedia reported the information*. (This might provide the basis for Schank's claim that falsehoods are *derived from* our stock of stored truths.) There may, of course, be situations where this occurs, but no plausible psychological theory can insist that all information stored in LTM is of this kind; we frequently fail to remember where we got a particular piece of information. In such cases it is the *information*, not the *source + report*, that we normally retain in long term memory. There is evidence that Schank agrees, for he represents the sentence 'John read about Nixon in the Encyclopedia' as follow (Schank 1975, p. 61):

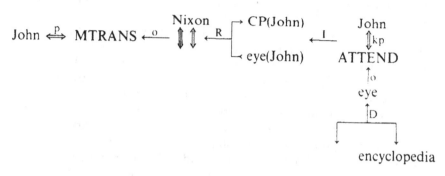

Schank adds that 'What John MTRANsed here were assorted unknown facts about Nixon'; he does not say that John MTRANSed the fact that the encyclopedia was reporting facts about Nixon. Since the putative facts may be incorrect, but may nonetheless be accepted by John, the 'postulate' that Long Term Memory contains only truths is untenable. In terms of our example, we should say also that at least some of what goes into John's Long Term Memory is not knowledge.

Why, then, does Schank endorse the curious doctrine that Long Term Memory contains only truths? The primary reason, I suggest, is that he takes himself to be proposing a knowledge representation scheme. In Schank's words, '"Know" is represented as "being in the LTM of"' (Schank 1975, p. 62). Moreover, I suggest, Schank realizes that knowledge requires truth. Thus, in order to accommodate these two ideas – (1) that a knowledge representation scheme is being proposed, and (2) that knowledge requires truth – it is stipulated that the system's Long Term Memory only contains truths. From here it is not too difficult to conclude (as Schank in fact does conclude) that knowledge and belief are 'virtually identical'.

Although this treatment of knowledge representation is quite common in the artificial intelligence literature, it fares rather badly on two grounds. First, by requiring that all stored propositions be true, it ignores the question of how *mis*representation is possible, although this is a question that models of human cognition can scarcely afford to dismiss. And second, it fails to recognize that knowledge representation, properly conceived, involves considerably more than just the well-organized storage of true propositions. To determine just what else is needed comes as no easy task, as post-Gettier epistemology has made clear. But knowledge representation systems that ignore this question are, I submit, parading under a false banner.

Earlier, it was mentioned that CD theory provides a computational advantage for translation from one language to another. The primitive ACTs of CD theory are also interesting insofar as they allow for a common representation of sentences that have significant overlapping conceptual content. This too has a computational advantage, insofar as allowable inferences associated with ACT primitives only need to be stored once in the system. For example, (1) 'John gave Mary a book', (2) 'Mary received a book from John', (3) 'John bought Mary a book' and (4) 'John stole a book for Mary' would all be diagrammed using the ATRANS primitive (for abstract transfer of possession). This ATRANS primitive serves as the common connecting point for probable inferences concerning transfer of possession (Who has the object now? Who had it before? Did John want Mary to have a book?), thereby obviating the need to store the same inference rules redundantly. Of course, the four sentences in this example have important differences of meaning also. Such differences would tend to be brought out by different Instrumental case diagrams (indicating the means by which the ACT was accomplished).

Despite the inferential (computational) advantage accruing to ACT primitives, there are times when this approach does not work very well. For example, one of the inferences from EXPEL is that the EXPELled object was previously INGESTed. But the sentence 'John spat at Mary' is represented in terms of John's EXPELling saliva (Schank 1975, p. 58), although in most instances saliva is manufactured, not INGESTed. It is hardly surprising that a mere eleven ACT primitives should fail to capture the core meaning of most natural-language action verbs. The problem becomes particularly acute, however, for action terms which operate against a background of social institutions and conventions. As Schank acknowledges, 'if we have 'John kissed Mary', our mapping of kiss into 'MOVE lips towards' will not simplify the problem one bit' (Schank 1975, p. 81). Similar points could be made about 'The policeman gave me a parking ticket' and 'My friend has been married and divorced three times'. In all such cases, ACT primitives appear to be of little service; what is needed in these particular cases is knowledge of appropriate social institutions.

Schank does not indicate how he thinks we come to possess our representation language. Suppose, as some writers have, that it is innate. In that case, one would expect its ACT categories to be universal. This need not imply that all the categories of CD are employed in every possible culture: in discussing the notion of transfer of ownership, Schank remarks that 'it is possible to conceive of a culture and therefore a language that would have a different set of those abstract relations or none at all (and thus no ATRANS)' (1975, p. 55). In such an instance, the universal ACT primitive ATRANS would simply not get actualized. But another speculation suggests that CD might not turn out to be universal after all: 'If in fact, there exists a culture where life is viewed as a continuum rather than a series of distinct actor-action events, Conceptual Dependency would not do as a conceptual model of such a culture' (Schank 1973a, p. 206). In that case, Schank's recourse would presumably be either to hold (1) the (very unparsimonious) view that each of us has multiple innate representation languages, perhaps only one of which actually gets employed by a given individual, or (2) that the representation language is not innate. On the latter alternative, one's representation language would presumably be acquired in a linguistic environment, which raises the suspicion that it may not really be a necessary condition for the understanding of natural language (cf. Fodor 1975, Chap. 2, for further arguments). For if the representation language itself could be acquired (without an underlying language), why could a natural language not be acquired this way also?

3. CONCEPTUAL SYNTAX

Despite the subordination of natural-language syntax to meaning in Schank's sentence analyzer, there is considerable emphasis given to the formal structure of Conceptual Dependency diagrams. Here are some examples (Schank 1975, pp. 38-9):

(1)   PP <==> ACT

(2)   ACT <--$\overset{O}{}$-- PP

(3)   ACT <--$\overset{D}{}$-- $\begin{array}{l} \longrightarrow PP_1 \\ \\ \longrightarrow PP_2 \end{array}$

(4)   ACT <--$\overset{R}{}$-- $\begin{array}{l} \longrightarrow PP_1 \\ \\ \longrightarrow PP_2 \end{array}$

(5)   ACT <--$\overset{I}{}$-- $\begin{array}{c} \wedge \\ \parallel \\ \parallel \\ V \end{array}$

Rule (1) says that Picture Producers (usually, animate agents) can perform actions; Rule (2) means that ACTs can have objects; Rule (3) means that ACTs can have directions (a variable in place of PP_1 or PP_2 indicates an unknown position). Rule (4) indicates that ACTs can have recipients. And Rule (5) says that ACTs have instruments that are themselves complete (completeness is shown by the double lines between two arrowheads). Rules (2) through (5) collectively represent conceptual cases – modifiers of ACTs – and a specific number of them (either two or three) is required by every ACT.

In some instances, the CD syntax rules *permit* a particular structure; in other cases they *require* it. One such requirement involves the Instrumental case. Returning to the CD representation of 'John ate a frog', notice that while the Instrumental case depiction is a reasonable inference, it does not represent information explicitly given in the sample sentence (John could have done this even though he possessed no hands). In fact, although Schank will insist that ACTs always have instruments, he frequently omits their depiction in instances where the instrument was not expressly specified, and cannot be known with virtual certainty.[7] If the instrument is not filled in by the *analysis* of a sentence into CD, it can be obtained by an inference mechanism that relies on default judgments.

Whether or not instrumental ACTS are explicitly shown, however, the requirement that every ACT must have an Instrumental case encounters a familiar logical difficulty.[8] Since the instrument of an ACT is itself a complete (and distinct) conceptualization, the occurrence of one ACT will actually require an infinity of ACTs. For example, suppose that John eats ice cream, and that the instrumental ACT is his moving a spoon to his mouth. Now, the conceptual representation of 'John moves a spoon to his mouth' will itself require an instrument, e.g., 'John activates the muscles in his arm', and so on. The problem is that if the performance of any given one ACT presupposes an infinity of ACTs, no ACTs will be possible at all. Schank, unfortunately, views the Instrumental case requirement only as providing a notational inconvenience:

Since an analysis of this kind is not particularly useful and is quite bothersome to write, we do not do so. Rather, whenever we represent a conceptualization we only diagram the main conceptualization and such instrumental conceptualizations as might be necessary to illustrate whatever part we are making (Schank 1975, p. 33; cf. Schank 1973a, p. 201).

He continues:

[T]he ACT in a conceptualization is really the name of a set of *sequential* actions that it subsumes (and are considered to be part of it). These instrumental conceptualizations *are not causally related* since they are *not actually separable* from each other. In actuality, they express one event and are thus considered to be part of one conceptualization. The rule is then, that one conceptualization (which may have many conceptualizations as part of it) is considered to be representative of one event (*Ibid.*, p. 34, italics added).

It is certainly plausible to maintain that the name of an event somehow encompasses its constituents, as the phrase 'the third game of the 1988 World Series' might subsume a variety of events making up that baseball game. It is true also that in ordinary circumstances we do not carry the analysis of an act into its constituents very far. But these points do not obviate the fact that the Instrumental case requirement is logically committed to an infinity of constituents for any ACT. Each of those constituents must in turn be an ACT performed by an agent. Moreover, it is not at all clear what Schank means in claiming that the subsumed instrumental conceptualizations are not 'actually separable', since he also maintains that they are sequential. If they are sequential, they certainly are separable, and they should therefore at least be candidates for causal interaction. In short, the universal requirement of Instrumental cases is highly problematic.[9]

4. PERCEPTION AND IMAGE-REPRESENTATION

As noted earlier, MTRANS involves the movement of a conceptualization into an agent's CP, IM, or LTM, either from the CP of some other agent, or perhaps through memory or sense perception. So, if Mary informed Bill that his car had been wrecked, a conceptualization is 'transferred' from Mary's CP to Bill's, although the term 'transfer' is something of a misnomer, since the information does not vacate Mary's CP in going to Bill's. On the other hand, if Bill momentarily noticed some event that he was later able to recall, there would presumably have been some 'movement' of information into LTM once the noticed event was no longer in Bill's consciousness.

Schank's treatment of perception raises some very interesting and difficult issues. Consider his representation of the sentence 'John saw Bill swimming' (Schank 1975, p. 61):[10]

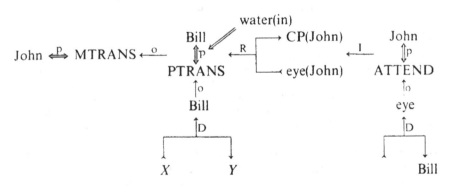

Given Schank's account of various ACT terms, this diagram appears to say that John transferred from his eye to his Conceptual Processor the conceptualization that Bill was swimming.[11] It should be remembered that this is intended, not as an account of perception *simpliciter*, but rather as a description of how a layman represents the perceptual process. Of course, few laymen could be expected to use categories such as 'conceptual processor' and 'conceptualization' (see the end of

Section 5 below for further discussion), but perhaps the point here is just that John became aware that Bill was swimming, on the basis of seeing him. No doubt there is something right about this account, insofar as John's conceptualization was derived from sense perception.

At the same time, as one's account of perception becomes more sophisticated, some limitations of conceptual primitives emerge. It is important to bear in mind that, in Schank's account, the object of an MTRANS is always a conceptualization. But, according to the above diagram, the *conceptualization*, before going to the CP, was somehow *in the eye*! There is, I think, no need to be overly literal about what this means: it might involve a retinal image, or a series of images,[12] or perhaps even a percept or something of the sort. Nonetheless, even on this liberal reading, the MTRANS account of perception involves a major problem. The problem is that a conceptual representation must be *constructed from* the available sensory information;[13] it does not occur 'ready-made' at the sensory level. And what ends up being cognitively available to an agent is considerably *less than* what was given in perception. In the current example, visual information received by John includes such items as whether Bill was nude or wearing swimming trunks, whether he was in a lake or a pool, whether anyone else was near him, whether the sun was bright, etc. – none of which appears in the CD graph displayed above. I do not mean that this omission represents a mistake; no plausible CD diagram would include a description of everything 'contained in' the sensory data, for we are very seldom aware of everything we perceive. There is, in other words, a considerable gap between sensory reception and conceptual representation. Although the process by which the one gives rise to the other is not well understood, the phenomenon itself seems uncontroversial. What the MTRANS account fails to detail, or even to acknowledge, is the process by which a specific piece of information is extracted from the greater wealth of information available at the sensory level.

This point is important enough to warrant consideration from a slightly different point of view. A sensory representation, be it an image, image series, or percept, has the informational richness of a picture.[14] An interpretation of it leads to an informationally impoverished cognitive counterpart. And this interpretation requirement shows why a sensory content (imagistic or otherwise) is not by itself sufficient to yield the content of a Schankian conceptualization. If one asks, 'What proposition does this image (or sensory content) convey?', there

is no single answer, and *a fortiori* no single *correct* answer. The reason
is that propositions have truth values, whereas icons do not. As Jerry
Fodor has written:

To a first approximation, the kind of thing that can get a truth value is an assignment of
some property to some object. A representational system must therefore provide appropriate vehicles for expressing such assignments. Under what conditions, then, is a representation adequate to express the assignment of a property to an object? Well, one
condition which surely must be satisfied is that the representation specify *which* property
is being assigned and which object it is being assigned to. The trouble with trying to
truth-value icons is that they provide no way of doing the former (Fodor 1975, p. 181).

Fodor's idea is that a given image can represent any number of propositions. The *same* image (sensory content), for example, could yield the
proposition that Mary is fat, that Mary has a perm, that Mary is wearing
clothes, and so on. We may, of course, assign an interpretation –
perhaps consisting of a conjunction of propositions – to an sensory
representation, but the point is that the assignment involves extrasen-
sory factors.[15]

It appears once again that the attempt to account for perception in
terms of MTRANSing a conceptualization from a sensory component
to LTM has serious limitations. In part, the problem arises from at-
tempting to make conceptual primitives bear too much weight. But the
underlying issue is really just a version of a major issue in the study of
perception: How does sensory information mediate between the external world and a percipient's mental model thereof? No doubt it was
not Schank's intention to address this problem in any depth, and, as
noted earlier, it may be that his account does approximate the way in
which 'ordinary' people think about perception. No argument is provided, incidentally, to show that this is the case. In fact, it strikes me as
unlikely that the layman has any view at all about whether propositional
structures are contained, say, in a retinal image, or constructed from
that image. But if the layman opts for the first account, as is suggested
by Schank's analysis, the present discussion indicates that the 'common
sense' account cannot be extended very naturally into a more accurate
and complete version.

5. IS CD NECESSARY?

Does the use of CD graphs, including ACT primitives, make for a
reasonable viewing of the way in which human beings represent events?
Let us begin by canvassing some arguments on its behalf:

(1)   Sentences that we understand are generally not stored in the form in which we encounter them. 'If two sentences with different words mean the same thing, then it is not easy to recall which particular words were used after a certain time' (Schank 1975, p. 17).

(2)   Although sentences in a natural language may be ambiguous, there must be some way of representing unambiguously each possible meaning, since 'the original meaning that the speaker chose to impart was unambiguous' (Ibid., p. 15).

(3)   Human hearers are able to supply information that was not explicitly given in a natural language sentence. The inferential mechanisms that humans can apply to natural language sentences would not be economically accounted for in terms of natural language storage (Schank 1981, p. 16).

To take these points in order: it is true that understanders engage in automatic paraphrasing, and without special effort they cannot repeat verbatim much of what they have heard. But it does not *follow* that the paraphrase must be represented in anything like CD graphs. While CD representation certainly provides a possible account, it is not obviously preferable to some alternative. Might it not be the case that my representation of the meaning of natural language sentences is stored in the form of natural language expressions?

Whatever the ruling on this issue, however, the appeal to CD representation as a *required* vehicle for natural language understanding must face a logical dilemma. For, if understanding natural language requires us to map natural language expressions onto CD, then in what does our understanding of CD consist? Clearly, it cannot be maintained that we in turn map CD expressions onto some other type of representation, for an infinite regress would then be under way. So it must be possible for us to understand CD expressions without mapping them in turn onto a meaning representation language. But if we can understand CD representation without doing any sort of mapping, then why should it not be possible to understand natural language without doing any mapping either?

Fodor has considered this argument, and has offered a reply to it. He draws an analogy between a human's mapping of natural language onto an inner representation scheme, and a compiler's producing machine code from a higher-level language. Although a compiler (or interpreter) is required to render the higher-level language usable, there is obviously no need for a second compiler to make the object code usable. Fodor writes:

> What avoids an infinite regression of compilers is the fact that the machine is *built* to use the machine language. Roughly, the machine language differs from the input/output language in that its formulae correspond directly to computationally relevant physical states and operations of the machine . . . .
>
> [T]here are two ways in which it can come about that a device (including, presumably, a person) understands a predicate. In one case, the device has and employs a representation of the extension of the predicate, where the representation is itself given in some language that the device understands. In the second case, the device is so constructed that its use of the predicate (e.g., in computations) comport [*sic*] with the conditions that such a representation would specify. I want to say that the first is true of predicates in the natural languages people learn and the second of predicates in the internal language in which they think (Fodor 1975, p. 66).

This analogy between machines and humans breaks down in one crucial respect, however. For as Fodor himself has pointed out elsewhere (Fodor 1981, ch. 8), the meaning of anything couched in machine's 'representation language' is entirely parasitic upon the higher-level source code (whose meaning may in turn be dependent upon a programmer's intentions). A given bit pattern, in other words, might represent an ASCII alphabetic character, a positive integer in base ten, or a two's-complement negative number. There is nothing intrinsically representative about the machine-level 'language'. Yet a 'language of thought' such as Schank's (or, for that matter, Fodor's) must possess its representational power *independently* of any higher-level language, since it is supposed to be a precondition of learning or processing a higher-level (natural) language. Machine language, however, possesses no (classical denotative) semantics of its own; in a word, what the computer 'understands' has no meaning. What kind of understanding is this supposed to be? Needed, of course, is a convincing account of how Conceptual Dependency (or the Language of Thought) gets its reference to the world. This is the problem that John Haugeland dubbed 'the mystery of original meaning' (Haugeland 1985, pp. 119ff), and it remains a major stumbling block for theories of mind that appeal to a Language of Thought.[16]

Turning at last to the second argument for CD representation (concerning the need for unambiguous representation), although the various meanings of ambiguous sentences should be susceptible to unambiguous representation, it does not *follow* that the representation must be inter-lingual, no matter whether the ambiguity is syntactic or semantic in origin. The multiple interpretations of syntactically ambiguous sentences (e.g., 'Flying planes can be dangerous') as well as semantically ambiguous sentences (e.g., 'I went to the bank') can be specified unambiguously in English. In fact, we quite commonly do so.

The third point (concerning inference) has already been touched upon (see Section 2 above). There I argued that, although inferential parsimony was alleged to derive from a universal, language-independent representation scheme, neither inferential adequacy nor language-independence can in fact properly be claimed for it. Here I want to add that CD theory fails to provide a plausible account of inferences involving intensional contexts.

Consider the sentence 'John believes that the Evening Star is red'. Even though the Evening Star is identical to the Morning Star, the substitution of the phrase 'Morning Star' into our example sentence may not be truth preserving. As is well known, extensionally equivalent terms are not intersubstitutable in belief-contexts, or indeed in *any* contexts describing a psychological state. Notice also, however, that even with *in*tensional equivalence added, the terms may not be intersubstitutable in those contexts either; the sentence 'John believes that horses are four-legged and eat grass' does not entail 'John believes that horses are graminivorous quadrupeds', despite the relevant synonymies. This is not merely a point about the relationship between sentences, for there is a related psychological point here as well. Insofar as the ascription of beliefs to an agent provides a vehicle for explaining that agent's actions, we need to know, not just what the agent believes, but (so to speak) how he or she believes it. The mental representations of the two sentences about horses are presumably different[17] and can therefore be expected to produce somewhat different causal consequences. Thus, it should not be supposed that both descriptions of John's belief are equally apt.

The connection of these reflections with ACT primitives is as follows. Even if ACT primitives captured the meaning of natural language verbs, it does not follow that they can enter into the propositional content of anyone's psychological attitudes. Take, for example, Schank's CD representation of the sentence 'John remembered that he forgot to bring his sandwich to school' (Schank 1975, p. 60):

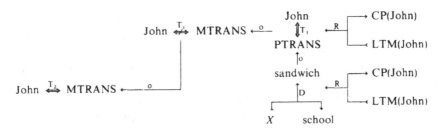

According to this diagram, the *content* of John's memory is approximately this: he remembered that he failed to MTRANS into his CP the fact of PTRANSing his sandwich to school. What has happened here is Schank has incorporated a theory about *how* people represent things into an account of *what they represent*. And in this case, the account is highly implausible. Memories, like beliefs, figure into explanations of action; hence, if John really remembered that he failed to MTRANS something, he might be expected, say, to issue a report couched in those terms. But, unless John happens to be one of Schank's disciples intent upon making an idiosyncratic point, he will do no such thing. I conclude that there is a large class of sentences–those describing the contents of psychological attitudes for which the use of ACT primitives in CD representations will not work. They simply do not accurately depict the contents of anyone's psychological states. Or, perhaps more accurately, they fail to allow for a distinction between *de dicto* and *de re* construals of those states.

6. CONCLUSION

There is no doubt that computer programs built upon Conceptual Dependency theory have produced (in carefully delimited microworlds[18]) some interesting and striking results. Viewed from a pragmatic perspective, this approach is salutary; it may, for example, lead to increasingly user-friendly machines with natural language interfaces. But the goal of many researchers in artificial intelligence, Schank included, is to produce a psychologically valid computer model of human mental processes. I have set forth a number of serious difficulties which Conceptual Dependency theory – the bedrock of Schank's approach – must face. These difficulties, I believe, collectively constitute a strong reason for doubting that Conceptual Dependency theory provides (a component of) a plausible theory of mental representation.

I shall conclude by reiterating three problems that strike me as most important. (1) The reduction of human actions to a small group of primitives has little promise of succeeding, as does the parallel project of reducing objects to properties; (2) Primitive ACTS cannot plausibly serve to capture the contents of intentional states; this provides a second reason for thinking that Conceptual Dependency diagrams cannot get by with ACT primitives everywhere replacing natural language action verbs; and (3) The kind of project envisaged by Schank ultimately requires a 'naturalized' semantics for the 'language of thought', whether that 'language' appears in a human being or a machine. Very little work has been done to date in this area, and in this respect, Schank's program is no worse off than many other computational theories of mind. I do not know whether such a project of 'naturalized' semantics can possibly succeed. If points (1) and (2) are correct, however, the 'language of thought' requiring a naturalized semantics will not look very much like the language of Conceptual Dependency Theory.

NOTES

[1] An ancestor of this paper was written while I was on sabbatical leave from the University of Michigan, Flint, during which time I held a fellowship in the Computer Science Department of Wright State University. Revisions were made while I held a Visiting Lectureship at the University of Waikato. I am grateful to these three institutions for their support, and to James H. Fetzer, David Hemmendinger, and Edwin Hung for helpful comments on earlier versions.

[2] CD theory has played a less explicit role in Schank's most recent work (Schank 1977, 1980, 1982, and 1986), where the aim has been to develop accounts of 'higher-level' knowledge structures. Nonetheless, much of CD theory is embedded in the later work as well; consequently, its difficulties tend also to be absorbed into the more recent accounts.

[3] *Time Magazine* (International Edition), July 24, 1989, p. 64.

[4] The number of primitives Conceptual Dependency theory has varied; at one time fourteen were employed. This is understandable, given Schank's experimental approach to the issue of representation.

[5] Christopher Riesbeck writes:

What is lacking is a well-defined internal structure for PPs [Picture Producers]. Presumably a PP is a bundle of features, but how many features there are, how many it takes for an object to qualify as a certain kind of PP, how features relate to each other, how features which are discrete relate to the perception of a world that is not, all these questions are unanswered (Riesbeck, in Schank 1975, p. 114).

Although Riesbeck registers no skepticism about the *possibility* of providing 'a well-defined internal structure for PPs', the history of unsuccessful attempts by phenomenalists to 'reduce' physical objects to collections of sensory data suggests that a workable "feature" account of PPs is not likely to be forthcoming.

[6] This kind of reflection led Fodor to argue for 'methodological solipsism', one point being that psychological explanations involve opaque construals of mental states (Fodor 1981, Chapter 9). If you and I are presented with different examples of a metallic substance, gold in color, we may both acquire the belief that 'My sample is genuine gold'. And *pace* Schank, this belief may go into both of our LTMs even though I was viewing iron pyrite, and you were viewing the genuine article. In this case my LTM contains a false belief, while yours contains a true one.

[7] For example, the representation of 'John punched Mary' would show John's moving his fist as the instrumental ACT, while the CD representation of 'John went to New York' would not specify the instrumental ACT (he might have taken a plane or a bus or a train, etc.).

[8] The universal requirement of an Instrumental case was explicitly absent in Schank's early discussions. See Schank 1972, especially pp. 572 and 574.

[9] It should be remembered that Conceptual Dependency theory is intended, in part, as a model of human psychology. But no psychological argument is provided for claiming that we must represent every action as having an instrument. Here, defenders of 'basic actions' might extend their ontological claims into the psychological realm, the idea being that basic actions constitute a necessary ingredient in our representation of actions.

[10] Notice that no distinction is drawn here between (1) 'John saw Bill swimming', and (2) 'John saw that Bill was swimming'. In fact, Schank's version of CD theory does not appear to distinguish these two expressions. Since the object clause of (1) is the object of an MTRANS, it can go into LTM, and therefore serve an object of knowledge. But this must mean that the object clause of (1) is being regarded as propositional.

[11] Swimming, of course, means more than moving oneself about in the water, but Schank employs the current shorthand just for the purpose of illustration.

[12] See, for example, Dretske (1981, ch. 6, p. 145). The entire Chapter 6 of his book is an excellent and fascinating study of perception from the standpoint of information theory.

[13] In the example under discussion, much of the sensory information is visual, but important clues may also include proprioceptive data. Information concerning turning of the head, for example, is valuable for determining whether it is the perceived object or the percipient that is moving.

[14] This analogy is suggested by Dretske, *op. cit.*, pp. 137-143, and does not imply that sensory representations need be imagistic.

[15] It is worth noting that other sorts of representation schemes are subject to the same point. The inscription 'my banjo', for example, could be taken as a referring phrase, or as a series of alphabetic characters. Context and convention, not the 'representation itself' are the crucial determiners.

[16] For interesting, related discussions of this issue, see Fetzer (1988a, 1989) and Searle (1980).

Fodor has recently tackled the problem of a naturalized semantics (Fodor 1987, Chapter 4), espousing a version of the causal theory of content. The causal connection between an object (e.g., horse) and an appropriate internal token ('horse') may be mediated by intentional links. This would appear to undercut the claim that a naturalized semantics has been achieved. Fodor deals with this issue by claiming that 'For purposes of semantic naturalization, *it's the existence of a reliable mind/world correlation that counts, not the mechanisms by which that correlation is effected*' (p. 122, Fodor's italics). Who says so? It looks to me as if this is pure stipulation, and that semantic naturalization is achieved by leaving something essential—a description of the causal mechanisms—out of the story. Once the underlying intentional mechanisms are described, however, the claim to semantic naturalization for internal tokens loses its plausibility.

[17] Even if they were the same, however, it would not follow that the respective beliefs were the same. As Putnam has repeatedly urged— most recently in Putnam 1988—agents' beliefs are a function, not only of mental representation, but of the contexts in which agents are embedded.

[18] Dreyfus 1979 has built an extensive case for his contention that the results obtained in such microworlds do not admit of generalization, and do not constitute an appropriate model for human mental processes.

REFERENCES

Dennett, Daniel C. and Douglas R. Hofstadter (eds.): 1981, *The Mind's I*, Basic Books, New York.

Dretske, Fred I.: 1981, *Knowledge and the Flow of Information*, The MIT Press, Cambridge.

Dreyfus, Hubert L.: 1979, *What Computers Can't Do: The Limits of Artificial Intelligence* (revised edition), Harper Colophon Books, New York.

Fetzer, James H.: 1988a, 'Signs and Minds: An Introduction to the Theory of Semiotic Systems', in *Aspects of Artificial Intelligence*, Kluwer Academic Publishers, Dordrecht, pp. 133–161.

Fetzer, James H. (ed.): 1988b, *Aspects of Artificial Intelligence*, Kluwer Academic Publishers, Dordrecht.

Fetzer, James H.: 1989, 'Language and Mentality: Computational, Representational, and Dispositional Conceptions', *Behaviorism* 17, 21–39.

Fodor, Jerry A.: 1975, *The Language of Thought*, Thomas Y. Crowell Company, Inc, New York.

Fodor, Jerry A.: 1981, *Representations*, The MIT Press, Cambridge.

Fodor, Jerry A,: 1987, *Psychosemantics*, The MIT Press, Cambridge.

Haugeland, John: 1985, *Artificial Intelligence: The Very Idea*, The MIT Press, Cambridge.

Putnam, Hilary: 1987, *Representation and Reality*, The MIT Press, Cambridge.

Rieger, Charles J. III: 1975, 'Conceptual Memory and Inference', in Roger Schank, *Conceptual Information Processing*, Elsevier, Amsterdam.

Schank, Roger: 1972, 'Conceptual Dependency: A Theory of Natural Language Understanding', *Cognitive Psychology* 3, 552–631.

Schank, Roger: 1973a, 'Identification of Conceptualizations Underlying Natural Languages', in Schank and Colby, *Computer Models of Thought and Language*, W. H. Freeman and Company, San Francisco, pp. 187–247.

Schank, Roger C. and Kenneth Mark Colby: 1973b, *Computer Models of Thought and Language*, W. H. Freeman and Company, San Francisco.

Schank, Roger: 1975, *Conceptual Information Processing*, Elsevier, Amsterdam.

Schank, Roger and Robert Abelson: 1977, *Scripts, Plans, Goals and Understanding*, Lawrence Erlbaum Associates, Hillsdale, New Jersey.

Schank, Roger: 1980, 'Language and Memory', reprinted in Barbara J. Grosz, Karen Spark Jones, and Bonnie Lynn Webber: 1986, *Readings in Natural Language Processing*, Morgan Kauffman Publishers, Inc., Los Altos, California, pp. 171–91.

Schank, Roger C. and Christopher Riesbeck: 1981, *Inside Computer Understanding*, Lawrence Erlbaum Associates, Hillsdale, New Jersey.

Schank, Roger C.: 1982, *Dynamic Memory*, Cambridge University Press, Cambridge.

Schank, Roger C.: 1986, *Explanation Patterns*, Lawrence Erlbaum Associates, Hillsdale, New Jersey.

Searle, John R.: 1980, 'Minds, Brains, and Programs', reprinted as Chapter 22 of Dennett and Hofstadter, 1981.

Dept of Philosophy
University of Michigan, Flint
Flint, Michigan 48502
U.S.A.

DAVID COLE

FUNCTIONALISM AND INVERTED SPECTRA

ABSTRACT. Functionalism, a philosophical theory, has empirical consequences. Functionalism predicts that where systematic transformations of sensory input occur and are followed by behavioral accommodation in which normal function of the organism is restored such that the causes and effects of the subject's psychological states return to those of the period prior to the transformation, there will be a return of qualia or subjective experiences to those present prior to the transform. A transformation of this type that has long been of philosophical interest is the possibility of an inverted spectrum. Hilary Putnam argues that the physical possibilty of *acquired* spectrum inversion refutes functionalism. I argue, however, that in the absence of empirical results no *a priori* arguments against functionalism, such as Putnam's, can be cogent. I sketch an experimental situation which would produce acquired spectrum inversion. The mere existence of qualia inversion would constitute no refutation of functionalism; only its persistence after behavioral accommodation to the inversion would properly count against functionalism. The cumulative empirical evidence from experiments on image inversion suggests that the results of actual spectrum inversion would confirm rather than refute functionalism.

Functionalism is attractive because it solves certain ontological problems of type-type identity theory while at the same time satisfying the intuitions which made some behavioristic analyses of mental states plausible, holding that there are essential connections between context/stimuli, behavior, and mental states. The connections are causal and thus functionalism reflects the new respectability of causality in philosophical theories. But functionalism is not bound by what now appears to have been a bugbear of behaviorism, namely the methodological prohibition of the inner.

I shall argue here that functionalism is also closely connected with specific experimental outcomes: functionalism predicts that where systematic transformations of sensory input occur and are followed by behavioral accommodation in which normal function of the organism is restored such that the causes and effects of the subject's psychological states return to those of the period prior to the transformation, there will be a return of qualia to those prior to the transform. Qualia are the conscious subjective sensory experiences characteristically had in perception but also present in hallucination and afterimages. Here a

J. H. Fetzer (ed.), Epistemology and Cognition, 85–100.
© 1991 Kluwer Academic Publishers. Printed in the Netherlands.

systematic transformation is one that preserves information and so is reversible, such as shifting all auditory input up in pitch an octave, for example, by using a frequency doubler.

A transformation of this type that has long been of philosophical interest is the possibility of an inverted spectrum. This possibility has been of interest especially for epistemological reasons: it poses a problem for our *knowledge* of other minds. How can I know that those who behave, in all respects, just as I do have subjective mental experiences that are the same (type identical) with my own? Might they not have quite different qualia? The intuitive possibility of an inverted spectrum thus appears as a counterexample to behaviorism. But the alleged possibility of undetectable variation in subjective states, such as the inverted spectrum, also raises questions regarding the semantics of color words. It suggests that the meaning of these terms is not provided by the subjective and this is supportive of logical behaviorism.

More recently, critics of functionalism allege that the problem posed by the possibility of inverted spectra carries over to this successor of behaviorism. Among these critics is Hilary Putnam (1981), who argues that the physical possibility of acquired spectrum inversion refutes functionalism. I shall argue, however, that functionalism makes specific empirical predictions regarding Acquired Inversion of the Qualia Spectrum (AIQS), and that in the absence of empirical results no a priori arguments against functionalism, such as Putnam's, can be cogent. I will sketch an experimental situation which would produce AIQS, and I will suggest that prior experience with visual image inversion appears to confirm functionalism. My argument and the existing evidence suggests that while AIQS is both logically and physically possible, its mere existence would constitute no refutation of functionalism; only its persistence after behavioral accommodation to the inversion would properly count against functionalism. The cumulative empirical evidence from related experiments thus suggests that spectrum inversion would confirm rather than refute functionalism.

The form of functionalism that I take to be empirically corroborated is pure functionalism. By contrast, some, such as Shoemaker, have allowed that the possibility of the inverted qualia spectrum suggests that functionalism should be weakened to recognize not just functional properties but also underlying physiological properties as determinants of the character of qualia. Stephen White (1986) contends that this departure from pure functionalism is unsatisfactory as a solution to the problem it is meant to solve, and I argue here that the abandonment of pure functionalism is not necessary.

Functionalism, in its strong pure form, is thus committed, on my view, to the thesis that the causal roles of psychological states make them the states they are, not just as a matter of linguistic analysis or merely as a contributor to the observed public behavior of the organism, but also as the determinant of the subjective character of the states. Function determines qualia. What the mental states of bats do thus determines what it is like to be a bat.

1. EMPIRICAL CONSEQUENCES OF METAPHYSICAL THEORIES

To the extent that the mind-body problem is a metaphysical problem and functionalism is an attempted solution to this metaphysical problem, functionalism is a metaphysical theory. And given that functionalism is naturalistic and indeed is a very general conceptual framework upon which specific cognitive psychological theories may be built, functionalism is metaphysics naturalized. But functionalism itself nevertheless appears to be extremely far removed from the empirical consequences of any particular psychological theory that might be functionalistic in its broad approach. Indeed, functionalism might be held to be compatible with any empirical psychological data whatsoever: for any functionalist theory conflicting with specific data, there is some other equally functionalistic theory with differing specific functional analyses which is compatible with that data. This should not be surprising, for the type-type identity theory that functionalism arguably displaces does not have any specific empirical consequences in the absence of specific identities of particular mental events with particular neuronal events beyond the very general consequence that the anencephalic must be mindless.

Moreover, although it is general, this nevertheless *is* an empirical consequence of identity theory: 'no brain, no pain'. Metaphysical theories, in characterizing the underlying reality of mental phenomena, make general claims about the forms that empirical phenomena can take. Thus, functionalism is not alone in having at least some specific empirical consequences. Rival metaphysical theories of mind and body, however, also appear to me to entail specific consequences. Cartesian interactionist dualism, for example, creates the metaphysical possibility that a mind can switch its causal relation from one body to another in the absence of any physical change to those bodies. If such switching were observed, it would, it seems to me, clearly confirm dualism. A rival mind/brain identity theory, on the other hand, might rule out such a metaphysical possibility; and if bodies were observed suddenly having acquired new minds, it would disconfirm materialism. But bodies are not observed to suddenly become possessed of new minds, nor do some of us occasionally awaken with new bodies as a result of some metaphysical malfunction.

Dualism also has the consequence that physical changes of the brain cannot affect central mental processes (such as cognition or thought itself), mental ability, dispositions to infer or to associate, or personality characteristics. Dualists suppose that these are not physical processes. This dualistic thesis also has empirical consequences. Dualism can explain some of the effects of alcohol consumption – double vision, slurred speech, loss of coordination – because these effects essentially involve sensory and motor processes that depend upon afferent and efferent neuronal transmission of information, where those physical processes are affected by alcohol. But how is dualism to account for the effects of alcohol on central mental processes? Alcohol reduces inhibitions, weakens the will, interferes with inference, has dose-specific effects on association and creativity, and so forth. Since these cognitive processes are supposed by the dualist to be nonphysical, the psychological effects of alcohol disconfirm dualism. Similar implications hold for many other psychoactive drugs and also for psychosurgery (e.g., prefrontal lobotomy). If these physical alterations of the brain were to affect only perception and motor processes, then dualism would be confirmed and materialism would be disconfirmed. But this is not what is observed.

Independently of this general claim that metaphysical theories of mind have empirical consequences, the particular theory of functionalism is seen by both critics and defenders as having consequences with regard to subjective experiences, i.e., qualia. What I believe has not been noticed is the extent to which these consequences are susceptible to empirical test and the extent to which functionalism is related to prior empirical work on the subjective character of perception.

2. PUTNAM'S ARGUMENT REGARDING ACQUIRED INVERSION OF THE QUALIA SPECTRUM

The problem of the inverted spectrum has a much longer history than does functionalism. The possibility is raised by Locke.[1] The inverted spectrum appears to be an undetectable conceptual possibility concerning the content of other minds. But then again it appears to be more than just a conceptual or metaphysical possibility; given a bit of knowledge about how the eye actually responds to chromatic stimuli, it appears to be a physical possibility: the neuronal connections to the cones in the retina could be permuted (genetically, micro-surgically, or even by disease).

Putnam exploits the physical reality of this possibility. And his argument introduces an interesting variation upon such a possibility. Most previous discussion had centered on the possibility of innate spectrum inversion involving persons who had different visual color qualia from birth and thus through the period of language acquisition. Putnam shifts attention to acquired spectral inversion (AIQS), contending that AIQS is at least a problem and perhaps even a refutation of functionalism when functionalism is conjoined with realism regarding qualia.[2] Putnam notes that one could actually come to experience spectral inversion (through some form of neurological modification). It is not just a skeptical or epistemological problem regarding other minds, but a real physical possibility one could oneself experience, and be quite certain one had experienced. With linguistic adjustment and subsequent amnesia, one could display absolutely complete behavioral adaptation.

Putnam states his variation on the classical problem of the inverted spectrum (which he says he has "used for many years in lectures") as follows:

> ...imagine your spectrum becomes inverted at a particular time in your life and you remember what it was like before that. There is no epistemological problem about 'verification'. You wake up one morning and the sky looks red, and your red sweater appears to have turned blue, and all the faces are an awful color, as on a color negative (1981, p. 80).

Putnam goes on to underscore that this is a real physical possibility: "In this case, it seems that one even knows what must have happened. Some 'wires' must have gotten 'crossed' in the brain" (1981, p. 80). Thus these new qualitative states have half the functional character of the old ones: the subjectively red state is caused by conditions that used to produce the subjectively blue state. So now subjectively red states become reliable indicators of objects one used to call 'blue'.

Now Putnam only needs to suppose that the effects of the new qualitative states come to be those of the old qualitative states – e.g., one learns to say 'That's blue' when in the qualitative state which previously led one to say 'That's red'. And the new qualitative states have almost the functional properties of the old states. They differ in that one presumably still notices the difference and occasionally remarks how weird it all is that one's qualitative states are not what they were. Putnam then administers the alleged *coup de grace* for functionalism:

> If this functional role were *identical* with the qualitative character, then one couldn't say that the quality of the sensation had changed. (If this is not clear, then imagine that after the spectrum inversion, and after learning to compensate for it linguistically, you experience an attack of amnesia which wipes out all memory of what colors used to look like. In this case it would seem as if the sensation you are *now* calling a 'sensation of blue' could have almost exactly the functional role that the sensation you used to call the 'sensation of blue' used to have, while having a totally different character). But the quality *has* changed. The quality doesn't seem to be a *functional* state in *this* case (1981, p. 81).

At least one tacit premise of Putnam's argument is intuitively plausible, yet on reflection, questionable: he supposes that the qualia remain unchanged through behavioral adaptation. But this is surely an empirical question. It is plausible that immediately after permutation of the retinal neurons there would be AIQS. But the subject would notice the change at this time and presumably would manifest the change in behavior in many different ways. This is completely compatible with functionalism; indeed, functionalism has the consequence that there must be a qualitative difference given that both the inputs (causes) and outputs (effects) from the visual processing system have been altered.

It seems clear that AIQS with behavioral compensation is a counterexample to functionalism only if the adaptation is complete. Putnam only mentions that the imagined AIQS subject has "learned to compensate for it linguistically". The functionalist should be unperturbed unless the adaptation is complete and includes more than just surface linguistic behavior: response times must settle back down to pre-inversion levels, and non-linguistic responses also must adapt where these include performance on color sorting tasks, associations with colors, emotional affect of colors, and color proximity judgments. All these must be as before AIQS for an old functional role to be assumed by an allegedly new qualitative state. To suppose that a functional role is exhausted by overt linguistic response to stimuli is not to take functionalism seriously.

So let us present Putnam's case with the thoroughness that is required of a challenge to functionalism on the basis of AIQS. Let us suppose that with amnesia the adaptation to AIQS is absolutely complete and thus that the post-neuron-permutation qualitative states come to play exactly the same functional role as the pre-neuron-permutation states. Let us then consider Putnam's claim that these post-permutation and adaptation qualitative states would be different from those before. What is the basis for this claim? This clearly presupposes the thesis that qualitative states are immutable through functional change. But this is the very issue that is in dispute. Thus Putnam's argument begs the question.

Furthermore, Putnam's claims to the contrary notwithstanding, verificationism does rear its ugly head. We now imagine ourselves as persons who behave exactly as do normal persons, whose observable color responses are normal, and who deny and do not believe that we now or ever have been the subject of different color qualia. How can we possibly tell whether our qualia are like those other people have or those that we have had prior to the unusual events in the preceding scenario? The only answer would appear to be that others have good evidence that before the behavioral accommodation and the amnesia, our behavior and color experience was not normal. Yet to suppose that this can solve our current epistemological problem is clearly to suppose the truth of the qualia immutability thesis.

3. EXPERIMENTS WITH RETINAL IMAGE INVERSION

In addition to begging the question against the functionalist, the assumption of the immutability of qualia throughout functional change does not appear to be borne out in studies of a different phenomenon bearing interesting similarities to AIQS. Empirical evidence regarding this related phenomenon, retinal image inversion, suggests that this premise may be false as well. There has been a long series of experiments undertaken to investigate the effects of inversion of the image on the retina. Both human and animal subjects have been used; our interest attaches to human subjects, as in the work of George Stratton and his successors.[3] The apparatus itself is relatively simple, merely involving special goggles or spectacles.

Inversion of the retinal image has the immediate qualitative effect all might expect: things look upside down. Performance on tasks involving motility is severely degraded. Subjects have difficulty grasping objects and manipulating them. Adaptation to the spectacles is thus itself a spectacle. But perceptual demands of everyday life and contrived tasks force adaptation. Subjects do adapt, albeit slowly and with difficulty. One subject[4] even demonstrated the extent of his adaptation by riding a motorcycle through a city, although it is unclear what perceptual abilities other than vision might facilitate such a performance (Kohler 1962, p. 64).

What of the qualia? Subjects have reported that the experience is very unpleasant and disturbing. More interesting are the reports that the qualia change in the course of these experiments. As adaptation occurs, it appears that things appear less strange. Stratton even reported that sometimes the world ceased to appear upside down but actually came to appear uninverted. That is, the qualia are not immutable through adaptation. Subjects also have reported that upon removal of the inverting spectacles, things briefly appear inverted. Wallach et al. 1963 report quite rapid partial behavioral and subjective adaptation to rotations of the visual image just by having subjects look at their own feet. Unfortunately, these self-report data are not reported by all subjects, and are debated by psychologists (cf. Kaufman 1974 and Rock 1975). So these results are not by themselves to be taken as a clear-cut confirmation of functionalism. They should, however, undermine any merely intuitive confidence we might have had in the immutability thesis. Also we should note that there has been variance in the experimental protocols, the duration of wearing the spectacles, and the extent of behavioral adaptation achieved. To the extent that adaptation affects the qualitative character of experience, therefore, functionalism is supported. And, more weakly, since no investigator found that complete behavioral adaptation occurred with no effect on qualia, functionalism achieves a form of Popperian corroboration by means of these experiments.

Intriguingly, Stratton himself seems to have taken his results to be support for something like the position now called 'functionalism'. In Stratton 1909, he argues that psychology involves an autonomous level of causal explanation that is not identical with the neurophysiological. These causal processes are not in general available to consciousness: "A host of real relations thus apply to mental data, without necessarily having any conscious presence or representation among the data" (p. 82). Unfortunately, the term 'functionalism' has been applied to a host of positions. At the time Stratton was working in psychology, functionalism denoted a neo-Darwinian position that treated mental processes as mere contributors to global survival fitness of the organism (e.g.,"thought serves the coordination of muscle contractions") rather than exploring the causal relations between mental states that modern functionalists and Stratton advocate.

One thing to be noted about inverted image experiments is that they confront troublesome problems that would not arise in spectrum inversion. The color spectrum is unique to one sense modality, vision. But spatial orientation involves not only vision but also auditory localization, kinesthetic sense, proprioception and balance. In fact, the relation between these senses has been the primary interest of many researchers within this area. This interest stems in part from Berkeley's claim that touch predominated over vision in the creation of psychological space.[5] But it thus may well be more difficult to achieve the alteration of qualitative spatial representation in the experiments that have been performed than it would be in the case of spectral inversion. For the character of spatial representations appears to be determined by several modalities. To merely invert one of these produces conflicts not just with prior visual experience, but also with current information from the other modalities.

Thus, consideration of experiments that produce less intermodal conflict is desirable. Here again there is gratification for functionalists. For example, Kaufman reports that Taylor wore contact lenses that caused horizontal lines to appear bent:

Although when first viewed through the [lenses] the line appeared to be bent, after scanning the line by moving the eyes it gradually came to appear to be straight. In one experiment, 20 seconds of scanning was sufficient to produce complete straightening of the line (Kaufmann 1974, p. 424).

These results were replicated by Festinger et al. (1967). They confirm an effect originally reported by J. J. Gibson (1933). These results also refute the general thesis that qualia are immutable through adaptation. Now let us consider the thesis as applied to perceived color.

4. EXPERIMENTS WITH COLOR STIMULUS MODIFICATION

The modification of color vision thus presents a simpler test than image inversion of the consequences of behavioral adaptation for the thesis of the immutability of qualia because spectrum inversion does not produce intermodal conflicts. While as far as I know no experiment has been performed on spectrum inversion itself, various experiments have been performed investigating the effects of modification of the light spectrum reaching the eyes of subjects on qualia. In fact, these experiments were initiated as an outgrowth of the inverted image experiments of Stratton and his successors described above. This is because those experiments employed prisms to invert the image, and the prisms introduce color fringes as the various chromatic bands of the spectrum are differentially diffracted. It had been noted in passing in the early experiments with these goggles that subjects reported that these fringes 'disappeared' during the period of sustained wearing of the goggles (Kohler 1962, pp. 64–68). The color qualia were not immutable.

While other aspects of such experiments, especially those having to do with aftereffects, have been the subject of controversy, there is a consensus on the mutability of qualia during the course of the stimulus alteration. Goggles used in these experiments have been equipped with color filters so that each lens is divided down the middle, with the left half of the lens tinted one color and the right another (Kaufman 1974, p. 521f). Goggles rather than more ordinary tinted spectacles are used so that subjects cannot see around the edge of the lens. An example is provided by Celeste McCollough (1965), who wore red and blue-green filters for 75 days on her right eye only, with the left eye occluded except during special tests. She was thereby able to test for interocular differences in color discrimination ability during the test. She reports that behavioral adaptation was quite good (although the right fovea showed less sensitivity than the left to both red and to blue-green light (1965, p. 377). Of interest here is her report of the subjective color qualia:

During the first few weeks the spectacles were worn, the colors of the spectacles appeared to become progressively less saturated. . . . When the colored filters were placed before the left eye, objects seen through each filter seemed to be just as highly colored as they had appeared to the right eye at the beginning of the experiment (1965, p. 370).

Thus the thesis of the immutability of color qualia through stimulus transformations appears to be false. Again, the questions being addressed in the research mentioned here did not concern the global theory of functionalism. Like other experiments in psychology, it was concerned with more detailed description of adaptation, with attempts to account for the adaptation and, in particular, with the description and explanation of aftereffects observed following removal of the spectacles.

Indeed, from the standpoint of those merely wishing for corroboration or disconfirmation of functionalism, these experimental situations are excessively complex, involving, e.g., split visual fields. Functionalism is corroborated by the more mundane and familiar fact that quite often the wearing of merely uniformly tinted glasses initially is quite noticeable, producing color qualia alteration, and also interferes with color judgment. But with time the tint becomes unnoticed and does not interfere with color judgment (apart from the reduction of luminance). These familiar facts of adaptation to color alteration by spectacles may seem somewhat removed from the possibility of acquired spectrum inversion but the distance involved here is not as great as may first appear.

5. EMPIRICAL CONSEQUENCES OF FUNCTIONALISM FOR SPECTRUM INVERSION

Spectral inversion is an empirical problem in the same sense as is the inverted retinal image. Functionalism is a philosophical or high level theory that nevertheless *prima facie* makes specific empirical predictions in the case of sudden spectral inversion: if spectral inversion were to occur, either (1) behavioral adaptation would eventually be complete and subjective adaptation would then also be complete (qualia would change to those had prior to the inversion); or, (2) behavioral adaption would never be complete and qualia would not revert to those of pre-inversion. That is to say, the truth of functionalism seems to rule out just the one case Putnam mentions where behavioral adaptation is complete, yet qualia remain inverted. And we have seen that supposing that this last would be the outcome begs the question and attempts to settle an empirical question *a priori*.

Spectral inversion is not just a conceptual possibility or even the bizarre and extremely remote medical possibility of Putnam's own scenario. One can sketch a fairly straightforward experimental design to produce spectral inversion and test its consequences. Like the experiments in inverted image and color-filtering goggles described above, this experimental design modifies the character of the information reaching the sense organs of the subject rather than surgically altering the subject. Whether and when it produces AIQS, a qualitative subjective effect, is an independent matter and, indeed, would be the subject of the investigation.

Let the subject wear electronic spectacles. A color television camera could be mounted atop the subject's head and lightweight color video displays, e.g., lcd's, would be positioned before each eye (or before one eye with the other eye occluded). The color spectrum of the image seen by the subject can then be electronically inverted. Putnam mentions that in his scenario we are to imagine the qualia as those of a color negative. And it is straightforwardly possible to make the visual stimuli be those of a color negative. Presumably, the qualia initially follow suit.

Until recently, there would have been a difficult problem of focusing, which must be done by the camera (the eye itself must focus on the CRT). This would now be ameliorated by recently developed and generally available automatic focusing methods, perhaps with a manual override controlled by the subject. Despite the parallel Putnam draws with a color negative, we do not wish to invert luminance, making dark areas light and vice versa; we wish merely to invert the spectrum. The inversion will leave the spectrum center-point unchanged, but ideally will replace violet with red. The center of the visual spectrum is approximately 5550 Angstroms, a yellow-green. This is close to the emission characteristic of the 'Green' phosphors used in standard RGB color cathode ray tubes. Thus a very simple modification of a standard CRT can produce a reasonable approximation of spectrum inversion: reverse the wires to the 'Red' and 'Blue' cathodes. Such an alteration should be more than adequate to test the hypothesis of the immutability of qualia through adaptation, and thus functionalism. Let the subject then wear such electronic spectacles or blindfolds at all times during the experiment.

It now becomes important to distinguish the qualia of the subject from the character of the stimulus. The experimental arrangement sketched would produce Visual Image Spectral Inversion – that is, the alteration of the stimulus. And initially it is certainly plausible, and would presumably be borne out by the subject's behavior and reports, that such an alteration would have the subjective effect Putnam supposes would occur in his scenario – AIQS. What remains unclear and would be the subject of such an investigation is the truth of the thesis of the immutability of qualia through functional adaptation.

So it would now remain to experimentally determine what happens as adaptation occurs. Since an ordinary environment appears to make relatively slight demands on color sightedness (the adept color blind can conceal their disabilities in many ordinary situations), we would need to take special measures to promote adaptation. Adaptation can be assisted (and assessed) by color training sessions involving color samples and tasks with ordinary objects. After training to linguistically respond to color patches correctly, we would also need training and assessment of performance on tasks such as "Pick out the ripe banana"; "Describe the colors in this scene"; "How does this color make you feel?" "Does this person have jaundice?"; "Which pants go with this suit?"; "Is this a good color for breakfast cereal?". These sessions would force, to the extent possible, accommodation of the perceptual change. To discover what methods of training will most rapidly and most thoroughly produce behavioral adaptation is itself an empirical matter, but it is important that as complete an adaptation as is possible be accomplished. Other than expense and convenience, there is no need to optimize the timeframe.

It may appear that testing the effects of spectral inversion has become possible only with very recent technology. But a second possible protocol would be just to present recolored objects to a normally sighted individual. Subjects would spend all their time in a color-modified environment where familiar objects were recolored. The subject would view color-altered paintings of exterior and interior scenes. It would be especially important that the color of important and familiar objects be carefully modified: food (using food colors), other humans (using makeup), and the subject's own body. This experiment could have been performed in Locke's time. In our own time, extensive use could also be made in an experimental environment of an electronically modified television that inverts the color spectrum and displays a wide-ranging yet interesting range of material involving objects familiar to the subject. Selections from ordinary television programming ought to suffice, with the subject required to correctly answer color-related questions during the viewing in an otherwise darkened or color modified environment.

These experiments alter the colors reaching the subject from an otherwise normal environment. The experiments could have four possible outcomes: either complete behavioral adaptation or not; and, in each of those cases, either subjective adaptation (qualia reversion) or not. Thus the outcome of incomplete behavioral adaptation with complete subjective adaptation would *prima facie* be the most surprising. But perhaps it would be the most revealing: it could not only be compatible with functionalism but might also provide some interesting specificity in relation to a functionalist theory of sensation. One could hold that just those areas where behavioral adaptation did occur were important for the functional characterization of color sensation. Those behaviors that did not adapt would thereby be shown unnecessary for determining the subjective character of color perception.

Of the three other possible experimental outcomes, only one could count against pure functionalism: complete behavioral adaptation with no concomitant qualia reversion. (This is the outcome that Putnam claims – without empirical evidence – to be the result in his thought experiment scenario.) The other two possible outcomes of actual experiments would confirm functionalism. It would be irresponsible to predict these experimental outcomes *a priori*, but given experience with retinal image inversion, line straightening, and color modification, it would be rash to wager against an outcome compatible with functionalism.

NOTES

[1] *An Essay Concerning Human Understanding*, Bk. II, Chapter 32, section 14.

[2] It is unclear to me exactly what qualia realism amounts to. It is also not clear to what extent Putnam views his argument as a refutation of functionalism, a theory which he did much to develop. It may well be that he believes that the real (so to speak) problem lies with realism and that a suitably metaphysical anti-realist home can be found for functionalism. But if so, it would not be the functionalism that I defend here, which is straightforwardly committed to the real existence of other minds and their subjective sensations and states, including qualia.

[3] Such experiments began in the last century, pioneered first by von Helmholtz, and later by George M. Stratton at the University of California. Replications and variations were performed by J.J. Gibson and Theodor Erismann in 1928. Work with two subjects was reported by Ewert in 1930; and more recent work has been performed by Fred Snyder, Ivo Kohler, and others.

[4] Apparently more than one subject in inverted image experiments chose to ride a motorcycle to demonstrate his successful adaptation. In 1963 I watched a film that had been produced (presumably in the 1950's) by the Moody Institute of Science in Chicago. This film depicted an inverting goggle-wearing subject riding a motorcycle through a slalom course. I do not know whose work was being reported nor if this film is still available. In any case, as I remember it the subject in the Moody film was American, whereas the subject Kohler describes took part in Erismann's experiments in Innsbruck, Austria, and rode his motorcycle through Innsbruck. I assume they were distinct.

[5] Cf. Kaufman (1974), pp. 416–19; and Rock (1966) and (1975).

REFERENCES

Block, N. J., and J. A. Fodor: 1972, 'What Psychological States are Not', *Philosophical Review* **81**, 159–81.

Clark, Austen: 1985b, 'Spectrum Inversion and the Color Solid', *Southern Journal of Philosophy* **23**, 431–43.

Clark, Austen: 1985a, 'Qualia and the Psychophysiological Explanation of Color Perception', *Synthese* **65**, 377–405.

Ewert, P. N.: 1930, 'A Study of the Effect of Inverted Retinal Stimulation upon Spatially Coordinated Behavior', *Genet Psych Monogr* **7**.

Festinger, V., C. A. Burnham. H. Ono, and D. Bamber: 1967, 'Efference and the Conscious Experience of Perception'. *Journal of Experimental Psychology*. Monograph Supplement **74**, number 637.

Gibson, J. J.: 1933, 'Adaptation and After-Effect in Perception of Curved Lines', *Journal of Experimental Psychology* **16**, 1–31.

Gibson, J. J.: 1950, *Perception of the Visual World*. Houghton Mifflin, Boston.

Gibson, J. J.: 1966, *The Senses Considered as Perceptual Systems*. Houghton Mifflin. Boston.

Harris, C. S.: 1963, 'Adaptation to Displaced Vision: Visual. Motor or Proprioceptive Change?' *Science* **3**, 71–72.

Harris, C. S.: 1961, 'Perceptual Adaptation to Inverted. Reversed and Displaced Vision'. *Psychological Review* **72**, 419–44.

Harris, C. S. and A. R. Gibson: 1968, 'Is Orientation-specific Color Adaptation in Human Vision due to Edge Detector. Afterimages. or "Dipoles"?', *Science* **162**. 1056–7.

Held, Richard: 1964, 'Plasticity in Sensory-Motor Systems', *Scientific American* **213**. 84–94.

Horgan, Terence: 1984, 'Functionalism, Qualia, and the Inverted Spectrum'. *Philosophy and Phenomenological Research* **44**, 453–69.

Kaufman, Lloyd: 1974. *Sight and Mind*. Oxford U. P.. New York.

Kitcher, Patricia: 1982. 'Two Versions of the Identity Theory'. *Erkenntnis* **17**. 213–28.

Kohler, Ivo: 1964, *The Formation and Transformation of the Perceptual World*. trans. H. Fiss, International Universities Press. New York.

Kohler, Ivo: 1962, 'Experiments with Goggles'. *Scientific American*, pp. 61–72.

Kripke, Saul: 1971, 'Naming and Necessity', in D. Davidson and G. Harman (eds.). *Semantics of Natural Language*, D. Reidel. Boston, pp. 253–355.

Lewis, David: 1980, 'Mad Pain and Martian Pain', in Block (ed.). *Readings in the Philosophy of Psychology*, Vol. I., pp. 216–22.

McCollough. C.: 1965a. 'The Conditioning of Color Perception'. *American Journal of Psychology* **78**. 362–68.

McCollough. C.: 1965b. 'Color Adaptation of Edge-detectors in the Human Visual System', *Science* **149**, 1115–16.

Putnam. Hilary: 1981, *Reason. Truth and History*. Cambridge University Press. New York.

Rock, Irvin: 1966, *The Nature of Visual Perception*. Basic Books. New York.

Rock, Irvin: 1975, *An Introduction to Perception*. Macmillan. New York.

Shoemaker, Sydney: 1975, 'Functionalism and Qualia', *Philosophical Studies* **27**, 291–315.
Shoemaker, Sydney: 1982, 'The Inverted Spectrum', *Journal of Philosophy* **79**, 357–81.
Snyder, Fred. W. and N. H. Pronk: 1952, *Vision with Spatial Inversion*, University of Wichita Press.
Stratton, George M.: 1896, 'Some Preliminary Experiments on Vision without Inversion of the Retinal Image', *Psychological Review* **3**, 611–17.
Stratton, George M.: 1897, 'Vision without Inversion of the Retinal Image', *Psychological Review* **4**, 341–60.
Stratton, George M.: 1909, 'Correction of Rival Methods in Psychology', *Psychological Review* **16**.
Taylor, J. G.: 1962, *The Behavioral Basis of Perception*, Yale University Press.
Wallach, H., J. H. Kravitz, and J. Lindauer: 1963, 'A Passive Condition for Rapid Adaptation to Displaced Visual Direction', *American Journal of Psychology* **76**, 568–78.
White, Stephen L.: 1986, 'Curse of the Qualia', *Synthese* **68**, 333–68.

Department of Philosophy
University of Minnesota
Duluth, MN 55812
U.S.A.

PAUL   THAGARD

CONCEPTS AND CONCEPTUAL CHANGE*

ABSTRACT. This paper argues that questions concerning the nature of concepts that are central in cognitive psychology are also important to epistemology and that there is more to conceptual change than mere belief revision. Understanding of epistemic change requires appreciation of the complex ways in which concepts are structured and organized and of how this organization can affect belief revision. Following a brief summary of the psychological functions of concepts and a discussion of some recent accounts of what concepts are, I propose a view of concepts as complex computational structures. This account suggests that conceptual change can come in varying degrees, with the most extreme consisting of fundamental conceptual reorganizations. These degrees of conceptual change are illustrated by the development of the concept of an acid.

1. INTRODUCTION

According to Ian Hacking (1975), current analytic philosophy is the "heyday of sentences". Whereas seventeenth-century thinkers talked of ideas, contemporary philosophers take sentences to be the objects of epistemological investigation. Knowledge is true justified belief, so increases in knowledge are additions to what is believed. Epistemology, then, consists primarily of evaluating strategies for improving our stock of beliefs, construed as sentences or as attitudes toward sentence-like propositions.

In the cognitive sciences, however, the intellectual terrain is very different. In cognitive psychology, the question of the nature of concepts receives far more attention than the question of belief revision. Researchers in artificial intelligence often follow philosophers in discussing belief revision, but they also pay much attention to how knowledge can be organized in concept-like structures called *frames* (Minsky 1975; for reviews see Thagard 1984b, 1988). Nevertheless, even a philosopher like Alvin Goldman (1986), who takes cognitive science very seriously, places belief revision at the center of his epistemology, paying scant attention to the nature of concepts and the question of conceptual change. Gilbert Harman has written both on epistemic change (1986) and on the nature of concepts (1987), but has not much discussed the relevance of the latter topic to the former. Historically

101

J. H. Fetzer (ed.), Epistemology and Cognition, 101–120.

oriented philosophers of science such as Kuhn (1970) have suggested
the importance of conceptual change but have not provided accounts of
conceptual structure that are sufficiently developed for epistemological
application.

   I shall argue that the nature of concepts and conceptual change is in
fact an important epistemological topic and that drawing on ideas from
the cognitive sciences can provide an account of conceptual change
adequate for epistemology and the philosophy of science. After considering an argument that there is nothing more to conceptual change
than belief revision, I contend instead that belief revision cannot be
understood without paying attention to questions of conceptual change.
I survey some recent proposals about what concepts are and outline a
view of concepts as complex computational structures. Finally, the
relevance of this account of concepts to epistemological issues is shown
by reviewing the changes that have taken place in the history of the
important scientific concept of an acid.

   First a note to prevent terminological confusion. Researchers in cognitive psychology and artificial intelligence tend to use the terms 'knowledge' and 'belief' differently from philosophers who often characterize
knowledge as true justified belief. Their use of 'knowledge' is closer to
philosophers' use of 'belief'. Cognitive scientists have also taken to
using the term 'epistemology' very broadly to cover anything having to
do with knowledge in a diluted sense that does not have anything to
do with justification. In this paper I generally use 'knowledge' and
'epistemology' in their traditional philosophical senses that presuppose
questions of justification.

2. BELIEF REVISION AND CONCEPTUAL CHANGE

The central question in current epistemology is when we are justified
in adding and deleting beliefs from the set of beliefs judged to be
known. Without denigrating this question, I propose that epistemology
should also address the question: What are concepts and how do they
change? Concepts are relevant to epistemology if the question of conceptual change is not identical to the question of belief revision. But
maybe it is; consider the following argument.

> The issue of conceptual change is a red herring. Whenever
> a concept changes, it does so by virtue of changes in the

beliefs that employ that concept (or predicate, if you are thinking in terms of sentences). For example, if you recategorize whales as mammals rather than fish, you have made an important change in the concept *whale*. But this amounts to no more than deleting the belief that whales are fish and adding the belief that whales are mammals. Your concept of mammal may also change by adding the belief that whales produce milk, but this merely follows from the other belief addition. So as far as epistemology is concerned, conceptual change is redundant with respect to the central question of belief revision.

This argument shows, at least, that anyone who thinks conceptual change is important has to give an account of it that goes beyond mere belief revision.

The problem with the argument is that it assumes that the principles according to which beliefs are added and deleted operate independently of considerations of conceptual structure. If you are a Bayesian, for example, belief revision is just a matter of changing probability distributions over the set of propositions. But suppose that you want to take a more psychologically realistic approach to belief revision, one that could account for why some revisions are harder to make than others and why some revisions have more global effects. It may be that such facets of belief revision can only be understood by noticing how beliefs are organized via concepts. Perhaps there is a difference between deciding that whales are mammals and deciding that whales have fins, a difference that can only be understood in terms of the overall structure of our conceptual scheme, relating *whale* to *mammal* in ways more fundamental than simply having the belief that whales are mammals. For the moment, this is only a possibility, not a refutation of the argument that conceptual change is just belief revision. But it is enough to suggest that it is worth exploring the cognitive science literature on concepts for suggestions about how conceptual structure could matter to belief revision.

3. WHAT ARE CONCEPTS FOR?

Before proceeding further, some clarification is in order concerning concepts and predicates, and sentences and propositions. Sentences are syntactic entities, marks on paper. Among their constituents are predicates such as 'whale' in the sentence 'Gracy is a whale'. In contrast, I shall treat concepts and propositions as mental representations, with concepts corresponding to predicates and propositions corresponding to sentences. This mentalistic interpretation is not the only one possible: a Platonist could treat concepts as the meaning of predicates and propositions as the meaning of sentences independent of what is in anybody's head. Instead of discussing abstract meanings, I follow researchers in psychology and artificial intelligence in supposing that concepts are mental structures analogous to data structures in computers.

Psychologists have many reasons for being interested in the nature of concepts. Whereas the epistemologist's primary concern is with the question of justification, the psychologist must try to account for many different kinds of behavior. Here is a list, undoubtedly incomplete, of various roles that concepts have been deemed to play, using the concept *whale* as an example.

(1) *Categorization.* Our concept *whale* enables us to recognize things as whales.

(2) *Learning.* Our concept *whale* must be capable of being learned, perhaps from examples, or perhaps by combining other existing concepts.

(3) *Memory.* Our concept *whale* should help us remember things about whales, either in general or from particular episodes that concern whales.

(4) *Deductive inference.* Our concept *whale* should enable us to make deductive and inductive inferences about whales, for example, enabling us to infer that since Gracy is a whale, she has fins.

(5) *Explanation.* Our knowledge about whales should enable us to generate explanations, for example saying that Gracy swims *because* she is a whale.

(6) *Problem solving.* Our knowledge about whales should enable us to solve problems, for example, how can we get an errant whale out of the harbor.

(7) *Generalization.* Our concept *whale* should enable us to learn new facts about whales from additional examples, for example, to form new general conclusions such as that whales have blubber under their skin.

(8)   *Analogical inference.* Our concept *whale* should help us to reason using similarities: if you know that dolphins are quite intelligent and are aquatic mammals like whales, then perhaps whales are intelligent too. Metaphor should also be supportable by the concept, as when we say that an overweight person is a whale.

(9)   *Language comprehension.* Our understanding of sentences such as 'Gracy is a whale' depends on our knowing something about the concept *whale.*

(10)   *Language production.* We need to be able to utter sentences like 'Gracy is a whale' and 'Whales are less friendly than dolphins'.

Ignoring the last two language issues, which introduce problems not directly connected to belief revision, we can examine whether the first eight roles require that belief change pay attention to conceptual structure. Categorization might be seen as a straightforward case of belief application: you believe that any large sea-object that moves and blows water into the air is a whale, so you categorize the large blob in the ocean producing spray as a whale. You thereby add the belief 'the blob is a whale' to your set of beliefs. But categorization is rarely so simple as this deduction, since unexceptionable rules are hard to come by. Submarines are also large sea-objects that move and can blow water into the air. So in categorizing the blob as a whale rather than as a submarine you will need to decide which concept fits the blob better, and fitting the concept may be more than a matter of simple belief application (see the discussion of categorization in Holland, Holyoak, Nisbett, and Thagard 1986).

Identifying the blob as a whale presupposes that you have already formed the concept of a whale, but what does this amount to? The belief-revision approach to epistemology never addresses the question of the origin of the concepts (or predicates, if you prefer) that are essential components of beliefs. Without the concept of a whale you could never form the belief that Gracy is a whale. I recently learned the concept of a narwhal, which like a whale is a cetacean and a large sea-creature, but has a long ivory tusk. Now, with the help of the tusk criterion and a picture of a narwhal I saw in my dictionary, I can potentially form the belief 'the blob is a narwhal'. But how are such concepts formed? The psychological and computational literature on concept formation suggests two principal ways: by learning from examples and by combining previously existing concepts (see Holland et al., chap. 7). Neither of these is a simple matter of adding new beliefs. In particular, forming new concepts by combining old ones requires that the concept have much structure, because the new concepts are not simple sums of the old (Thagard 1984a, 1988, chap. 4; Holland et al., chap. 4). To form, for example, the concept *walking whale* we have to decide how to reconcile what we know about whales with what we know about walking, perhaps by concluding that whales merely imitate walking by floating with their tails near the bottom of the ocean and wiggling their fins.

Is memory important for epistemology? For Harman (1986) and Goldman (1986) it professedly is, yet neither considers the role that concepts have been conjectured to play in memory. We need to be able to remember beliefs in order to use them to revise others, and conceptual organization can be highly relevant to memory. If spreading activation of concepts is a crucial way in which beliefs get accessed, as in the PI system (Thagard 1988), then the organization of concepts matters to memory and hence to belief revision based on memory.

The defender of a pure belief revision approach to epistemology might say that at least the next three roles in my list – deductive inference, explanation, and problem solving – do not require any attention to the conceptual structure. Explanation and problem solving are approximated by deduction, and deduction is just a matter of deriving the consequences of a set of beliefs. In a real system, however, there must be constraints on what gets deduced to avoid the explosion of exponentially increasing numbers of beliefs: a system that expands its data base by inferring from A to A&A, A&A&A, etc., will quickly be swamped. One way of constraining deduction is to draw inferences only from a subset of beliefs deemed to be active, and one way of controlling the activation of beliefs is through the activation of concepts to which they are attached (Thagard 1988). Moreover, some deductive inferences may be performed by processes that directly use conceptual structures rather than typical rules of inference. If the structure for whale contains the information that a whale is a kind of mammal, then information stored with the structure for mammal can then be 'inherited' by whale. A frame system can infer that whales produce milk by virtue of the *kind* link between the whale frame and the mammal frame. What is inferred is the same as what a logic system would conclude using standard deduction from sentences, but the procedure is more direct. Hence deduction – and perforce explanation and problem solving – may be served by additional conceptual structure.

Generalization, such as inferring from some examples that whales have blubber, may also benefit from conceptual structure. We can infer a generalization from fewer instances if we know something about the variability of the kinds of things under consideration (Holland et al. 1986, chap. 8). For example, a few instances of whales that have blubber under their skin may be enough to convince you that all whales have blubber under their skin, because kinds of mammals, cetaceans, and sea-creatures do not vary much in their subcutaneous attributes. In contrast, if you see a few whales swimming in circles near volcanoes you will be hesitant to infer that all whales swim in circles near volcanoes because your background knowledge tells you nothing about the variability of the behavior of mammals, or cetaceans, or sea-creatures near volcanos. Crucial to such inferences is knowing what kinds of thing whales are, and this could be part of the structure of the concept *whale*.

Finally, analogical inference may well require much conceptual structure for several of the reasons already mentioned. Use of an analog in inference, problem solving, or explanation requires retrieving it from memory, which can depend heavily on the structure of concepts (Thagard, Holyoak, Nelson, and Gochfeld 1990). Mapping from one analog to another to determine what corresponds to what can require judgments of semantic similarity that also depend on conceptual structure (Holyoak and Thagard 1989).

None of the remarks just made is conclusive. We do not have a definitive theory covering the areas of cognition mentioned above. But there are enough psychological and computational experiments to suggest that the postulation of conceptual structure may be important for understanding many cognitive phenomena relevant to belief revision. Now let us look at some recent proposals concerning what concepts might be. I shall briefly consider recent suggestions by Edward Smith, connectionists, and George Miller.

4. WHAT ARE CONCEPTS?

Smith (1989) reviews recent experimental and theoretical research in cognitive psychology on the nature of concepts, starting with the traditional view that concepts can be defined by giving necessary and sufficient conditions for their application. This view has two major problems: (1) it is nearly impossible to find defining conditions for non-mathematical concepts, and (2) concepts show typicality effects. Apples and peaches, for example, are more typical fruits than figs or pumpkins. Typicality effects have led psychologists to consider concepts in terms of prototypes, or best examples. Something is categorized as a fruit if it is sufficiently similar to our prototype of a fruit (see also Lakoff 1987 for a discussion of prototypes), and typicality is a function of degree of similarity to the prototype.

The account of concepts as prototypes has, however, encountered some theoretical and empirical difficulties of its own. Armstrong, Gleitman, and Gleitman (1983) have found typicality effects even in crisp mathematical concepts: 3 is a more typical odd number than 359. Smith argues that a concept includes a *core* as well as a prototype, where the core is more diagnostic than the prototype even though the prototype may be useful for quickly identifying instances. Thus the core of *odd number* would be defined mathematically in terms of divisibility, even if we quickly decide that something is an odd number by matching it against prototypes. In non-mathematical concepts, cores will not be strict definitions, but will nevertheless serve to give concepts stability. Following Murphy and Medin (1985), he observes, however, that there is more to categorization than simply matching to a prototype, since causal reasoning can play a role. For example, if you see a man at a party jump into a swimming pool, you may categorize him as drunk, not because jumping into swimming pools matches your prototype drunk, but because the hypothesis that he is drunk explains his behavior.[1] As I suggested above, explanation is one of the roles that concepts must serve, so more than the prototype or prototype + core theories is needed.

Computational implementations of prototypes have centered on Minsky's (1975) notion of a frame. Frames are symbolic structures that specify for a concept various slots and default values for a slot. For example, a frame representing the concept *whale* would have a slot *size* with the value *large*. Default values are not definitional but merely express typical expectations. Recently, a very different kind of computational approach has been proposed by *connectionists*, who theorize using networks modeled loosely on the brain. Rumelhart, Smolensky, McClelland, and Hinton (1986) advocate a view of schemas (concepts) as patterns of activation distributed over neuron-like units in a highly connected network. A concept is not a structure stored in the brain the way a data structure is stored in a digital computer. Rather, it emerges when needed from the interaction of large numbers of connected nodes.

The connectionist view of concepts appears promising for accounting for subtle categorization effects. A network could, for example, acquire the concept of a whale by being trained on examples of whales, learning to identify blobs as whales without acquiring explicit slots or rules that state typical properties of whales. No single unit corresponds to the concept whale, since information about whales is distributed over numerous units. Work in progress is investigating how concepts as learned patterns of activation can even be organized into kind and part-whole hierarchies. Memory also appears tractable from a connectionist viewpoint, since retrieving information about a concept should happen automatically when the right pattern of activation arises. Another appealing aspect of the the connectionist approach is that it in principle has no problem with partially non-verbal concepts such as 'red' or 'the taste of gorgonzola cheese' since these also can be patterns of activation acquired by training.

Nevertheless, connectionists cannot be said to have a full theory of concepts, since no account has been given of:

(1)   how concepts can be formed by combination rather than from examples;

(2)   the use of concepts in relatively sequential processes such as explanation, problem solving, and deduction;

(3)   how distributed representations of concepts can be used in a wide range of inferential tasks including complex generalizations and analogies; and

(4)   how distributed representations can be used in a general theory of language production and comprehension.

Perhaps progress is imminent on all these fronts, but for now we cannot rely only on connectionist ideas for help in understanding the nature of concepts. Although connectionists show us how to understand prototypes as patterns of activation derived from examples, they have a daunting task in showing how such concepts can generate explanations as in the above case of the drunk in the swimming pool.

A different although perhaps ultimately complementary view comes from the work by George Miller and his colleagues on the structure of the mental lexicon (Miller et al. 1988; Miller and Johnson-Laird 1976). WORDNET is an electronic lexical reference system based on psycholinguistic theories of the organization of human lexical memory. A concept is represented by a set of synonyms, and synonym sets are organized by means of kind, part-whole, and antonymy relations. Kind and part-whole relations are fundamental to the organization of the lexicon because they generate hierarchies. For example, a whale is a kind of cetacean, which is a kind of mammal which is a kind of animal, which is a kind of living thing. A toe is part of a foot, which is part of a leg, which is part of a body. Kind and part-whole hierarchies serve to structure most of our conceptual system, providing backbones off of which other conceptual relations can hang. Although well-known to psycholinguists, the importance of these hierarchies has been neglected by philosophers who have tended to speak of 'conceptual schemes' entirely in the abstract. Hierarchical organization of concepts is very important for understanding the notion of a conceptual revolution (Thagard in press).

WORDNET now includes many thousands of entries, including verbs and adjectives as well as nouns. One advantage of working on such a large scale is that the differences between the kinds of lexical items become readily apparent. Kind and part-whole hierarchies apply well to nouns, but adjectives are primarily organized into antonymic clusters such as that posed by the extremes *wet-dry*. Verbs do not have part-whole hierarchies, and their kind hierarchies seem to differ from the kind hierarchies of nouns in ways that are still under investigation. Whereas most work on the nature of concepts has been restricted to nouns, a general theory should attend to other parts of speech as well.

WORDNET's semantic relations are not intended to exhaust the meaning of a concept. Miller and Johnson-Laird (1976) have a procedural theory of meaning that associates concepts with computational routines, often tied to perception, for identifying instances of a concept. But they say (p. 696) that semantics also requires placing concepts and sentences in the context of a larger system of knowledge and belief. I presume this larger context would include information of the sort that can be used for generating explanations and performing the other roles of concepts discussed above. Conceptual information should therefore be tied to world knowledge such as that drunks tend to act wildly, which, in conjunction with the characterization of jumping into the swimming pool as acting wildly, could give rise to the explanatory hypothesis that the man in the swimming pool was drunk. I shall now propose how this kind of knowledge can be integrated with other considerations of conceptual structure.

5. CONCEPTS AS COMPLEX STRUCTURES

No one currently knows how concepts are stored in the brain. Perhaps they are patterns of activation of neurons as the connectionists suggest, or maybe some more complex organization and distribution exists. Without worrying about neural implementation, we can nevertheless consider how concepts are organized and serve to play the numerous roles listed above. I am not saying that connectionism and neuroscience are irrelevant: we are still in the early stages of cognitive science and should not tolerate imperialistic limitations on kinds of approaches. My proposals will be at the level of traditional symbolic artificial intelligence, but are meant to suggest targets for subsequent connectionist and neurological analysis. In contrast to the sometimes acrimonious debate between proponents of symbolic AI and purportedly subsymbolic connectionism, I see cognitive science as using a continuum of complementary computational methods.

What is the concept of a whale? Let us start with WORDNET-style lexical organization. Information about *whale* could include something like the following:

WHALE
A kind of: cetacean, mammal, sea-creature.
Subkinds: humpback-whale, blue-whale, killer-whale, sperm-whale, white-whale, beluga-whale, etc.
Parts: fins, blubber, bone, blow-hole, tail.

A WORDNET entry can in addition include lists of synonyms, antonyms, and wholes. For a full representation of the concept, we can supplement this representation with pointers to individual whales like Gracy that comprise the known instances of whales. The concept of whale should, in addition, provide access to various general facts about whales that are important for conversing and reasoning about whales. It should therefore be connected with rules such as the following:

(R1) If x is a whale, then it swims.
(R2) If x is a whale, and x surfaces, then x blows water through its blow-hole.

Holland, Holyoak, Nisbett, and Thagard (1986) discuss the relevance of rules for concepts. Notice that Rl is easily represented as a slot in a Minsky-style frame:

WHALE:
Locomotion: swims.

In contrast, R2 with more complicated conditions and the complex relation *blows water through* is less amenable to treatment as a slot. It would also pose problems for simple connectionist learning schemes that form patterns of activation merely from features. The word 'whale' is unusual in lacking synonyms and antonyms, which abound especially for adjectives. The concept *whale* should also help to provide access to instances of whales such as Gracy.

My proposal then is to think of concepts as complex structures akin to frames, but (1) giving special priority to kind and part-whole relations that establish hierarchies; and (2) expressing factual information in rules that can be more complex than simple slots. Schematically, a concept can be thought of as a frame-like structure of the following sort:

CONCEPT:
A kind of:
Subkinds:
A part of:
Parts:
Synonyms:
Antonyms:
Rules:
Instances:

The presence of rules shows how concepts can be used in deduction, explanation, and problem solving. For suggestions about how concepts as complex structures can figure in generalization, analogy, and other forms of inference, see the discussion of the PI cognitive architecture in Thagard (1988).

We are still far from having a genuine theory of concepts, but the enriched account offered so far makes possible a start on considering how conceptual structure can be relevant to epistemic change. I shall now show how the above view points to different kinds of conceptual change that would be opaque from the point of view of belief revision alone.

6. DEGREES OF CONCEPTUAL CHANGE

The lesson I want to draw from the previous discussion of the nature of concepts is that not all beliefs are equal from the point of view of conceptual structure. In particular, beliefs about kind and part-whole relations are especially important, because those relations organize concepts. Hence revisions of beliefs about these relations will be more momentous than routine changes. Deciding that whales are mammals and not fish is a significant alteration in our kind hierarchy.[2]

It would be futile to try to offer criteria for identity of concepts that attempt to specify when a concept ceases to be the concept it was. We cannot even give such criteria for mundane objects like bicycles: if I change the tires on my bicycle, is it the 'same' bike? What if I change the wheels, or the frame, or all of the above? But without giving a definition of sameness for bicycles, we can nevertheless rank degrees of change. Replacement of the parts mentioned are all changes in my bicycle, but it seems clear that changing the frame is a more severe change than the wheels, which is more severe than changing the tires. Similarly, we can characterize different kinds of conceptual change and see that some are more serious than others.

Taking a concept as a kind of complex structure described above, we can list at least the following kinds of conceptual change, which are roughly ordered in terms of degree of increasing severity. My list considers additions, but could easily be expanded to include deletions too.

(1)   Adding a new instance, for example that the blob in the distance is a whale. This involves a change to the structure of the concept *whale*, but is relatively trivial like adding a pennant to a bicycle.

(2)   Adding a new weak rule, for example that whales can be found in the Arctic ocean.

(3)   Adding a new strong rule that plays a frequent role in problem solving and explanation, for example that whales eat sardines.

The terms 'weak' and 'strong' indicate the importance of the rule for problem solving. Thus the distinction between (2) and (3) is pragmatic:

if you are an Eskimo or Russian fisherman, (2) might be a stronger
rule. For a discussion of pragmatics and rule strength, see Holland et
al. (1986).

(4)   Adding new part-whole relation, for example that whales
         have spleens.

(5)   Adding new kind relations, for example that a dolphin is a
         kind of whale.

(6)   Adding a new concept, for example, *sea-elephant*.

The additions outlined in (1)–(5) only become possible when one has
formed a concept of whale as a distinct kind of entity. Concepts can
be added for a variety of reasons. In the eighteenth century, heat and
temperature became different concepts, a process psychologists call
differentiation (Wiser and Carey 1983; Carey 1985). In the nineteenth
century, scientists realized that electricity and magnetism were fundamentally the same and produced the *coalesced* concept of electromag-
netism. In addition to differentiation and coalescence, new concepts
can be introduced for explanatory reasons, for example, when the
concept *sound wave* was formed as part of the explanation of why
sounds behave as they do (Thagard 1988).

(7)   Reorganizing hierarchies by *branch jumping*, that is, shifting
         a concept from one branch of a hierarchical tree to another.

We saw that kind relations organize concepts in tree-like hierarchies.
A very important kind of conceptual change involves moving a concept
from one branch of the tree to another. Such branch jumping is common
in scientific revolutions. For example, the adoption of Copernican
theory required the reclassification of the earth as a kind of planet,
when previously it had been taken to be *sui generis*. Similarly, Darwin
recategorized humans as a kind of animal, when previously they were
taken to be a different kind of creature. This jump is illustrated in
Figure 1. Thagard (in press) describes cases of branch jumping in the
chemical revolution that involve both kind and part-whole hierarchies.

(8)   *Tree switching*, that is, changing the organizing principle of
         a hierarchical tree.

Darwin not only reclassified humans as animals, he changed the
meaning of the classification. Whereas before Darwin *kind* was a notion
primarily of similarity, his theory made it a historical notion: being of

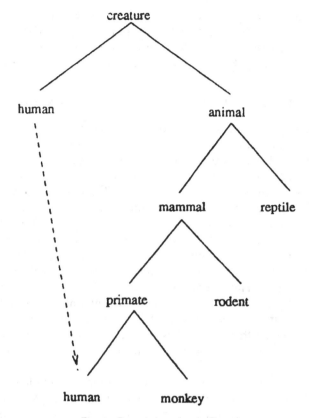

Fig. 1. Branch jumping in Darwin.

common descent becomes at least as important as being in the same kind as surface similarity. Einstein's theory of relativity changed the nature of part-whole relations, by substituting ideas of space-time for everyday notions of space and time.

If one does not attend to conceptual structure, and thinks only in terms of belief revision, the importance of the last five kinds of conceptual change will be missed. Although (1)–(3) can be interpreted as straightforward kinds of belief revision, (4)–(8) cannot. In particular, branch jumping and tree switching are changes that are very difficult to make on a piecemeal basis. Darwin did not simply pick away at the creationist conceptual structure: he produced an elaborate alternative edifice that supplanted it as a whole. Adopting a new conceptual system is more holistic than piecemeal belief revision. A theory of explanatory coherence that shows how such holistic replacements can take place is developed elsewhere (Thagard 1989, Ranney and Thagard 1988).

7. ILLUSTRATION: THE CONCEPT OF AN ACID

I have been primarily illustrating conceptual change so far using the concept whale, but now want to consider a scientific example that is embedded in a richer theoretical context. Today the concept of an *acid* is known to everyone, but that was not always so (for a good historical review, see Walden 1929). The originating Latin term (*acidus*) just means sour, and was applied to sour things like vinegar, whose Latin word *acetum* comes from the same root as *acidu*, and to lemon juice. What we now think of as the acid components of these substances, acetic acid and citric acid, were not identified until much later. Only in the middle ages did alchemists isolate what we now call nitric acid and sulphuric acid. The French term 'acide' arose in the sixteenth century and the English term 'acid' in the seventeenth, as an adjective meaning sour but also as a noun vaguely denoting a class of sour substances. It seems that the earliest concept of an acid was for sour substances whose subkinds included vinegar and nitric and sulphuric acids.

As far back as Democritus, however, the attempt was made to explain why some things are sour. He offered the atomistic explanation that how something tastes is caused by the shape of the atoms that make it up (Sambursky 1956, p. 122). Similarly, in the seventeenth century, Nicholas Lemery proposed that the properties of acids derive from the sharp, spikey form of the corpuscles that make them up. In the phlogiston theory, which dominated mid-eighteenth century chemistry, acids were taken to be simple substances while what we now conceive of as their constituents were understood as compounds. For example, sulphur was thought to be a compound of oil of vitriol (sulphuric acid) and phlogiston.

The first general theory of acids originated with Lavoisier who thought that the central property of acids was that they contain oxygen. In fact 'oxygen' derives from Greek words meaning 'sour producing'. There was no place in his system for the concept of phlogiston, and acids were viewed as compounds rather than simple substances: sulphuric acid is a compound of sulphur, oxygen, and hydrogen. For Lavoisier, oxygen was more than just a constituent of acids: it was the *principle* of acidification, that is, what gave acids their sourness and other central properties. The transition from the phlogiston view of acids to Lavoisier's was not a matter of piecemeal belief revision, but required the development and acceptance of a whole new system of kind and part-whole relations (Thagard in press).

Lavoisier's theory was demolished, however, in 1815 when Humphrey Davy showed that muriatic acid – what we now call hydrochloric acid – consists only of hydrogen and chlorine. He and Liebig contended that hydrogen, rather than oxygen, was essential to the constitution and effects of acids. This idea was put on a quantitative basis by Arrhenius in 1887 when he proposed that acids are substances that dissociate to produce hydrogen ions. More general conceptions of acids were proposed by Brönsted, Lowry, and Lewis in the 1920s. The Brönsted–Lowry account characterizes an acid as a substance that donates protons, so that having hydrogen as a part is no longer essential. Lewis's account counts still more substances as acids, since acids are characterized as any substances that can accept an electron pair. Chemistry textbooks typically present all three of the Arrhenius, Brönsted–Lowry, and Lewis accounts as useful approximations. Each theory has correlative accounts of the nature of bases and salts. There is no attempt to state a rigid definition of what acids are.

For the understanding of conceptual change, several stages in this development are very interesting. Sometime around 1700 the modern concept of acid as a special class of substances with properties other than sourness came into use. *Acid* and *sour* became differentiated. Important changes have taken place in the part-whole relations of the concept, from the idea that acids have sharp atoms, to the idea that oxygen is their most important part, to the idea that hydrogen is essential, to current ideas that describe acids in terms of protons and electrons rather than elements. The rule that acids typically have hydrogen as a constituent is far more important than the observation, dating from at least the seventeenth century, that acids turn litmus red. The litmus rule has been useful to generations of chemistry students, but plays no role in locating the concept of acid in conceptual hierarchies or in generating explanations of the experiments involving acids.

Over the centuries, there has been a dramatic increase in the number of substances counted as acids, from the few known to the medievals to well over a hundred counted by modern chemists. One interesting consequence of the modern theories is that water can be counted as both an acid and a base, since depending on what substance it combines with it can either donate or accept protons and electrons. Also of interest is the subclassification of acids, adding important new sub-kinds such as amino acids. What has occurred in the development of the concept of acid is clearly far more complicated than the refinement of necessary and sufficient conditions for the term 'acid': definition and theory go hand in hand. Merely talking of belief revision would obscure the fact that the concept of acid has changed remarkably in its structural relations to other concepts while enjoying a certain stability: we still count vinegar and lemon juice as acidic.

8. CONCLUSION

I conclude, therefore, that an understanding of conceptual development in science and everyday life is an essential part of epistemology. Merely attending to belief revision will miss crucial aspects of epistemic change. I have only alluded to the cases that seem to me to show this most decisively: scientific revolutions, in which whole systems of concepts get altered or replaced (Thagard in press). Even in more mundane cases of epistemic change, we ought for various psychological and epistemological reasons to take seriously the role of concepts, both their formation and their effects on organizing and affecting the revision of beliefs. Hence conceptual change is more than belief revision, and epistemology needs a theory of concepts just as much as does psychology.

NOTES

* I am grateful to Michael Ranney and Gilbert Harman for comments on an earlier version of this paper.

[1] Smith (in press) calls this inference 'reverse deduction', but philosophers since Peirce have called it *abduction*. See Thagard (1988a, chap. 4).

[2] The momentousness of a belief revision is affected, of course, by more than these conceptual relations. Some beliefs are very important to us because they are closely related to our personal goals, while other beliefs are important because they are densely related to many other beliefs.

REFERENCES

Armstrong, S., L. Gleitman and H. Gleitman: 1983, 'What Some Concepts Might Not Be', *Cognition* **13**, 263–308.

Carey, S.: 1985, *Conceptual Change in Childhood*, MIT Press, Cambridge, Massachusetts.

Goldman, A.: 1986, *Epistemology and Cognition*, Harvard University Press, Cambridge, Massachusetts.

Hacking, I.: 1975, *Why Does Language Matter to Philosophy?*, Cambridge University Press, Cambridge.

Harman, G.: 1986, *Change in View: Principles of Reasoning*, Cambridge University Press, Cambridge.

Harman, G.: 1987, '(Nonsolopsistic) Conceptual Role Semantics', in E. LePore (ed.), *Semantics of Natural Language*, Academic Press, New York, 55–81.

Holland, J., K. Holyoak, R. Nisbett and P. Thagard: 1986, *Induction: Processes of Inference, Learning, and Discovery*, MIT Press/Bradford Books, Cambridge, Massachusetts.

Holyoak, K. and P. Thagard: 1989, 'Analogical Mapping by Constraint Satisfaction', *Cognitive Science* **13**, 295–355.

Kuhn, T.: 1970, *Structure of Scientific Revolutions*, 2nd edition, University of Chicago Press, Chicago (first published 1962).

Lakoff, G.: 1988, *Women, Fire, and Dangerous Things*, University of Chicago Press, Chicago.

Miller, G. A., C. Fellbaum, J. Kegl and K. Miller: 1988, 'WORDNET: An Electronic Lexical Reference System Based on Theories of Lexical Memory', *Revue Québécoise Linguistique* **17**, 181–213.

Miller, G. and P. Johnson-Laird: 1976, *Language and Perception*, Harvard University Press, Cambridge, Massachusetts.

Minsky, M.: 1975, 'A Framework for Representing Knowledge', in P. H. Winston (ed.), *The Psychology of Computer Vision*, McGraw-Hill, New York, pp. 211–77.

Murphy, G. L. and D. L. Medin: 1985, 'The Role of Theories in Conceptual Coherence', *Psychological Review* **92**, 289–316.

Ranney, M. and P. Thagard: 1988, 'Explanatory Coherence and Belief Revision in Naive Physics', *Proceedings of the Tenth Annual Conference of the Cognitive Science Society*, Erlbaum, Hillsdale, NJ, 426–32.

Rumelhart, D., P. Smolensky, G. Hinton and J. McClelland: 1986, 'Schemata and Sequential Thought Processes in PDP Models', in J. McClelland and D. Rumelhart (eds.), *Parallel Distributed Processing: Explorations in the Microstructure of Cognition* Vol. 2, MIT Press/Bradford Books, Cambridge, Massachusetts, pp. 7–57.

Sambursky, S.: 1956, *The Physical World of the Greeks*, Routledge and Kegan Paul, London.

Smith, E.: (1989), 'Concepts and Inductions', in M. Posner (ed.), *Foundations of Cognitive Science*, MIT Press, Cambridge, Massachusetts.

Thagard, P.: 1984a, 'Conceptual Combination and Scientific Discovery', in P. Asquith and P. Kitcher (eds.), *PSA 1984*, Vol. 1, Philosophy of Science Association, East Lansing, Michigan.

Thagard, P.: 1984b, 'Frames, Knowledge, and Inference', *Synthese* **61**, 233–59.

Thagard, P.: 1988, *Computational Philosophy of Science*, MIT Press/Bradford Books, Cambridge, Massachusetts.

Thagard, P.: 1989, 'Explanatory Coherence', *Behavioral and Brain Sciences* **12**, 435–467.

Thagard, P.: (in press), 'The Conceptual Structure of the Chemical Revolution', *Philosophy of Science*.

Thagard, P., K. Holyoak, G. Nelson and D. Gochfeld: 1990, 'Analogical Retrieval by Constraint Satisfaction', *Artificial Intelligence* in press.

Walden, P.: 1929, *Salts, Acids and Bases*, McGraw-Hill, New York.

Wiser, M. and S. Carey: 1983, 'When Heat and Temperature Were One', in D. Gentner and A. Stevens (eds.), *Mental Models*, Hillsdale, New Jersey, pp. 267–97.

Cognitive Science Laboratory
Princeton University
221 Nassau St.
Princeton, New Jersey 08542
U.S.A.

WILLIAM BECHTEL AND ADELE A. ABRAHAMSEN

BEYOND THE EXCLUSIVELY PROPOSITIONAL ERA[1] •

ABSTRACT. Contemporary epistemology has assumed that knowledge is represented
in sentences or propositions. However, a variety of extensions and alternatives to this
view have been proposed in other areas of investigation. We review some of these
proposals, focusing on (1) Ryle's notion of *knowing how* and Hanson's and Kuhn's
accounts of theory-laden perception in science; (2) extensions of simple propositional
representations in cognitive models and artificial intelligence; (3) the debate concerning
imagistic versus propositional representations in cognitive psychology; (4) recent treat-
ments of concepts and categorization which reject the notion of necessary and sufficient
conditions; and (5) parallel distributed processing (connectionist) models of cognition.
This last development is especially promising in providing a flexible, powerful means of
representing information nonpropositionally, and carrying out at least simple forms of
inference without rules. Central to several of the proposals is the notion that much of
human cognition might consist in *pattern recognition* rather than manipulation of rules
and propositions.

1. INTRODUCTION

Knowledge is expressed in sentences, or in propositions that are sentence-like in important respects. This assertion appears rather obvious
and uncontroversial; it covers the two main versions of what we will
refer to as the *propositional view* of knowledge. It has been assumed
by contemporary epistemologists and also within the mainstream of
cognitive psychology, linguistics, artificial intelligence, and other cognitive sciences. Perhaps the propositional view of knowledge emerged as
the natural, favored view because propositions are so accessible to
reflection. We observe ourselves conversing, writing, and lecturing by
means of natural language, and make the inference that sentences or
sentence-like expressions are the medium of knowledge representation
and thought within the mind-brain as well as the medium of communication across individuals.

Some may object to combining sentences and propositions indiffer-
ently under the rubric 'the propositional view'. It has been a matter of
long debate within philosophy whether or not it is useful to posit
propositions, that is, entities that have a relation to sentences but are
more abstract (e.g., the same proposition would be expressed regardless

J. H. Fetzer (ed.), Epistemology and Cognition, 121–151.

of whether the active or passive voice were used). For our purposes, the distinction between sentences and propositions will not be important. Propositions are modeled after sentences, and share many of their important characteristics. Both are composed of symbols under the constraint of rules of formation (syntax). Both have (or can be viewed as having) truth value. Both can be regarded as timeless (although one might choose instead to focus on the auditory or graphic detail of a spoken or written sentence token). Finally, both are abstract in the sense that there is no iconic resemblance between the expression and its external referent (although propositions are abstract in additional ways as well).

Regardless of which version of the propositional view is taken, there are several strands of cognitive science research which suggest that a simple propositional format may be insufficient as a sole means of representing knowledge. In this paper, we will briefly review the focus on propositions within mainstream epistemology, as well as the claims some philosophers have advanced for considering nonpropositional formats for knowledge. We then summarize some of the theoretical and empirical work within other cognitive sciences which offers extensions and alternatives to a simple propositional approach to mental representations. A very recent advance is the most promising one: the development of *parallel distributed processing* models (also referred to as *connectionist* models, and closely related to neural network models).

Our goal here is not to demonstrate through argument that nonpropositional formats *must* be adopted. Rather, we wish to illustrate a variety of nonpropositional approaches, showing what they have to offer as alternative vehicles for knowledge representation. To adopt any of these alternatives is not a simple matter. There are serious unresolved questions regarding the roles that might still remain for propositions. For example, one view would be that some kinds of knowledge should be represented propositionally, and others nonpropositionally. A different view is that all knowledge can be given a relatively low-level nonpropositional representation, and that propositions are a way of expressing certain informational regularities in those representations.

Issues of this kind cannot be resolved at this time. However, an argument can be made that philosophers should be attentive to them. In one sense, what we are calling for is a naturalization of epistemology: we hold that epistemological analyses need to be compatible with the best current scientific accounts of human cognition. However, we are not proposing (as did Quine 1969) to make epistemology simply a chapter of empirical cognitive science. Epistemology's aim remains normative: to identify what should count as knowledge and to make recommendations as to how best to procure knowledge (see McCauley 1988). In this respect our endeavor is close in spirit to more traditional epistemology, such as that pursued by Aristotle, Descartes, and Hume, who drew freely upon the best science of their day in formulating their epistemological claims.

2. PROPOSITIONAL AND NONPROPOSITIONAL PARADIGMS IN PHILOSOPHY

Much of contemporary epistemology has been devoted to obtaining an adequate definition of knowledge, i.e., one that would cover all and only cases of knowledge. Most modern accounts of knowledge assume that knowledge minimally consists of *justified true belief*. Each of these three requirements points us toward propositional models of knowledge. Consider first the idea that knowledge requires belief. Belief is typically construed as a propositional attitude (Russell 1940), where a proposition is the object of the attitude. If Sarah believes that the cat is on the roof, her belief is *about* the proposition ⌐the cat is one roof⌐. According to the analyses of folk psychology, she could also have other attitudes towards this proposition: some epistemic (e.g., doubt), some emotional (e.g., fear). All require the existence of a proposition (although proponents of this approach might not be committed to the idea that a proposition is somehow represented in the head of the individual). The requirement that knowledge be true also seems to require that knowledge be propositional. Although there are different theories as to what truth consists in, truth values are generally held to accrue to propositions or sentences. It is not clear what other kinds of entities could be counted as true or false. Finally, justification is typically construed in terms of arguments; we are justified in our belief if we have a compelling argument that the proposition in question is true. There is variation in epistemological views about the nature of justification (e.g., foundationalism vs. coherentism), but they have in common that justification consists of arguments which in turn consist of propositions.

Epistemological analyses have focused exclusively on propositional knowledge. Within philosophy more broadly, however, there have been occasional contentions that knowledge may also be expressed in formats that are not propositional. Ryle (1949) objected to the preoccupation of philosophers with facts and theoretical knowledge and argued that acquiring propositionally encoded knowledge was only one aspect of human cognition. Examining a broader range of human practices that could be performed intelligently (or stupidly), he introduced a distinction between *knowing how* and *knowing that*. There are many things a person knows *how* to do (e.g., read a map) for which it is difficult if not impossible to state propositionally *what* the person knows. Ryle's approach to analyzing knowing how, of course, was behavioristic; he treated this knowledge as manifest in our actions and so not to be understood in terms of something hidden and internal (the ghost in the machine).

Ryle's notion of knowing how has received little attention in epistemology. One reason for this is that we do not have a clear notion of what is involved when someone acquires such knowledge. We can specify criteria in terms of which we decide whether someone has acquired this knowledge, but we are hard pressed to explain what has changed *in* the person when he or she has acquired the knowledge of how to perform a skill. As we shall indicate below, some psychologists have modeled this kind of knowledge by means of mental rules. Somewhat ironically, this was the sort of approach Ryle was opposing.

One context in which some philosophers have seriously explored the possibility of nonpropositional knowledge is in the analysis of perception. Wittgenstein (1953) was one of the first to explore this issue, probing at what the difference might be between *seeing* something, and seeing it *as* a particular kind of thing. Like Ryle, Wittgenstein raised doubts as to whether this difference could be explained in terms of differences occurring within the person, for example in terms of an act of interpretation, and focused instead on the behavioral manifestations of this difference.

The focus on perception has been most prominent in the challenges to the logical positivists' account of science. A major component of the positivist view was the claim that knowledge is anchored in observation statements – statements which directly report features of the observed world (or, in some cases, features of phenomenal experience). For the positivists, epistemic processes occurred once information was encoded linguistically or propositionally. The challenge to the positivists' position can be seen as claiming that a great deal of knowledge is involved in the primitive act of seeing prior to the point at which knowledge is encoded propositionally.

Hanson (1958) was one of the first to mount a sustained argument against the view of perception as a simple act of recording. He focused on conflicts in science in which, for example, one scientist would see the Golgi apparatus of the cell, whereas another would see an artifact due to methods of staining.[2] As an analogy, Hanson pointed to ambiguous figures such as the Necker cube (Figure 1), which can be seen in more than one way. Hanson rejected the view that all people see the same thing (for example, an arrangement of lines in two dimensions), with some proceeding to see the figure first as a cube looked at from the front, and others first as a cube viewed from above. Rather, he maintained, each individual directly sees the cube from one perspective, and may then switch to the other perspective. Hanson applies this idea to seeing objects in the domain of a science; for example, where the amateur simply sees an apparatus made of glass and other materials, the physicist sees an x-ray tube. The physicist does not first see as the layperson sees and then make an inference, but rather directly sees the x-ray tube. Moreover, this depends upon learning: "The layman must learn physics before he can see what the physicist sees" (p. 16). Hanson

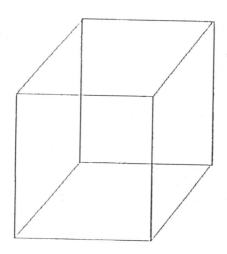

Fig. 1. Necker Cube.

characterizes this process as depending on the "knowledge, experience, and theories" (p. 18) that the physicist possesses, and so labels perception as 'theory-laden'. Knowledge, in his view, consists of propositions. Hence, seeing represents a bridge between the physical world and propositions, and learning to see as a scientist is primarily a matter of learning the appropriate propositions. (However, as we will see, there are other ways to model this knowledge, which would not have been familiar to Hanson.)

The notion that observation is theory-laden also figures centrally in Kuhn's (1970) account of normal science and of scientific revolutions; in fact, this is responsible for much of the controversy his work has generated. The reason is fairly obvious. Kuhn maintains that pre- and post-revolutionary practitioners of a science do not see the world in the same way (or do not even see the same world) and hence their accounts of the world are *incommensurable*. The two groups of scientists do not describe the world in ways that are intertranslatable, but each uses its own ways of describing the world to make its empirical predictions and to present the evidence for its theory. The supposed inability to compare two theories in terms of the different predictions the theories make appears to undercut the objectivity of science and generate relativism (an interpretation Kuhn ultimately rejected). For these and other reasons, Kuhn's notion of theory-laden observation generated considerable controversy.

In this controversy, a potentially more significant point may have been ignored. That is the fact that for Kuhn, learning normal science involves learning to see the world in particular ways. This is most clear in Kuhn's discussion of what a scientist must do to proceed through a revolution: "at time of revolution, when the normal-scientific tradition changes, the scientist's perception of his environment must be re-educated – in some familiar situations he must learn to see a new gestalt" (p. 112).

The idea that a scientist needs to learn to see the world in a particular manner suggests that a part of what a scientist knows consists in *knowing how to see* as a practitioner of that science would. Kuhn makes it clear that he does not see this learning as involving a translation manual whereby one learns to translate one's new scientific vocabulary into a preexisting observational vocabulary. Moreover, it is an activity that takes time. A student can memorize a textbook relatively easily, but knowing the propositions does not entail mastery of the science. Kuhn emphasizes the importance of student scientists learning by replicating paradigmatic work in the science. Much of the real learning in science is accomplished by apprenticeship – a student goes into the laboratory and there learns how to deal with the world as a practitioner of the discipline.

This aspect of Kuhn's account has been little developed, in part probably because it is so hard to say what the knowledge consists in if it is not something that is to be encoded propositionally. But at least he alluded to an important aspect of science on which few other philosophers have placed much importance. One of the benefits of extending the focus of epistemology beyond propositions is that ultimately we may be able to understand the kind of knowledge that underlies perceptual capabilities as well as the phenomenon of *knowing how*. However, actual exploration of what such representations might be like, and under what conditions they may be used, is work that has been carried out in cognitive science disciplines other than philosophy. In particular, cognitive psychologists engaged in very active debate and experimentation on propositional versus nonpropositional representations during the 1970s. To a lesser extent, the issue was pursued in artificial intelligence as well. We now turn to these efforts.

3. PROPOSITIONAL AND NONPROPOSITIONAL REPRESENTATIONS IN THE COGNITIVE SCIENCES

Most cognitive scientists involved in constructing models of knowledge representation have used some version of propositional representation. The earliest efforts tended to involve relatively unstructured declarative representations: sets of propositions in a format adapted in one way or another from first order predicate calculus. Within artificial intelligence, Black's (1968) question-answering system is an early exemplar. The question "Can the monkey get the bananas?", for example, was represented as

canult(monkey,has(monkey,bananas))

where 'canult' means 'can ultimately cause'. Within psychology, Kintsch (1974) represented text in terms of a propositional text base. Propositions had a uniform format: one predicate followed by one or more arguments. The predicates and arguments were viewed as underlying concepts which could be variably realized in natural languages, and were capitalized to distinguish them from the words that would be used in their realization. For example (p. 18), the sentence "The subjects were 20 female students." was represented as (STUDENT, SUBJECT) & (FEMALE, STUDENT) & (NUMBER, SUBJECT, TWENTY). Connections among propositions were captured by means of a repetition rule involving recurrent concepts such as STUDENT, and by embedding. For example, (BECAUSE, α, β) is a proposition that embeds two other propositions. A variety of empirical studies were undertaken, some providing evidence for propositional representation and others simply assuming it in the pursuit of other issues. For example, it was shown that a sentence expressing a single multi-argument proposition tended to be recalled as a unit, whereas a sentence equated for length but expressing several single-argument propositions had less stability in memory.

To actually sit down and work out an extensive propositional model of long portions of text is not a method of inquiry that philosophers would tend to carry out. Psychologists and computer scientists, in utilizing propositions as a tool for modeling, put themselves in a position to discover the opportunities and limitations of this tool. As a result of this kind of experience, they found that simply listing all of the applicable propositions was too impoverished an approach. Although they usually retained propositions in one form or another, modelers found it advantageous to modify the format of expression, and to add certain kinds of higher-order structure (at least to Kintsch's degree, and often considerably beyond that).

One of these alternative formats for propositional representation is the semantic network, in which nodes are connected by links, and one or both of these are labeled. Quillian's 1966 dissertation (see Quillian 1968) introduced this approach into the early artificial intelligence literature, and it was further developed by others in that field as well as in psychology. Some versions, in which predicate nodes are linked to argument nodes, have a predicate calculus flavor (e.g., Norman, Rumelhart, and the LNR Research Group, 1975). Semantic networks may in fact be equivalent to other kinds of propositional representations in the information they can express. We mention the network format, however, because it can be viewed as one predecessor to the PDP models discussed in the Section 5 of this paper, and because certain kinds of processes are most naturally understood in terms of networks (e.g., spreading activation; see Anderson 1983).

It did not take long before larger units of knowledge were made the focus of investigation. Propositional or network-propositional representations were used to build complex informational structures (sometimes referred to as *schemata*). In artificial intelligence, Minsky's (1975) *frames* and Schank and Abelson's (1977) *scripts* were particularly influential. Both provide a higher-order framework which organizes propositions into larger units, and specifies default values that are assumed (inferred) unless there is explicit information to the contrary. For example, the restaurant script specifies what one knows about going to a restaurant: that one is seated, obtains a menu, orders, eats the meal, obtains a bill, and finally pays for the meal. If there is a blackboard instead of menu, or payment precedes eating the meal, the defaults will be overwritten; otherwise the information in the script comes 'for free' when the frame or script is activated. Another variation on higher-order structure is the 'story grammar' approach proposed in psychology by Rumelhart (1975) and others. When propositional networks are used in these ways, they take on some of the functions and characteristics of pattern recognition systems.

A different kind of step away from a purely propositional approach is to use propositions to express procedures, rather than (or in addition to) declarative knowledge. Such propositions are referred to as rules, and appropriate sets of such propositions are rule systems. Generative grammars represent linguistic knowledge in this way (Chomsky 1957), although the rules are intended as abstract representations of 'competence' rather than models of 'performance'. Production systems, in contrast, are more often intended to model actual mental activity. Each rule in a production system is a production of the form "If X then Y," where X is some condition that must be met and Y is an action that is then carried out. Typically some of the rules are used to build and manipulate goal structures; an example from a production system for performing arithmetic is: "If the goal is to iterate through the rows of a column and the top row has not been processed, then the subgoal is to add the digit of the top row to the running total" (Anderson 1983, p. 8). Some procedural theorists, including Anderson, incorporate both declaratively-formatted knowledge and procedures in the architecture of their models; others attempt to produce purely procedural models. An innovative approach is to use a uniform representation which may be treated as either data or procedure (see Bobrow and Winograd, 1977; Norman, Rumelhart, and the LNR Research Group, 1975).

The approaches discussed thus far diverge in various ways from an unstructured, purely declarative orientation to propositional representation; nonetheless, they do remain within an overall propositional framework. This distinguishes them from an alternative tradition of focusing on mental images as a format for encoding knowledge. Most recently, this resulted in a very lively debate in the 1970s over the representational status of mental imagery, and the question of the sufficiency of propositions. Images are generally characterized as differing from propositions in that they are modality-specific, analog and iconic rather than abstract, discrete, and arbitrary in form (see, e.g., Anderson 1978). It is usually visual images that are focused upon; these need not be viewed as literal pictures, but would show certain isomorphisms with the visual world that would give them a spatial character. These distinctive properties of images led Paivio (1971) to posit a dual-code theory of memory, which holds that modality-specific representational formats are used to mentally encode knowledge. In particular, visual information is encoded in mental images, and sentential information is encoded in a verbal code that is auditory or articulatory in nature. The primary contrasting position is that abstract propositional representations are adequate to encode all kinds of knowledge, including visual and spatial knowledge, without themselves being visual or spatial in character.

To give the flavor of the kind of data that were in dispute, we will briefly describe a few of the early experiments. (They were followed by more clever studies that ruled out certain alternative explanations but are too complex to summarize here; see Kosslyn 1980). Moyer (1973) asked subjects to answer questions such as "Which is larger, moose or roach?". There was a linear relation between the disparity in size of the two animals and the time required to respond. Similar linear relationships between analog dimensions of difference and reaction time have been found for tasks such as scanning a mental image of a map (Kosslyn, Ball, and Reiser, 1978) and mentally rotating letters or other patterns (Cooper and Shepard, 1973). There is even evidence to suggest a role for analog (or at least spatially ordered) representation in carrying out inferences. Huttenlocher and Higgins (1971) presented subjects with three-term series problems. For example: "Tom is taller than Sam. John is shorter than Sam. Who is tallest?". By varying the order and wording of the premises, they were able to obtain reaction time patterns that suggested that subjects mentally ordered the terms in a spatial array (e.g., Tom–Sam–John). Not everyone accepted this interpretation (see Clark 1969), but the body of data from these and other studies presented a challenge to purely propositional approaches to mental representation that was not ignored.

Given results such as these, some investigators have concluded that an alternative form of representation, which Kosslyn (1980) calls *depictive* or *quasi-pictorial image representation*, is involved in tasks with a spatial or analog character. In one version, the long-term knowledge store itself uses different representation formats appropriate to the type of information. In a different version (Kosslyn 1980), a long-term representation which is more or less propositional in format is used to generate a depictive representation (visual image) in a short-term visual buffer; the image can then be manipulated by analog processes which produce reaction time functions such as those summarized above. In this version, the 'knowledge' itself is represented uniformly, but when that knowledge is activated there is diversity in the format of short-term representation. Very different ways of employing imagistic or spatial representations have been proposed by others (e.g., Johnson-Laird 1983, and Langacker 1986).

Defenders of a more traditional approach (e.g., Pylyshyn 1981) have insisted on the primacy of propositional representations. Anderson (1978) described a propositional representation and associated processes which could yield a linear function for mental rotation; however, given that the same kind of empirical data could be generated by either a propositional or an imagistic model, he argued that there were no definitive grounds for choosing between these two forms of representation. Palmer (1978) concluded his detailed discussion of representational formats similarly, suggesting that the question was one for physiological rather than cognitive psychology. Some have taken up that challenge. For example, Farah (1988) reviewed an impressive array of neuropsychological data that support the view that the representations involved in imagery are the same ones that are involved in perception. However, she declined to address the issue of whether these common representations are propositional or depictive in format. We ourselves do not wish to argue a position on this issue. The important point is that there is a class of empirical findings which are aptly captured by nonpropositional representations, and that these phenomena and the forms of representation posited to produce those phenomena should at least be given consideration.

In this section, we have just sampled from a large pool of investigations in psychology and artificial intelligence which suggest alternatives to simple propositional representation. However, there is one important idea which we just hinted at (in the context of frames and scripts). That is the idea that at least certain kinds of knowledge representation may best be approached as *patterns*. In the past, the notion of patterns tended to be raised only in the context of perception, not cognition. However, Rosch (1978) and others have proposed an approach to semantic categories that rejects the applicability of necessary and sufficient conditions, and treats categories rather like patterns. In the next section we describe this approach.

4. CONCEPTS AND CATEGORIZATION

The process of using concepts to categorize objects or events is clearly one of the most basic cognitive activities and traditionally has been approached from a propositional perspective. It has been characteristic of the propositional approach to categories to assume that instances of a category share common features; hence it has been presupposed that categories can be defined in terms of necessary and sufficient conditions for category membership. For example, the concept *bachelor* is taken to be defined in terms of the properties *unmarried* and *male*, which must be possessed by any individual in order to exemplify or count as an exemplar of the concept. This account has a long lineage; it stems from Socrates' quest for definitions and is now referred to as the *classical theory of categorization*. The classical account is one that coheres well with the propositional view of knowledge, for according to it, we can state the conditions for category membership in propositions, and so categorization can be thought of as governed by propositionally encoded knowledge.

The classical view, however, has recently undergone severe challenges which have ramifications for the broader view that knowledge is limited to propositional formats. Within philosophy, Wittgenstein (1953) initiated the challenge (see also Austin 1961). Wittgenstein questioned whether the categories delineated by concepts of ordinary language (e.g., 'game') possessed necessary and sufficient conditions, and suggested that instead instances of a category might only share a *family resemblance*. The challenge has been brought into the domain of empirical investigation through the endeavors of Eleanor Rosch and her colleagues. The key to Rosch's challenge was the discovery of facets of the manner in which humans perform categorization tasks which could not be readily explained on the view that human knowledge of a category consisted in knowing a classical definition of a category. A classical definition would treat a category as a set; within a set, any member would be deemed to be as good a member as any other. Building upon Berlin and Kay's (1969) work, which revealed the importance of focal colors in color perception, however, Rosch produced evidence that for a wide variety of categories, various instances of the category are treated differently (Rosch and Mervis, 1975; Rosch 1978). Some instances are found to be particularly good exemplars (e.g., robin is a good example of bird); Rosch introduced the term *prototype* for those. Other instances (e.g., owl and chicken) would be judged less good exemplars. Barsalou (1983) noted that this scale continued through instances that clearly lay outside the category, and introduced the term *graded structure*.

The evidence for graded structure amongst category members is quite robust, appearing under a variety of additional measures: (1) in determining whether an instance belongs in a category, reaction times are shorter for more prototypical instances; (2) people more readily supply prototypical instances when asked to name an instance of a category; (3) less prototypical instances are judged to be more similar to prototypes than vice versa; and (4) people will generalize information about a prototype to the whole category more readily than they will generalize information about a non-prototype (see Smith and Medin, 1981, for a review). Defenders of the classical view have suggested ways to reconcile the evidence about prototypicality with the classical view (e.g., by proposing that in addition to using necessary and sufficient conditions for category membership, we employ a variety of identification procedures which induce the prototype results; see Armstrong, Gleitman, and Gleitman, 1983). The prototypicality evidence, though, is clearly in tension with the view that categories are sets, and that our ability to categorize depends solely upon knowing conditions of set membership; this suggests that our knowledge of how to categorize may not be encoded in a propositional format.

One response to Rosch's work has been to suggest that the prototypicality results reveal something about how concepts are stored in the head. In particular, some psychologists have proposed that categories are represented mentally in terms of prototypes, and a metric in terms of which the similarity of new instances to the prototypes is judged. The idea is that we then categorize an object in terms of the prototype to which it is judged most similar. The view that our knowledge of categories is stored in terms of representations of prototypes and a similarity metric, however, confronted an obstacle which is familiar to philosophers from the work of Goodman (1955): there is no simple, objective basis for similarity judgments, because any two objects in the universe share an infinite number of properties and differ in an infinite number of properties. One must specify the respect in which two objects are to be judged as similar or different. Murphy and Medin (1985) recognized this difficulty, and proposed that only via *theories* can we determine which features are relevant in determining whether two objects are similar (see also Medin and Wattenmaker, 1986).

Positing a role for theories in processes of categorization is in many respects comparable to proposing that observation is theory-laden, for both moves introduce theories into what seem to be our lowest level cognitive processes. And, as in the case of the theory-ladenness view of observation, the introduction of a role for theories into categorization seems to reverse our intuitive understanding of how cognition occurs. Concepts have been taken to be our basic tools of thought, with our theoretical knowledge built up out of them. If concepts in turn depend upon our theoretical knowledge, then we have lost the foundation. Moreover, as theorists like Medin clearly recognize, if theories are to determine how we categorize objects, we clearly need some way to evaluate theories to determine which ones to use. Our decision about which theories to apply, however, cannot be made in a straightforward manner in terms of empirical evidence, since what we take to be empirical evidence depends upon how we categorize objects and hence on our theories.

The challenge that confronts those who regard categorization as theory-laden is to characterize the nature of the theories that inform categorization. Lakoff (1987) speaks of these structures as *idealized cognitive models* (ICMs), part of which can be represented propositionally, but part of which he maintains are nonpropositional. Even the parts that can be represented propositionally are represented in terms of frame structures (see above), and he views these frames as developed relative to one's purposes. For example, following Fillmore (1982), he construes the frame representing *bachelor* as dependent upon a conception of a human society in which there is an institution of marriage and a typical marriageable age. The model is *idealized* in that it identifies only some aspects of what might be relevant in judging marriageability, which provides one source for prototypicality results. The model fits some contexts well (e.g., a straight male who has never been married, is eligible to marry, and thought likely to be an attractive candidate for marriage) and others poorly (e.g., the Pope), thus inducing a graded structure to our categorization of bachelors.

The components of ICMs that Lakoff claims cannot be captured propositionally are image schemas (a notion he borrows from Langacker, 1986) and metaphoric and metonymic models. The notion of *metonymy*, of letting one aspect or part of something stand for the whole of it, or for other parts, figures centrally in Lakoff's account of categorization. It underlies our use of stereotypes, and so may play a significant role in our subsequent cognitive processing. He describes the case of the category *mother*, wherein the *housewife mother* commonly stands for the whole category, defines what a mother is supposed to be, and provides the basis for our reasoning about mothers. Working mothers are explicitly defined in contrast to this stereotype. One consequence of the role of ICMs in our categorization process for Lakoff is the emergence of radial categories. These are categories which possess a central instance and variations that are accepted by convention, but where there is no general rule that predicts which variations will be accepted (e.g., the Japanese classifier *hon* which is used for long, narrow objects, but is extended to cover hits in baseball, trips via airplanes, etc.). The central instances of these categories play an important role in our thinking, but Lakoff claims that our knowledge of these categories is not embodied in rules that tell us how to apply them.

One element that the prototype view of categories seemed to share with the classical view was the assumption that categorical concepts are relatively stable. Rosch maintained that inter-subject correlations in typicality judgments were extremely high. Recently, this view has been challenged by Barsalou (1986), who has shown much lower correlations both between subjects and within subjects over periods of one month. He also has provided evidence that people easily develop and use new categories (e.g., things to take canoeing in the Everglades), and that typicality judgments can be obtained for these categories. Barsalou thus argues that concepts are not structures stored in long-term memory, but are constructed from "large amounts of interrelated and 'continuous' knowledge" and tailored to current needs. If concepts are not structures in long-term memory, then neither presumably are propositions, since propositions are built out of concepts. This, of course, raises the question as to what the structure of long-term memory is, if it is not organized around concepts and propositions. The models we discuss in the following section provide one possible answer.

In this section we have reviewed some of the recent work on categorization which suggests that categories are not defined in terms of necessary and sufficient conditions but rely on a much more complex framework of knowledge. While many theorists who attempt to model this knowledge employ a symbolic framework, proposing rules to account for categorization performance, others (such as Lakoff) explicitly call for abandoning propositional representation. In a fairly extreme move, Barsalou suggests that concepts may be constructed as needed rather than stored in memory. Except for visual images, proposals as to the form that nonpropositional representations might take have been rare or insufficiently developed. In the next section we will describe a cognitive architecture which can indeed represent knowledge without resorting to explicitly encoded propositions, and has been developed in enough detail to support computer simulation.

5. CONNECTIONIST MODELS OF NONPROPOSITIONAL KNOWLEDGE

Connectionist models, which do not explicitly rely on propositions, actually had their origins prior to the era of modern cognitive science. Selfridge's (1955) pandemonium model and Rosenblatt's (1962) perceptron model were antecedents of such models. However, largely as a result of Minsky and Papert's (1969) demonstration of serious limitations in two-layer networks such as the perceptron, research diminished. It has, however, been revived in this decade with the development of what are referred to as *parallel distributed processing* (PDP) or *connectionist* models (Rumelhart, McClelland, and the PDP Research Group, 1986, and McClelland, Rumelhart, and the PDP Research Group, 1986; for discussion of philosophical implications of connectionism see Bechtel 1987). In this section we will introduce PDP type models and show how they can account for many cognitive phenomena, including categorization, without explicitly invoking inference relations between propositional structures. The PDP models can be viewed as a way of encoding knowledge in a nonpropositional format, and accessing it by a process that is more like pattern recognition than like inference.

PDP models are in part neurally inspired, although they are not meant to be accurate descriptions of actual neural processing. The goal in PDP networks is to show that network-type systems are capable of carrying out cognitive types of operations. These systems consist of a number of nodes or units, each of which has an activation value which is either discrete (e.g., 0 and 1) or continuous (e.g., from -1 to $+1$). Each unit is connected with a number of other units and, depending upon the weight of the connection (i.e., its current strength) and the activation of the current unit, serves to activate or inhibit these other units. The activation of a given unit is determined by a formula which takes into account the previous activation of the unit, the unit's resting level (i.e., the level that obtains in the absence of input), and various inputs to the unit. Processing in the system begins when activation is supplied to some or all of the units, and consists of units exciting and inhibiting each other until they reach a stable equilibrium. The activation of the units at equilibrium is the system's solution to the problem which was presented by specifying a particular array of input activations. Since it is the weights of connections between units that are critical in determining the behavior of such a system, learning can occur by providing a procedure for changing these weights. A variety of such procedures have been devised which enable systems to learn simply on the basis of information locally available (i.e., at the units connected by the weight that is to be changed).

In order to show how PDP-type models can provide an avenue for encoding knowledge nonpropositionally, we will briefly describe two PDP simulations.[3] The first simulation involves a two-layer network learning to recognize patterns, a process that could figure either in basic perception or in categorizing objects already perceived. The network consists of eight input units and eight output units, with each input unit connected to each output unit (see Figure 2). Activation of an output unit (a_j) is determined by a simple additive function that sums over the product of the input activations (a_i) and the weights of the connections linking them to the output units (w_{ji}):

$$a_j = \sum_i a_i w_{ji}.$$

The inputs presented to the network can be viewed as encodings of

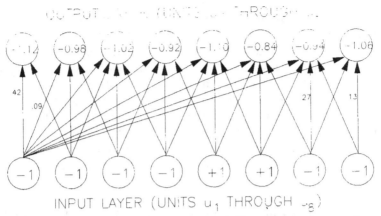

Fig. 2. Two-layer pattern recognition network. Not all connections are shown.

objects belonging to four different categories; here we will suppose (somewhat arbitrarily) that these are CUP, BUCKET, HAT, and SHOE. Table I shows the input patterns which correspond to a prototypical instance of each category, and the target output patterns that the network is trained to approximate. (These outputs can loosely be thought of as names for the four categories.) In training the network, the actual inputs and target outputs were distorted by a randomly chosen amount between 0.5 and −0.5 to capture the fact that we do not always encounter prototypical objects or undistorted names. Thus, where the pattern designated for the prototypical cup is

$$-1 \quad -1 \quad -1 \quad -1 \quad +1 \quad +1 \quad -1 \quad -1$$

an actual input on one trial might be:

$$-0.76 \quad -0.89 \quad -1.21 \quad -1.01 \quad 1.33 \quad 0.99 \quad -0.65 \quad -0.92.$$

TABLE I

Prototypical inputs and target outputs for two-layer pattern recognition network with eight units per layer (U1 through U8).

Object	Prototypical Inputs								Target Outputs							
	U1	U2	U3	U4	U5	U6	U7	U8	U1	U2	U3	U4	U5	U6	U7	U8
Cup	−1	−1	−1	−1	+1	+1	−1	−1	−1	−1	−1	−1	−1	−1	−1	−1
Bucket	−1	−1	+1	+1	+1	−1	−1	−1	−1	−1	−1	−1	+1	+1	+1	+1
Hat	−1	+1	+1	+1	−1	+1	−1	+1	−1	+1	−1	+1	−1	+1	−1	+1
Shoe	+1	+1	+1	+1	+1	+1	+1	+1	+1	+1	+1	+1	+1	+1	+1	+1

The network learns using the delta rule, which adjusts the weights (w_{ji}) of each connection leading to each output unit on each trial by an amount proportional to the difference between the actual output (a_j) and the target output (t_j) factored by the activation of the input unit (a_i) on that trial:

$$\triangle w_{ji} = 0.0125(t_j - a_j)a_i.$$

The network was trained over fifty epochs (i.e., training blocks); during each epoch it received a distorted version of each input and its corresponding target output once. The long training session was employed to enhance the quantitative accuracy of the output. The network very quickly acquired qualitative accuracy: by the fourth training epoch the activations of all output units were on the correct side of 0 (i.e., positive or negative as appropriate). After training, the network was tested on three different types of input. It was presented the actual prototype of each category, an instance randomly distorted in the way described above, and an instance for which the sign of one of the input units was reversed (see Table II). When presented with an actual prototype, the network produced an activity level for each output unit that was within 0.2 of the target level. When presented with a randomly distorted version of each input, the outputs were all within 0.5 of the target output. Finally, even when given a pattern in which one of the eight input values was reversed in sign from the prototype (making the pattern in that respect closer to the prototype of a different category),[4] it produced outputs that were usually within 0.5 of the target; all except one output (boldface) were on the correct side of 0.

It is clear that this simple network has learned to recognize and classify these simple patterns quite reliably. In general, this sort of pattern recognition is something that PDP networks are extremely good at. Even more impressive levels of performance can be achieved in networks that have intermediate layers of units (called *hidden units*). An example is Hinton's (1986) network for learning kinship relations. However, PDP type networks are able to exhibit other cognitive capacities than pattern recognition. The second simulation we shall discuss shows how simple forms of reasoning might be performed in a network where the knowledge upon which the reasoning is based is encoded nonpropositionally and where the type of reasoning that is accomplished would be more difficult to model in a propositional system. The network encodes a variety of properties exhibited by members of two gangs, the

TABLE II

Input and output activation levels for three sets of test instances using a two-layer pattern recognition network, following 50 training epochs based on target outputs in Table I.

Object	Layer	\multicolumn{8}{c}{Activation Levels for Input or Output Units U1 through U8}
		U1	U2	U3	U4	U5	U6	U7	U8
\multicolumn{10}{l}{a. Test instances are prototypes (see Table I for input activation levels).}
Cup	Output	1.12	−0.98	−1.02	−0.92	−1.10	−0.84	−0.94	−1.06
Bucket	Output	−0.99	−1.06	−0.98	−0.96	0.91	0.94	0.99	0.88
Hat	Output	−0.91	0.96	−0.87	1.05	−0.84	1.06	−0.90	0.92
Shoe	Output	0.99	0.94	1.05	1.07	0.93	1.03	0.92	1.15
\multicolumn{10}{l}{b. Test instances are prototypes with random distortion.}
Cup	Input	−0.76	−0.51	−0.82	−1.11	1.47	0.82	−0.83	−0.90
	Output	−0.81	−0.90	−0.71	−0.83	−0.77	−0.72	−0.62	−0.89
Bucket	Input	−1.00	−0.54	1.34	0.63	0.98	−0.59	−1.24	−0.81
	Output	−1.06	−0.81	−1.03	−0.68	0.63	1.00	0.70	0.88
Hat	Input	−1.18	0.62	1.20	0.87	−1.21	1.38	−1.02	1.48
	Output	−1.07	1.11	−1.01	1.22	−1.12	1.10	−1.18	0.92
Shoe	Input	1.42	1.44	0.64	1.31	0.72	1.24	1.03	1.19
	Output	1.20	1.28	1.25	1.39	0.81	1.00	0.77	1.15
\multicolumn{10}{l}{c. Test instances are prototypes with the sign of one input unit reversed (italicized). Only}
\multicolumn{10}{l}{one output unit was of the wrong sign (boldface).}
Cup	Input	−1.00	−1.00	−1.00	−1.00	.00	−*1.00*	−1.00	−1.00
	Output	−0.86	−1.39	−0.85	−1.41	−0.26	−0.78	−0.16	−0.89
Bucket	Input	−1.00	−1.00	−*1.00*	1.00	1.00	−1.00	−1.00	−1.00
	Output	−0.98	−1.24	−0.96	−1.22	0.30	0.06	0.39	**−0.03**
Hat	Input	−1.00	−*1.00*	1.00	1.00	−1.00	1.00	−1.00	1.00
	Output	−1.20	0.38	−1.14	0.49	−0.74	0.87	−0.75	0.68
Shoe	Input	−*1.00*	1.00	1.00	1.00	1.00	1.00	1.00	1.00
	Output	0.13	0.75	0.21	0.85	0.38	1.18	0.41	1.15

Jets and the Sharks: their gang affiliation, their age, highest level of education, marital status, and occupation (see Table III). Each central node in the network represents a particular gang member, and the peripheral nodes represent the properties. The connections between the nodes encode how the entities and properties are related.[5] The gang member's name is treated as one of the properties, and it is only the properties that, in the simulation, are viewed as entering consciousness. The unit for the gang member is included to facilitate

TABLE III

Characteristics of individuals belonging to two gangs, the Jets and the Sharks. (From 'Retrieving General and Specific Knowledge From Stored Knowledge of Specifics' by J. L. McClelland, 1981, *Proceedings of the Third Annual Conference of the Cognitive Science Society*. Copyright 1981 by J. L. McClelland; reproduced here by kind permission of the author.

Name	Gang	Age	Education	Marital Status	Occupation
Art	Jets	40's	J.H.	Single	Pusher
Al	Jets	30's	J.H.	Married	Burglar
Sam	Jets	20's	COL.	Single	Bookie
Clyde	Jets	40's	J.H.	Bookie	
Mike	Jets	30's	J.H.	Single	Bookie
Jim	Jets	20's	J.H.	Divorced	Burglar
Greg	Jets	20's	H.S.	Married	Pusher
John	Jets	20's	J.H.	Married	Burglar
Doug	Jets	30's	H.S.	Single	Bookie
Lance	Jets	20's	J.H.	Married	Burglar
George	Jets	20's	J.H.	Divorced	Burglar
Pete	Jets	20's	H.S.	Single	Bookie
Fred	Jets	20's	H.S.	Single	Pusher
Gene	Jets	20's	COL.	Single	Pusher
Ralph	Jets	30's	J.H.	Single	Pusher
Phil	Sharks	30's	COL.	Married	Pusher
Ike	Sharks	30's	J.H.	Single	Bookie
Nick	Sharks	30's	H.S.	Single	Pusher
Don	Sharks	30's	COL.	Married	Burglar
Ned	Sharks	30's	COL.	Married	Bookie
Karl	Sharks	40's	H.S.	Married	Bookie
Ken	Sharks	20's	H.S.	Single	Burglar
Earl	Sharks	40's	H.S.	Married	Burglar
Rick	Sharks	30's	H.S.	Divorced	Burglar
Ol	Sharks	30's	COL.	Married	Pusher
Neal	Sharks	30's	H.S.	Single	Bookie
Dave	Sharks	30's	H.S.	Divorced	Pusher

information processing, but is not directly accessible. All information about a gang member's properties are encoded by excitatory connections (weight 1.0) between the unit representing the gang member and the units representing his properties (see Figure 3). Since the properties can be grouped into mutually incompatible sets (e.g., single, married, and divorced), these units are negatively connected to one another (weight = −1.0). (In order to simulate various modes of reasoning, we

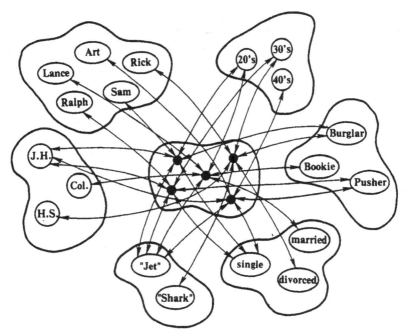

Fig. 3. The units and connections for the Jets and Sharks simulation, based on the information in Table 3. (From "Retrieving General and Specific Knowledge from Stored Knowledge of Specifics" by J. L. McClelland, 1981, Proceedings of the Third Annual Conference of the Cognitive Science Society. Copyright by J. L. McClelland; reproduced here by the kind permission of the author.)

modified the Rumelhart and McClelland model by removing inhibitory connections among the names which their model included.)

The network is intended to be a model of how information is stored in memory. Unlike traditional computer memory, this memory is content addressable: one probes the network by supplying an input to one or more nodes, and the processing within the network then reconstructs other information. For example, one might probe the network by supplying an input to the node for the name *Art*. The processing within the network will then result in the activation of the properties possessed by Art (i.e., that he is a Jet, that he is in his fifties, that his highest level of education was junior high, that he is single and a pusher). This is accomplished by the spreading of activation from Art's name node to the node for Art himself, and from that node to the nodes for Art's other properties. Here the network simply recovers the sort of information that might have been stored symbolically in a proposition. But the network is interactive: the activation of one node serves to excite or inhibit other nodes to which it is positively or negatively connected. Thus, when the nodes for Shark and Art's other properties are excited, each of them in turn serves to excite the nodes representing all the individuals sharing that property. The result is that the nodes for those individuals who share many properties with Art (Clyde and Ralph) will also be highly activated and this will serve to activate their name units, although not to the same degree as Art's name node (e.g., after 80 cycles of processing, Art's unit was activated at the 0.80 level, while Clyde and Ralph were activated at the 0.28 level). This activity of the model might be viewed as the process by which, when thinking of one individual, we are reminded of those who are similar to that individual. This would be a process that would take much computation if the information were stored propositionally, but is a natural product of processing in this network.

Since we can input values on any of the properties, we can simulate a variety of kinds of reasoning with this network. For instance, if we activate the unit representing the property of being a Shark, the system will activate the most typical properties of Sharks as well as the names of the most typical Sharks. In this case the network identified the typical Shark as being in his thirties, college-educated, married, and a pusher. Two gang members (Phil and Ol) fit this profile exactly, so their name units were the most active (0.32). Two others (Don and Ned) fit this profile in all respects but profession, and their units were also quite active (0.27). One can also query the network with a pair of properties, such as being in one's twenties and being a pusher. The network will then activate the name units of the candidates most likely to fit that scenario as well as their other properties. Three individuals (Gene, Fred, and Greg) met this description, and their names were activated.[6]

The categorization model and the Jets and Sharks model are 'toy' models that were designed simply to demonstrate how a network can exhibit cognitive capabilities. But that does not diminish their interest. They show how perceptual recognition and categorization might involve information that is stored in a nonpropositional format, how information might be stored in a long-term memory nonpropositionally, and how, in virtue of being encoded in this manner, simple tasks that seem to involve reasoning might be accomplished. Moreover, when we consider the performance achieved in these simple models and the challenges that would be involved in developing rule-based systems to perform these tasks, it appears that the nonpropositional mode of representation used in PDP simulations may actually facilitate simulation of reasoning. An especially impressive example is Hinton's (1986) network, which extracted the kinship structure of two families from a series of pairwise relations between individuals (e.g., "Charlotte has aunt Jennifer"). After learning, the network was able to infer relationships it had not been taught.

6. HOW FAR MIGHT NONPROPOSITIONAL KNOWLEDGE GO?

In the last three sections we have sketched how nonpropositional models of knowledge are being explored in recent cognitive science. One common criticism of nonpropositional models generally and PDP models in particular is that they are not powerful enough for modelling the kinds of complex reasoning and inference characteristic of human reasoning (see Fodor and Pylyshyn, 1988). Epistemologists might well respond in a similar manner, holding that the sort of knowledge in which they are interested is high level knowledge such as that involved in scientific theories, and that here propositional representation is required. One response of PDP researchers is to attempt to develop PDP models that do carry out higher level cognitive activities (e.g., Hinton's 1986 kinship model). This is clearly an important avenue to pursue, but there is another response possible, one which comports well with the main thrust of this paper. That is to emphasize the importance of the knowledge formats involved in seemingly *low-level processes* like perception and pattern recognition for our overall cognitive lives. In an earlier section we noted Ryle's emphasis on *knowing how* and Hanson's and Kuhn's discussion of the importance of perception in the conduct of science. Now that cognitive science has also developed analyses that seem to indicate a role for nonpropositional representations and, with the advent of PDP, has developed a system for modelling knowledge nonpropositionally, we may be better able to appraise how powerful nonpropositional representations might actually be.

In a recent programmatic work, Howard Margolis (1987) has proposed that cognition consists simply in a sequence of patterned responses to cues, with the recognition response to one cue serving as part of the cue for the next state. His endeavor is multi-faceted. On the one hand, he argues that this approach harmonizes with the phenomenology of cognition. We typically experience ourselves making a sequence of judgments without being aware of the principles that governed the steps. We sometimes try to explain these judgments by identifying principles that might have figured, but these, he maintains, are constructions we have learned to make *ex post facto*. The judgments themselves might well be propositional outputs of a nonpropositional pattern recognition system. Further, he offers an account of studies showing that people violate normative principles of reasoning, such as Wason's (1969) demonstration that on his four-card problem subjects seemed to fail to recognize the applicability of *modus tollens* inferences. Margolis proposes that the cues, especially cues regarding the scenario being presented, are ambiguous and so subjects exhibit different patterned responses. Finally, he outlines accounts of major discoveries in science (e.g., Copernican astronomy and Darwinian natural selection) as involving the development of new responses to patterns followed by the development of justificatory reasons. He accounts for the revolutionary character of these developments in terms of the difficulty for both the individual and the scientific community of replacing old pattern responses with new ones.

The idea that reasoning might best be modelled in terms of pattern recognition represents a radical departure from the view that reasoning depends upon formal manipulation of propositions in the manner of symbolic logic. An even more intriguing extension is the idea that our knowledge of formal logic might consist in pattern recognition capacities. In introductory logic courses we typically teach elementary forms of sentential logic by presenting the principles by which we can evaluate whether simple forms are valid or invalid. These principles are stated propositionally. Many students, however, do not grasp these abstract principles; they instead rely on examples and handle new cases by referring back to examples. One of us (Bechtel) has occasionally taught students who begin to identify forms and judge their validity accurately only after long practice using computer-aided instruction. What they seem to acquire through this process is the capacity to recognize different forms, a form of *knowing how*. It is not at all obvious that what they have learned is encoded propositionally. In formal logic these forms constitute inference rules that are employed to construct proofs. To teach proof construction, it is common for the instructor to do a variety of proofs to illustrate the procedure. Initially, however, many students are bewildered as to why different strategies are followed[7] and are prone to apply a rule like *modus ponens* simply because the previous steps license it even when doing so does not facilitate completing the proof. This is what we would expect if what they had learned was to recognize contexts in which *modus ponens* could permissibly, although not necessary aptly, be applied. Over time what students develop is a better sense of when it is fruitful to apply particular rules. From a pattern recognition perspective, this involves expanding the original pattern recognition capacity so as to become sensitive to new cues regarding the contexts in which the inference is profitable. What this suggests is that knowledge of formal logic may involve a form of *knowing how* that relies on pattern recognition capacities. Since pattern recognition is precisely the sort of activity a PDP system is good at, and that is difficult for a rule-based propositional system, this suggests that knowledge of logic may involve nonpropositional knowledge. (For further development, see Bechtel and Abrahamsen, 1990.)

This account parallels in many respects Dreyfus and Dreyfus's (1986) account of expertise. They maintain that in various domains (e.g., chess), expertise may consist not so much in being able to carry out complex inferences (expert chess players do not seem to carry out more calculations in planning their moves than beginning or competent chess players), but in focusing immediately on the most plausible class of moves to consider. This, they suggest, may rest on the ability to recognize situations as similar to ones encountered previously so as to focus immediately on moves that were successful or unsuccessful on previous situations. The knowledge on which they rely may thus be pattern recognition knowledge and not propositional knowledge. This analysis of expertise has been extended to the domain of nursing by Benner (1984), who argues that nurses begin by learning rules, achieve competence by developing abilities to form plans and use rules in the course of a plan, but achieve expertise only by developing skills to recognize situations and the courses of action appropriate to them. This knowledge seems only to be learned in the course of several years of practice, and is limited to the specialty in which the nurse practices.

7. CONCLUSION

Our goal in this paper has been to argue that by focusing only on propositionally represented knowledge, epistemologists may have overly impoverished their analyses of knowledge. Recent work in cognitive science suggests that knowledge may be represented nonpropositionally. Performance on some cognitive tasks provides evidence that we may at times utilize nonpropositional visual images at least in working memory. Recent work on concepts and categorization points to the fact that the ability to categorize depends upon fairly complex knowledge, which may be encoded more like patterns than like sets of propositions. Finally, work on connectionist systems provides an important new approach to encoding information nonpropositionally and using this encoding in perception, categorization, and simple reasoning.

We are not arguing that there is no place for propositionally encoded knowledge. In particular, language is a propositional system and we most frequently communicate knowledge linguistically. Even here, however, much work in AI suggests that we may embed these propositions in richer structures such as frames or schemas and that our ability to employ these structures in reaching new conclusions may depend on these more complex structures. As another example, one may hold the view that conscious mental activity involves making judgments whose content is expressed in propositions. Even if this view is correct, it may be that the transitions between propositions are governed by other principles which are not encoded propositionally but in pattern-recognition systems.

At its inception, cognitive science relied heavily on the propositional models that figured prominently in philosophical accounts of mental states. Cognitive science, though, may be prepared to make a return contribution to philosophy by opening up the possibility of representing information in nonpropositional formats and by modelling human cognitive capacities in those terms. Epistemology, if it seeks to give a general account of human knowledge, may do well to attend to these developments in cognitive science and consider whether it is time to move beyond an exclusively propositional view of knowledge. Such an approach will require a fundamental reanalysis of what knowledge is, since the conditions of belief, truth, and justification are tied to the propositional framework. However, having an account of human knowledge which coheres with our best theories of human cognition may make it worth the cost.

NOTES

[1] The preparation of this article was supported in part by National Institutes of Health Grants No. NICHD-19265 and NICHD-06016. We would like to thank Rita Anderson, David Blumenfeld, Robert McCauley, and Patricia Siple for helpful discussions on points in this paper.

[2] This example was not contrived by Hanson. In the late 1940s the reality of the Golgi apparatus was in dispute, with major investigators including Albert Claude and George Palade, both later Nobel Laureates, arguing for the artifactuality of the Golgi.

[3] These simulations were run with software provided with McClelland and Rumelhart (1988). They are reasonably simple to set up and can be run on a standard IBM compatible personal computer.

[4] This models the situation in which an instance of one category (e.g., a hat) has a feature (e.g., a strap that looks rather like a handle on a bucket) that makes the hat, in that respect, look more like a bucket than a typical hat.

[5] Because it lets individual nodes serve representational functions, this simulation is termed *localist*. The previous simulation, in which it was patterns of activation over units that served representational functions, exemplified a *distributed* model. While localist models are easier to manage, most PDP theorists regard distributed models as more plausible.

[6] The processing in the network also had some interesting side-effects. The initial processing in the network activated the units for all individuals who were either in their twenties or pushers, with greatest activation for those meeting both descriptions. These units then served to activate property nodes which were compatible with each of the activated individuals, while the property nodes in each cluster served to inhibit each other. The result was a profile of other properties that tended to go along with either being in one's twenties or being a pusher–being a Jet, being in one's twenties, and having a high-school education. One other individual (Pete) fit all of these other specifications, except he was a bookie, not a pusher. Hence, his name unit was also active, although to a somewhat lesser degree than the other three.

[7] It is common for students to ask why a particular move was made and for the professor to supply reasons articulated in the form of propositions. The critical question is whether answers supplied to these questions reflect propositionally encoded knowledge that guides the professor's practice or are constructed to explain what the professor did.

REFERENCES

Anderson, J. R.: 1978, 'Arguments Concerning Representations for Mental Imagery', *Psychological Review* **85**, 249–77.

Anderson, J. R.: 1983, *The Architecture of Cognition*, Harvard University Press, Cambridge.

Armstrong, S. L., L. R. Gleitman and H. Gleitman: 1983, 'On What Some Concepts Might Not Be', *Cognition* **13**, 263–308.

Austin, J. L: 1961, *Philosophical papers*, Oxford University Press, Oxford.

Barsalou, L. W.: 1986, 'The Instability of Graded Structures: Implications for the nature of concepts', in U. Neisser (ed.), *Concepts and Conceptual Development: Ecological and Intellectual Factors in Categorization*, Cambridge University Press, Cambridge, England.

Bechtel, W.: 1987, 'Connectionism and the Philosophy of Mind: An Overview', *Southern Journal of Philosophy* **26**, Supplement, 17–41.

Bechtel, W. and A. A. Abrahamsen: 1990, *Connectionism and the Mind: An Introduction to Parallel Processing in Networks*. Basil Blackwell, Oxford.

Benner, P.: 1984, *From Novice to Expert: Excellence and Power in Clinical Nursing Practice*, Addison-Wesley, Boston.

Berlin, B. and P. Kay: 1969, *Basic Color Terms: Their Universality and Evolution*, University of California Press, Berkeley.

Black, F.: 1968, 'A Deductive Question-Answering System', in M. Minsky (ed.), *Semantic Information Processing*, MIT Press, Cambridge, Mass., pp. 354–402.

Bobrow, D. G. and T. Winograd: 'An Overview of KRL, A Knowledge Representation Language', *Cognitive Science* 1, 3–46.

Chomsky, N.: 1957, *Syntactic Structures*, Mouton, The Hague.

Clark, H. H.: 1969, 'Linguistic Processes in Deductive Reasoning', *Psychological Review* 76, 387–404.

Cooper, L. A. and R. N. Shepard: 1973, 'Chronometric Studies of the Rotation of Mental Images', in W. G. Chase (ed.), 'Visual Information Processing', Academic Press, New York.

Dreyfus, H. L. and S. E. Dreyfus: 1986, *Mind Over Machine, The Power of Human Intuition and Expertise in the Era of the Computer*, Free Press, New York.

Farah, M. J.: 1988, 'Is Visual Imagery Really Visual? Overlooked Evidence from Neurophysiology', *Psychological Review* 95, 307–17.

Fillmore, C.: 1982, 'Frame Semantics', in Linguistic Society of Korea (ed.), *Linguistics In The Morning Calm*, Hanshin, Seoul, pp. 111–38.

Fodor, J. A and Z. W. Pylyshyn: 1988, 'Connectionism and Cognitive Architecture: A Critical Analysis', *Cognition* 28, 3–71.

Goodman, N.: 1955, *Fact, Fiction, and Forecast*, Harvard University Press, Cambridge, Massachusetts.

Hanson, N. R.: 1958, *Patterns of Discovery*, Cambridge University Press, Cambridge, England.

Hinton, G.: 1986, 'Learning Distributed Representations of Concepts', *Proceedings of the Cognitive Science Society*, Erlbaum, Hillsdale, New Jersey.

Huttenlocher, J. and E. T. Higgins: 1971, 'Adjectives, Comparatives and Syllogisms', *Psychological Review* 78, 487–504.

Johnson-Laird, P. N.: 1983, *Mental Models*, Harvard University Press, Cambridge, Massachusetts.

Kintsch, W.: 1974, *The Representation of Meaning in Memory*, Erlbaum, Hillsdale, New Jersey.

Kosslyn, S. M.: 1980, *Image and Mind*, Harvard University Press, Cambridge, Massachusetts.

Kosslyn, S. M., T. M. Ball and B. J. Reiser: 1978, 'Visual Images Preserve Metric Spatial Information: Evidence from Studies of Image Scanning', *Journal of Experimental Psychology: Human Perception and Performance*, 4, 47–60.

Kuhn, T. S.: 1970, *The Structure of Scientific Revolutions* (2nd ed.), University of Chicago Press, Chicago.

Langacker, R.: 1986, *Foundations of Cognitive Grammar*, Volume 13, Stanford University Press, Stanford.

Lakoff, G.: 1987, *Women, Fire, and Dangerous Things*, University of Chicago Press, Chicago.

Margolis, H.: 1987, *Patterns, Thinking, and Cognition. A Theory of Judgment*, University of Chicago Press, Chicago.

McCauley, R. N.: 1988, 'Epistemology in an Age of Cognitive Science', *Philosophical Psychology*, **1**, 143–52.

McClelland, J. L. and D. E. Rumelhart: 1988, *Explorations in Parallel Distributed Processing. A Handbook of Models, Programs, and Exercises*, MIT Press/Bradford Books, Cambridge, Massachusetts.

McClelland, J. L., D. E. Rumelhart and the PDP Research Group: 1986, *Parallel Distributed Processing: Explorations in the Microstructure of Cognition. Vol. 2, Psychological and Biological Models*.MIT Press/Bradford Books, Cambridge, Massachusetts.

Medin, D. L. and Wattenmaker: 1986, 'Category Cohesiveness, Theories, and Cognitive Architecture', in U. Neisser (ed.), *Concepts and Conceptual Development: Ecological and Intellectual Factors in Categorization*, Cambridge University Press, Cambridge, England, pp. 25–62.

Minsky, M. A: 1975, 'A Framework for Representing Knowledge', in P. H. Winston (ed.), *The Psychology of Computer Vision*, McGraw-Hill, New York, pp. 211–77.

Minsky, M. A. and S. Papert: 1969, *Perceptrons*, MIT Press, Cambridge, Massachusetts.

Moyer, R. S.: 1973, 'Comparing Objects in Memory: Evidence Suggesting an Internal Psychophysics' *Perception and Psychophysics* **13**, 180–84.

Murphy, G. L. and D. L. Medin: 1985, 'The Role of Theories in Conceptual Coherence', *Psychological Review* **92**, 289–316.

Norman, D. A., D. E. Rumelhart and the LNR Research Group: 1975, *Explorations in Cognition*, Freeman, San Francisco.

Paivio, A.: 1971, *Imagery and Verbal Processes*, Holt, Rinehart and Winston, New York.

Palmer, S. E.: 1978, 'Fundamental Aspects of Cognitive Representation', in E. Rosch & B. B. Lloyd (eds.), *Cognition and Categorization*, Erlbaum, Hillsdale, New Jersey, pp. 259–303.

Pylyshyn W.: 1981, 'The Imagery Debate: Analogue Media versus Tacit Knowledge', *Psychological Review* **88**, 16–45.

Quillian, M. R.: 1968, 'Semantic Memory', in M. Minsky (ed.), *Semantic Information Processing*, MIT Press, Cambridge, Massachusetts, pp. 227–70.

Quine, W. V.: 1969, 'Epistemology Naturalized', in W. V. Quine (ed.), *Ontological Relativity and Other Essays*, Columbia University Press, New York, pp. 69–90.

Rosch, E. H.: 1978, 'Principles of Categorization', in E. Rosch and B. B. Lloyd (eds.), *Cognition and Categorization*, Erlbaum, Hillsdale, New Jersey.

Rosch, E. H. and C. B. Mervis: 1975, 'Family Resemblances: Studies in the Internal Structure of Categories', *Cognitive Psychology* **7**, 573–605.

Rosenblatt, F.: 1962, *Principles of Neurodynamics*, Spartan, New York.

Rumelhart, D. E.: 1975, 'Notes on a Schema for Stories', in D. G. Bobrow and A. M. Collins (eds.), *Representation and Understanding*, Academic Press, New York.

Rumelhart, D. E., J. L. McClelland and the PDP Research Group: 1986, *Parallel Distributed Processing: Explorations in the Microstructure of Cognition. Vol. 1, Foundations*, MIT Press/Bradford Books, Cambridge, Massachusetts.

Russell, B.: 1940, *An Inquiry into Meaning and Truth*, George Allen & Unwin, London.

Ryle, G.: 1949, *The Concept of Mind*, Barnes and Noble, New York.

Schank, R. C. and R. Abelson: 1977, *Scripts, Plans, Goals, and Understanding*, Lawrence Erlbaum Associates, Hillsdale, New Jersey.

Selfridge, O. G.: 1955, 'Pattern Recognition in Modern Computers', *Proceedings of the Western Joint Computer Conference*.

Shepard, R. N., and J. Metzler: 1971, 'Mental Rotation of Three-dimensional Objects', *Science* **171**, 701–703.

Smith, E. E. and D. L. Medin: 1981, *Categories and Concepts*, Harvard University Press, Cambridge, Massachusetts.

Wason, P. C.: 1969, 'Regression in Reasoning?', *British Journal of Psychology* **60**, 471–80.

Wittgenstein, L.: 1953, *Philosophical Investigations*, Macmillan, New York.

William Bechtel
Department of Philosophy
Georgia State University
Atlanta, GA 30303-3083
U.S.A.

and

Adele A. Abrahamsen
Department of Psychology
Georgia State University
Atlanta, GA 30303-3083
U.S.A.

PART II
SEMANTICS AND KNOWLEDGE

NEAL JAHREN

CAN SEMANTICS BE SYNTACTIC?*

ABSTRACT. The author defends John R. Searle's Chinese Room argument against a particular objection made by William J. Rapaport called the 'Korean Room'. Foundational issues such as the relationship of 'strong AI' to human mentality and the adequacy of the Turing Test are discussed. Through undertaking a *Gedankenexperiment* similar to Searle's but which meets new specifications given by Rapaport for an AI system, the author argues that Rapaport's objection to Searle does not stand and that Rapaport's arguments seem convincing only because they assume the foundations of strong AI at the outset.

1. INTRODUCTION

The purpose of this paper is to examine part of a recent reply made by William J. Rapaport (1988a) to John R. Searle's Chinese Room argument (1980, 1982, 1984). My goal is to defend the thesis of the Chinese Room against Rapaport's reply. Searle's argument is directed against a position that he calls 'strong Artificial Intelligence' (AI). In general, strong AI is the thesis that when a digital computer is running the appropriate program, it can manifest a mind much the same as a brain does. Strong AI is opposed to 'weak AI', which says that computer programs can be useful and/or interesting simulations of mentality but are not themselves mentality. The Chinese Room is an argument that strong AI is false; Rapaport argues to the contrary. I argue in turn that Rapaport's reply does not prove his thesis.

Rapaport's objection raises questions that are foundational to the philosophical issues surrounding AI. Most important of these are the relationship between AI and (strictly) human mentality, and the nature of the operational tests that would determine whether a computer has a mind. As I differ with Rapaport on some of these foundational issues, I shall have to spend some time presenting and defending my own stance in addition to evaluating Rapaport's arguments. For the remainder of this introduction, I shall lay out some starting points that I hope will be noncontroversial.

First, however, I have two notes about terminology. (1) For the sake

155

J. H. Fetzer (ed.), Epistemology and Cognition, 155–174.
© 1991 *Kluwer Academic Publishers. Printed in the Netherlands.*

of brevity I shall simply use the rubric 'computer' to designate a machine in the act of running its program. The hardware itself, of course, can do nothing without a program, nor can the software do anything without being run. Thus when I say 'computer', I mean the software-being-run-by-the-hardware (Rapaport 1988a, pp. 81–82). Also (2), when I say 'strong AI', I am referring specifically to the thesis that a computer can (in principle) have a human mind (i.e., a mind that functions as does a human mind). I take this position against the stance that other types of mentality more applicable to AI might exist, e.g.,

...the proper conclusion to draw might be that AI strives to develop machines that can solve problems in ways that are not accessible to human beings, in which case it might be maintained that the aim of AI is the creation of new species of mentality. (Fetzer 1989, p. 38)

It is important for the reader to keep this in mind as Rapaport does not accept this definition (Rapaport 1988a, 1988b). Instead, he seems to hold that there are forms of computational symbolic processing that are not human mentality but are 'mentality' nevertheless. Later, I shall argue for my narrow interpretation, and I shall also evaluate the impact of my arguments on the status of other forms of 'mentality' which AI might comprise. To answer the question of whether computers can be minded, we must lay some ground rules about what minds do. The arguments given by both Searle and Rapaport concern natural-language understanding. While minds do more than understand natural language, I shall take natural-language understanding to be a necessary condition for mindedness. Furthermore, if we view natural language as a series of signs used by a system, I shall take the sine qua non of natural-language understanding to be an ability to take those signs to stand for something else (see Fetzer 1988). Namely, for the system to understand natural language, it must be capable of making a semantic interpretation of natural-language terms that involves taking them to stand for something in the world. I here use the term 'sign' in the technical sense derived from Peirce (cf. Fetzer 1988). Rapaport, on the other hand, uses the terms 'concept' and 'object of thought' in his writings on semantics (Rapaport 1981, 1985b, forthcoming). Since the latter terms function for a mind in a capacity to stand for other things, I take them to be interchangeable with 'sign' for the level of generality I consider here. Thus, my criteria would state that the system must interpret its concepts or objects of thought as standing for something else.

This paper is structured as follows. In the present section, I present both Searle's and Rapaport's arguments about strong AI. Next, I discuss the relationship between AI and mentality and I then describe Rapaport's example of a system for computational natural-language understanding. Following that, I discuss the matter of operational tests for natural-language understanding, and finally, I shall use this prior material to evaluate Rapaport's argument.

2. ARGUMENT AND COUNTERARGUMENT

Both of the arguments that I wish to examine in this paper are *Gedankenexperimente*. In different ways, both authors wish to replicate the condition of a computer that processes one set of symbols according to instructions that are encoded in another. Searle's argument has come to be called 'The Chinese Room', and Rapaport calls the part of his reply I focus upon 'The Korean Room'. This section is devoted to a presentation of their respective arguments.

The Chinese Room

Searle imagines that he is locked in a room with an instruction manual, written in English, for manipulating Chinese characters. Searle himself does not understand Chinese, nor does the manual translate for him, but he is to recognize and manipulate the symbols according to their formal properties. Chinese speakers from outside the room pass samples of Chinese writing to Searle, who forms new strings of Chinese characters, cookbook style, according to the instructions. Searle hypothesizes that the instruction manual could conceivably be so well written that his 'responses' would be identical with those of native Chinese speakers. Searle, however, doesn't understand a word of Chinese – he is merely following well-written instructions (Searle 1980, pp. 284–85; 1982; 1984, pp. 31–33ff).

The heart of Searle's argument is the distinction between syntax and semantics (see Fetzer 1988, 1989, and references within). Computer programs, like Searle's instructions, specify data processing on a purely syntactic (or formal) level, but a human who carried out such computations would understand nothing. Therefore, Searle argues, syntactic manipulation of formally specified symbols will not convey any semantic interpretation (and consequently no understanding) to the agent performing the manipulation. As Searle puts it, "As long as the program is defined in terms of computational operations on purely formally defined elements, what the [Chinese Room] suggests is that these by themselves have no interesting connection with understanding" (Searle 1980, p. 286). It is important to recognize that Searle's argument applies only to machines that obey purely formal principles. He admits that machines that obey semantic rules would not be covered by his premises (Searle 1980, pp. 286, 298).

This last point has become a major point of contention in discussions of AI. Partially because of Searle's argument, Moor (1988, p. 43) has proposed that strong AI be defined as the thesis that "it may be possible to construct high-level semantics from low-level syntax". On this reading, the question of whether computation can be a philosophically interesting equivalent of mentality requires that we determine whether a running program is 'merely formal' at all levels, or if it will make semantic interpretations at some level. Rapaport's argument is designed to show that 'semantic programs' can exist.

Before turning to Rapaport's argument, I should like to make explicit what I am not arguing in this paper. First, I am not endorsing Searle's solution to the nature of mind. Except for the foundation laid at the beginning, I am not arguing anything positive about that issue; to do so would be beyond my ken. I use Searle's Chinese Room argument only as a basis for my negative thesis: namely, that Rapaport has not shown that computers can be minded. Also, Rapaport thinks that Searle requires a system to have direct epistemic contact with the world before it can be a mind (1988a, p. 120). I am uncommitted on whether Searle says this or not, but I believe my argument is consistent with Rapaport's position, so it is all one to me. Finally, I cannot claim to have argued against strong AI generally, but only to have given reason to believe Rapaport's method will not provide for any sort of natural-language understanding that would support strong AI. It may well be – although I do not believe it – that some other syntactic computational system will be able to succeed where I argue that Rapaport has failed.

For the remainder of this paper I shall distinguish John R. Searle who writes philosophy at Berkeley from Searle the inhabitant of the Chinese Room by referring to the latter as Searle-in-the-room. (This terminology is borrowed from Rapaport 1988a and Moor 1988.)

The Korean Room

The Korean Room argument is presented in Rapaport (1988a) in the course of a reply to Searle's Chinese Room argument. It is best described by its author (Rapaport, however, credits the suggestion of this argument to Albert Hanyong Yuhan):

Imagine a Korean professor of English literature at the University of Seoul who does not understand spoken or written English but who is, nevertheless, a world authority on Shakespeare. He has established and maintains his reputation as follows: He has only read Shakespeare in excellent Korean translations. Based on his readings and, of course, his intellectual acumen, he has written, in Korean, several articles on Shakespeare's play[s]. These articles have been translated for him into English and published in numerous, well-regarded, English-language, scholarly journals, where they have been met with great success. (Rapaport 1988a, p. 114)

Notice that the issue is not whether the Korean professor understands English; indeed, he most obviously does not. Instead, Rapaport argues that the Korean professor understands Shakespeare, as evinced by the reception his work gets from the scholarly community. Thus, we should also say that a computer that successfully runs a natural-language understanding program understands natural language, since to say this, according to Rapaport, is to say that the Korean professor understands Shakespeare, not a Korean translation of Shakespeare.

To understand exactly where Rapaport is countering Searle, one must place Rapaport's argument within the context of his entire paper (1988a). Rapaport has described an algorithm that is completely syntactic; nevertheless working through this algorithm in response to natural-language information would appear to constitute 'understanding' for the system that carries it out. The Korean Room argument is designed to support his thesis that the 'understanding' conveyed by this process is genuine, mentalistic understanding. This is the claim I wish to evaluate here.

To keep the different meanings straight, I shall hereafter refer to the 'understanding' which Rapaport's system has as understanding$_R$, and to the interpretations it assigns to symbols as semantic$_R$. Likewise, I shall refer to human understanding as understanding$_H$, and to the interpretations humans make as semantic$_H$. To reformulate the question I examine with my terminology, I shall evaluate the Korean Room as an argument that understanding$_R$ is equivalent to understanding$_H$, and that, as a result, strong AI is true. On this reading, Rapaport's challenge

to Searle comes down to a claim that human natural-language understanding can be reduced to the sort of syntactic manipulation that
computers can perform (cf. Moor 1988; Rapaport 1988a, p. 81). Remember, though, that I am using a very strict criterion for 'strong AI',
Rapaport's writing indicates that he would not necessarily accept my
definition; thus I shall spend the next section arguing for it. I shall also
propose exactly what the relationship between understanding$_R$ and
understanding$_H$ should be if strong AI (as I construe it) were true.

3. SHARPENING THE ISSUES

I believe that for 'strong AI' to be a philosophically interesting position,
it must confine itself to only human mentality when it asserts that
computers can exhibit mentality. Rapaport disagrees. Instead, he talks
about an abstraction called 'mentality' which both humans and computers can implement. We will return to this part of Rapaport's philosophy
later; for now I wish only to point out that for Rapaport, even if
computers implement 'mentality' (qua abstraction) in a completely different way than humans do, it is still mentality. For instance:

Let us return to the . . . point, that machine and human mentality are not the same but
might be different implementations of abstract mentality. Does this show that strong AI
is wrongheaded? Perhaps; but only if the AI is *very* strong, i.e., that *human* intelligence
is its goal. . . . In any case, as a philosopher and an AI researcher, I am more interested
in 'computational philosophy' than in 'computational psychology'. That is, I am more
interested in computational theories of *how mentality is possible* independently of any
implementing medium than I am in computational theories of what *human* mentality is
and how in fact it is implemented. (Rapaport 1988b, p. 595; see also 1986b, p. 14)

This is an all but explicit statement of what Flanagan (1984, pp. 228–29)
calls 'suprapsychological AI', which he defines as the idea that every
AI program manifests 'intelligence', but maybe not (always) human
intelligence. The trouble with suprapsychological AI is that it is philosophically uninteresting. As Flanagan notes,

Suprapsychological AI . . . simply proposes to extend the meaning of the term 'intelligence' in a way which allows computer scientists to be its creators. What remains philosophically controversial about suprapsychological AI, namely, that some appropriately
programmed computers actually instantiate human intelligence, can be dealt with by

talking about strong psychological AI. (Flanagan 1984, pp. 228–29; where by 'strong psychological AI', Flanagan means the same restricted definition I use here)

Essentially, this comes down to a conflict over words. Rapaport and other suprapsychological AI researchers would like to weaken the definition of 'mentality' while I wish to retain a stronger definition. Some AI researchers may respond that I am being chauvinistic by insisting that 'mentality' equals human mentality.[1] Maybe so, but the interesting question is not whether computers can process information in highly complex ways (because they obviously can), but whether any of those forms of information processing will give rise to phenomena such as consciousness and personhood. Human mentality is the only form of information processing (if, indeed, it is information processing at all) known to give rise to these phenomena, and I lay the burden of proof on the AI community to show that other forms of 'mentality' do as well. In the absence of such proofs, tampering with the term 'mentality' seems rather a way for AI researchers to evade the underlying questions. The new denotation allows 'mentality' to be attributed to computers regardless of whether they are conscious 'persons', while the use of the old word continues to convey the impression that gives computers the appearance of being conscious 'persons'. Thus, I maintain that 'mentality' should remain strictly tied to mindedness in a human sense, and I shall use the term to mean this for the rest of this paper. When I draw conclusions, I shall comment on how they bear on 'other types' of mentality, e.g., 'computational mentality'.

Given this strict interpretation, some computational natural-language understanding algorithm must, in fact, be understanding$_H$ if strong AI is true. How should we determine if understanding$_R$ is understanding$_H$? I propose that they must be equivalent according to what I shall call the 'Thesis of Functional Equivalence'. And I take the Thesis of Functional Equivalence to be that a computational system is minded to the extent that the information processing it performs is functionally equivalent to the information processing performed in a mind. (I take this to be an extension of Fetzer's notion of replicating mental states as opposed to simulating them; see Fetzer 1988, pp. 154–55.) To say that two mappings from one set of symbols to another are functionally equivalent implies that given the same input they will produce the same output. They do so, however, because these mappings themselves can be transformed into one another. For example, solving a matrix equation is said to be equivalent to solving a system of linear equations because there exist well defined rules for transforming a set of linear equations into a matrix equation. Each successive change in the matrix could just as well be a corresponding change in the system of linear equations. It is this relation of mutual derivability between linear systems and matrices that makes them 'functionally equivalent', in my sense. That they always return the same answer is inferable from this fact, not vice versa. (For linear equations and matrices, see Venit and Bishop 1985, especially chap. 2.)

What I am arguing here is that a strong AI (in the restricted sense) reading of understanding$_R$ vis-á-vis understanding$_H$ – and possibly the whole strong AI project as well – is underpinned by the idea that understanding$_H$ can be specified by a set of functions, functions that could be transformed into a set of functionally equivalent functions that are effectively computable (e.g., executable by a Turing Machine). I imagine that if Rapaport were to accept my definition of strong AI, he would also assent to the Thesis of Functional Equivalence as a measure of its success. For instance: '. . . I am arguing that there can be . . . a functional notion [of understanding], in fact, a computational one, that can be implemented in both computers as well as in human brains; hence, both can understand' (Rapaport 1985a, p. 343; cf. Rapaport 1988a, p. 88). Thus, given the definition of computer science as 'the study of what is effectively computable', Rapaport characterizes AI as 'the study of the extent to which mentality is effectively computable' (Rapaport 1988a, p. 91). The question remains of how we are to operationally evaluate two systems according to the Thesis of Functional Equivalence. I shall return to this in section 5, after explaining understanding$_R$ more fully.

Another advantage of the present approach – at least, so I will claim – is that the Thesis of Functional Equivalence and the semiotic foundations laid in Section 1 (i.e., that minds should take the signs they use to stand for something else) become our only forays into metaphysics. Since we are only looking at the abstract structure of information processing, we are spared the necessity of examining how brain states cause mind states and whether intentionality is a substance and so on *ad inconclusivium* (e.g., Searle 1982, 1984; Rapaport 1985a, 1986b, 1988b). What I intend to argue is that whatever the merits of Rapaport's system as an abstract description of mental processes, implementing understanding$_R$ on a computer will not lead to understanding$_H$.

4. RAPAPORT'S CONCEPTION OF NATURAL-LANGUAGE UNDERSTANDING

The purpose of this section is to explain Rapaport's theory of human natural-language understanding (Rapaport 1988a, Section. 3). This theory, when implemented in a computer, is what I refer to as 'understanding$_R$'. Computationally, understanding$_R$ is implemented using an AI package called 'SNePS' (see Rapaport 1986c, Sections 4.4–4.5; 1988a, Section 3.6; forthcoming, Section 5; and references within). Owing to the great complexity of the system, my own presentation is highly abbreviated. I include no more detail than is necessary for my discussion.

The first and in some ways most important part of a system utilizing this theory is a changeable data base from which the computer gets its information to draw inferences. A changeable data base would allow the computer to revise the information it has already stored when given new inputs (Rapaport 1988a, pp. 89–91; see also Moor 1988, p. 45); thus, it could 'learn' from experience (assuming, of course, that it can be influenced by the world).

The question of how the symbols are connected to the world, however, remains. The most obvious answer is that each individual term should be connected directly to the object it represents. Mentality, then, would seem to require direct access to the world. The prevailing opinion in philosophy for several hundred years, however, has been that not even human beings, the epitome of mentality, have such access. Thus, Rapaport correctly points out that if direct access were required, humans would not have minds either (Rapaport 1986a, p. 276; 1988a, pp. 105, 120).

Instead, Rapaport embraces the idea that minds have access only to 'internal representations' formed directly in response to sensory input from the world. While these internal representations need to be connected to the world (e.g., by causal interactions), the nature of that connection is not accessible to the mind. Indeed, Rapaport maintains it is irrelevant for purposes of explaining mentality (namely, Rapaport is a 'methodological solipsist'). In his own words, "The semantic link between word and object is never direct, but always mediated by a representation" (Rapaport 1988a, p. 105). As my earlier comments suggest, I take this particular statement to apply to both semantic$_R$ and semantic$_H$ links.

'Words' or 'concepts' and 'beliefs' are then represented by an 'Internal Semantic Network' (ISN), which is connected to these internal representations. The ISN is an abstract entity, but it can be implemented in a physical system. In his writing (e.g., 1986c, 1988a), Rapaport represents ISN's as a web of interconnecting lines or 'arcs' that meet at 'nodes'. In SNePS, the Network structure is propositional, i.e., the nodes of the ISN represent assertions made about these internal representations or about other nodes.

The semantics$_R$ of a term is given by its position within the entire network (cf. Rapaport 1988a, Appendix 2). For instance, 'red' could be asserted to be a subclass of 'colors' and a property of 'apples', 'tongues', and 'thimbleberries', and a corresponding ISN could be created so as to define the concept 'red' in terms of its relationship to these other concepts. In Rapaport's figures the arcs (which specify the relationships) are even given labels such as 'class', 'object', and 'proper name' (see especially Rapaport 1985b, Section 2).[2] Once completed, it should be possible to pick out each node uniquely by its position within the web. For Rapaport, such an 'internal semantics' – more or less the ability to pick out each concept and its associated word uniquely – is all that is required for a system to use a term coherently. Rapaport thus compares semantics$_R$ with Carnap's example of a railway map where the station names have been removed, but the line names have not (Carnap 1967, Section 14). Each station will still be uniquely identifiable as the convergence of a certain combination of lines. The important thing to remember is that, because all the concepts and words are ultimately connected to internal representations, forming a semantic$_R$ interpretation really amounts to more 'syntactic symbol pushing' (Rapaport 1986a, p. 276). Because ISN's can be built using only syntactic processes, it is possible to implement them on computers. Because ISN's and understanding$_R$ can be implemented on computers, discovering that understanding$_R$ is equivalent to understanding$_H$ would support strong AI.

There also seems to be evidence that Rapaport's conception of natural-language understanding does shed some light on how humans work with natural language. For example, my own criterion states that when I use the term 'alligator', I should know that it (qua sign) stands for something else, but let us examine the character of my knowledge. The word 'alligator' might be connected in my mind to visual images of alligators, like the ones I saw sunning themselves at the Denver Zoo some years ago. But imagine a case where I have no idea what an alligator is but have been instructed to take a message about an alligator from one friend to another. Now the types of representations to which the word 'alligator' is connected are vastly different in both cases. In the first, I understand 'alligator' to mean the green, toothy beast that was before me; in the second, I understand it to be only something my friends were talking about. But I would submit that the character of the connection is the same: it is only that in the former case there are richer representations of alligators (qua object) for me to connect to the sign 'alligator'. Despite this difference in richness of representation, I would maintain that in both cases I am taking the sign 'alligator' to stand for something else and thus am still exhibiting understanding$_H$.

My disagreement with Rapaport, then, is not with his theory that natural-language understanding$_H$ is accomplished with ISN's and internal representations. I am more concerned with whether implementing an ISN in a purely syntactic system (such as a computer) will lead to understanding$_H$. The question, as I see it, is whether the computer takes the information it stores in the ISN to stand for something else, as I do with the sign 'alligator'.[3]

5. THE ADEQUACY OF THE TURING TEST

In this section I discuss how we can operationally test for natural-language understanding in an automated symbol system. Rapaport relies heavily on the assertion – stated without argument – that a computer must possess understanding$_H$ to pass what is called 'the Turing Test' (Rapaport 1988a, p. 83).[4] Briefly, the Turing Test might be seen as saying that if one wants to find out whether a computer has a mind, see if it acts as if it has a mind. If the computer's verbal behavior matches that of a human, it is minded (Turing 1964).

But certainly one of the more plausible implications of the Chinese Room argument is that the Turing Test is not a good indicator of whether an information-processing system understands in the sense of understanding$_H$. The Chinese Room itself is a counterexample to the Turing Test since it passes, yet does not understand. Therefore, the Turing Test is unreliable as a test for mentality. Looking back, this is really not so surprising at all, since the Turing Test is really a test of whether the computer can make a person believe it understands natural language. However, 'I believe that p' does not imply 'p is true'.

Without the Turing Test to fall back on, we must supply some other criteria for evaluating whether understanding$_R$ is equivalent to human understanding. I propose here that we apply the Thesis of Functional Equivalence more or less directly. We should look for evidence that understanding$_R$ is or is not functionally equivalent to the way that humans process natural language.

Rapaport maintains that we should look at mental processes like natural-language understanding as abstractions that can be implemented in either human brains or digital computers. However, that implementing them in humans and computers leads to mindedness in both follows only if we supply the premise that computer implementations of abstract processes are functionally equivalent to human implementations. But this is exactly the thesis of strong AI on my reading: we have, in effect, assumed its foundation. It is unacceptable, then, to assume that implementation automatically equals equivalence, for the thesis of strong AI is precisely the point at issue here.

What support might Rapaport give for his assertion of equivalence between natural and computational implementations? Let us look at an example of a computer implementing a phenomenon that can also be implemented in nature: a hurricane (1986b, p. 13). Rapaport claims that a real-world hurricane and a computational simulation of a hurricane are both implementations of the abstraction 'hurricane'. They can be distinguished by the media in which they are implemented, but both are hurricanes nonetheless. In particular, he quotes James Gleick, who writes, "The substance of the [computer] model is the substance of the real world, more or less intact, but translated into mathematical equations. The model contains equations that behave very much like wind" (Gleick 1985, p. 35).

Now as a student of physics, I have a hard time accepting that equations behave in any way whatsoever.[5] Equations can be solved to yield numerical values, and certain equations might very well yield the same numerical values that would be returned by an array of measuring instruments as they monitor a real-world hurricane. But if understanding$_R$ is to understanding$_H$ as a computer generating numerals is to a howling windstorm, it casts doubt on how interesting this sense of equivalence could possibly be.

Here is the equivalence I can see between a computer-generated simulation of a hurricane and a simulation achieved by hundred-mile-an-hour winds: if I had before me two computers, one running a hurricane-simulation program and the other processing data being relayed to it by measuring instruments in a real-world hurricane, I couldn't tell which was which. Namely, the computational hurricane simulator could pass the Turing Test. The only independent criterion Rapaport supplies in support of his contention that understanding$_R$ is equivalent to under-standing$_H$ – or that any computational process is equivalent to its natural counterpart – appears to be their ability to pass the Turing Test (see 1988b, pp. 96–100; 1988b, p. 11). But Searle's counterexample shows that the Turing Test is fatally flawed.

Turing himself has seen fit to impugn those who deny the adequacy of his test on the ground that there might be something going on with the mind that we cannot see behaviorally (e.g., consciousness) with the label of 'solipsist'. After all, as he claims, we cannot be the machine ourselves, so how are we to know whether it is conscious or not (Turing 1964, pp. 17–18)? This gains prima facie plausibility from the way we attribute minds to other humans based only on overt behavior (cf. Rapaport 1988a, pp. 99–100; see also the 'other minds reply' in Searle 1980, pp. 297–98). I would claim, however, that in accordance with the Thesis of Functional Equivalence one can be the machine in the only theoretically relevant sense if one performs the same information pro-cessing that the machine does. Perhaps because the human mind is so poorly specified, at present we cannot do this for one another; however, it is the nature of computers to have the information processing they perform specified to the finest detail. Thus, not only should we be able to 'become' the machine by performing its functions, but this perspec-tive should actually allow us to see whether the effects of the machine's processes are at all comparable to what we experience during normal mentality. In taking this position I return to Searle's original idea (Searle 1980, p. 284): "A way to test any theory of the mind is to ask oneself what it would be like if one's own mind actually worked on the principles that the theory says all minds work on". In the next section, I shall follow this line of thought by undertaking a similar *Gedanken-experiment* in which understanding$_R$ is implemented in a modified Chinese Room.[6]

Incidentally, I also take the above discussion to be a defense against some arguments that have been advanced (e.g., Moor 1988; Cole 1984) that Searle-in-the-room is not an acceptable implementation of a com-puter program. I simply reply that Searle-in-the-room is performing the same information processing steps. Indeed, as Searle states, for the

Chinese speakers outside the room, he is simply instantiating a computer program they wrote (Searle 1980, p. 285), which becomes even more clear in the first part of his objection to the 'systems reply' (Searle 1980, p. 289).

6. THE CHINESE ROOM REVISITED

Suppose we return to the Chinese Room and alter the rules to reflect understanding$_R$: Let Searle-in-the-room be given record books on which he can write his own Chinese symbols. Moreover, let his instruction manual be revised so that it allows him to keep a record of specific symbols given him by the people stationed outside. This record must be kept in a certain specified order so Searle-in-the-room can keep track of it. The manual also says that under very specific conditions Searle-in-the-room should modify or delete part of the record, depending again on the symbols he has been given as input. Finally, let the manual instruct him on how to syntactically correlate the symbols in his record books with each other and with the symbols that have been passed in to him, and how to formulate strings based on all this information – strings that he will pass back out in return. Now let Searle-in-the-room be placed in the Chinese Room for a period of time, and let him engage in a vigorous exchange of Chinese writing with the Chinese speakers outside. Let him execute his new instructions faithfully. At the end of the time, it seems, Searle-in-the-room will have amassed more Chinese characters. But he will not have any more understanding of Chinese. Let us examine why this should be so.

Essentially, it is because Searle-in-the-room cannot distinguish between categories. If everything is in Chinese, how is he to know when something is a proper name, when it is a property, or when it is a class or subclass? In other words, how could he mentally reconstruct the ISN that the Chinese symbols represent so that he could determine the relations those symbols bear to each other?[7] In understanding$_R$, the interpretation of one term depends on its relation to the other terms in the network. But how is Searle-in-the-room to determine what these relationships are if this information is in Chinese? Remember that in the example of the railroad map, the names of the stations are removed, but the names of the rail lines are not. In other words, before one can interpret any of the terms in the network, one must have an interpretation for the type of connection that exists between them. For example, suppose Searle-in-the-room is given a sentence (in Chinese) about a boy named 'Chuck'. If he were implementing understanding$_R$, he would write in his notebook the appropriate Chinese symbols to represent (to a Chinese speaker) propositions about an object of the class 'boy' with a proper name 'Chuck'. But since Searle-in-the-room does not understand Chinese in the first place, how will he know that the Chinese symbols that represent the links in the network stand for 'object of the class' and 'proper name'? Rapaport's answer, based on how he answers similar questions (in 1988a, see pp. 98–99, Section 5), would presumably be that Searle-in-the-room could be given information in Chinese explaining what 'object of the class' and 'proper name' mean. It appears as though Rapaport goes by a theory of belief where 'naming is knowing': to know is to have a conceptual representation of the object of knowledge propositionally linked to the linguistic expression for it. For instance, he contends that a student would know that she is computing greatest common divisors when she is able to connect the action she is performing with the label 'greatest common divisors' (Rapaport 1988a, p. 118). Ultimately, such knowledge boils down to an ability to name the concept the system is working with. But if Searle-in-the-room doesn't understand Chinese, then how will he understand the explanations, or even know that something is being explained to him? The problem, as Fetzer (1989, p. 31) points out, is that it is impossible for every word in any given language to be defined without resorting either to circular definitions, which are unacceptable, or to an infinite regress, which is unilluminating. Thus, if Searle-in-the-room were to form propositions (in Chinese) to define the Chinese categories he uses (i.e., the 'organizing principles' of his notebooks), either the categories would have to be defined in terms of themselves – which would not help Searle-in-the-room one bit – or else he would have to form an infinite number of propositions! Once the language has been reduced to a set of primitive concepts, my modified Chinese Room suggests that more syntactic connections among these primitives will not allow any sort of semantic interpretation of other terms. A suprasyntactic interpretation of those primitives appears to be required. To return to my *Gedankenexperiment*, I argue that Searle-in-the-room cannot interpret any of the Chinese terms in the way he understands English terms without first freely translating at least as far as the categories (e.g., 'property', 'proper name'). But if he is translating, he is not following his instruction manual; and if Searle-in-the-room ceases to follow his instruction manual, he ceases to be an implementation of a computer program. In the final analysis, I believe Rapaport has reduced natural-language understanding to a group of categories. But these categories themselves must be understood in a suprasyntactic way before an interpretation can be given any of the individual terms. In my example, Searle-in-the-room is in a new spot, working with categories instead of individual terms, but he is stuck with the same old problem: unable to give a suprasyntactic interpretation to those categories, he cannot give any interpretation to the terms, either. Thus, I conclude that understanding$_R$ is not functionally equivalent to understanding$_H$, at least not when implemented in an exclusively syntactic system.

Furthermore, not only is understanding$_R$ not equivalent to understanding$_H$, but it is also clearly weaker. This is because understanding$_R$ involves only syntactic manipulations that humans can do, but understanding$_H$ involves making semantic$_H$ (i.e., suprasyntactic) interpretations that a system implementing understanding$_R$ cannot do. Thus, if Rapaport wants to say that understanding$_R$ represents a different type of mentality – say, 'computational mentality' – we can see that computational mentality is not only different from but also weaker than human mentality. Thus, to equate 'computational mentality' with mentality is to deny that mentality involves working with signs that the system itself interprets. But at the beginning I stipulated that interpreting the symbols that a system works with is the sine qua non of understanding and subsequently of mindedness. Thus, I maintain that calling 'computational mentality' a type of mentality would weaken the term 'mentality' unacceptably; or, if this definition were adopted, I would want to maintain that 'mentality' (in this weaker sense) is not what makes humans minded.

7. SO WHY IS THE KOREAN ROOM SO CONVINCING?

If the preceding argument has indeed shown that understanding$_R$ is not equivalent to understanding$_H$ even from an information-processing point of view, there is then the matter of why the Korean Room argument should be so convincing. After all, it does seem logical to say that the Korean professor of the story does understand Shakespeare rather than merely a Korean translation of Shakespeare.

My answer is that the Korean Room argument plays off our intuition that the Korean professor has a suprasyntactic understanding of what he is doing in the first place. Imagine that Rapaport's professor reads a Korean translation of Shakespeare's *Twelfth Night* (1601) and writes a brilliant interpretation of Viola's line 'I am not what I am' (IIIi, 141). Now it seems obvious that he is able to do this, if he is able to do this, because 'I am not what I am', as well as the rest of Shakespeare's corpus, is equally expressible in either English or Korean. Thus, we are justified in saying that the Korean professor understands Shakespeare, not just a Korean translation of Shakespeare. But the analogous statement for a natural-language understanding computer would be that understanding$_H$ is equally expressible through either human mentality or syntactic digital computation. Only with such a premise could we say that the computer understands$_H$ natural language rather than that it executes a syntactic simulation of natural-language use. But surely this premise is what Rapaport set out to prove. I conclude, then, that the Korean Room argument is persuasive only because Rapaport takes our intuition that the professor has a suprasyntactic understanding of Shakespeare and then assumes what he sets out to prove, i.e., this (suprasyntactic) understanding is understanding$_R$. He thereby begs the question.

It appears, then, that Rapaport's argument hinges on the assumption that humans implement natural-language understanding in the same way it would be implemented on a computer. This is, however, the premise that is controversial. I have argued, on the contrary, that if we imagine a person implementing understanding$_R$, it leads to no further understanding than the original Chinese Room, so I believe I have supplied independent grounds for rejecting Rapaport's assumption. This completes my defense of the Chinese Room.

It may be that some other syntactic algorithm might possibly allow a computer to perform information processing that is functionally equivalent to understanding$_H$. I cannot think of anything more that could be given a computer than Rapaport's system, but then again my experience with computers teaches me that most people are more clever with them than I am. Moreover, new kinds of machines might be built that can work with signs according to what they mean, and perhaps these machines could understand in the sense of understanding$_H$. Personally, my sympathies are with the existentialist camp, which holds that no deterministic system will ever be able to explain mentality. At the moment, however, it appears that human natural-language understanding results from some suprasyntactic capacity of the mind that cannot be specified through computational methods alone.

NOTES

* The author wishes to thank Brad Bergeron, David J. Cole, James H. Fetzer, Charles E. Jahren, Michael Losonsky, William J. Rapaport, and Robyn Roslak for reading earlier drafts of this paper and/or their general discussions on cognitive science and AI. An earlier version of this paper was given at the Student Conference of the Minnesota Philosophical Society, Bethel College, 1988.

[1] In these notes I respond to some objections that have been conveyed to me personally by Rapaport and Cole. Rapaport has objected that my argument here would be like saying that flying is only real when it is implemented on birds, and that if we build airplanes to implement flying, the possibility that airplanes might implement flying in a different way than birds do would mean that airplanes don't really fly. It seems that Rapaport relies on a metaphysical equivalence between natural phenomena and computational simulations that strikes me, at least, as rather bizarre.

Both birds and airplanes are able to physically move through the air under their own power; thus, we say they both fly. However, computational simulations do not produce the physical effects that natural phenomena do. (As Dretske puts it, "Computer simulations of a hurricane do not blow trees down".) Rapaport has objected, "They do, however, simulatedly blow down simulated trees" (1988a, p. 96). The problem with Rapaport's reply is that he must implicitly posit a metaphysical equivalence between those simulated trees and real trees or between the simulated blowing and real blowing, if the reply is to have any force. I am unwilling to grant that elevated metaphysical status to what is, after all, only a numerical computation in a machine. I will return to this point when I discuss the adequacy of the Turing test.

[2] Rapaport points out that the labels themselves are meaningless to the system. In fact, the labels can be user-defined to some extent. However, there are some predefined relations intrinsic to the system and the user-defined labels, and subsequently all the terms in the ISN will have to be defined in terms of these. (Cf. Rapaport 1985b, p. 44.)

[3] Rapaport has objected that I do not explain how it is possible for cognitive agents to take the symbols they use to stand for something else. I am afraid I cannot oblige him, since, as I have mentioned, I do not have my own theory of mind. (I mostly follow the existentialists in such matters, although I have some sympathies with the approach Fetzer takes in 1988 and 1989.) But since I experience myself to be a cognitive agent, and since I am taking the symbols I am writing at this moment to be standing for something else, I conclude that it is possible for cognitive agents to do so.

The question is whether the fact that cognitive agents do so could be explained purely by computation. I believe a computational model is viable only insofar as it explains the phenomena that I experience in my conscious mental life (e.g., taking signs to stand for something else). Rapaport, on the other hand, seems to think that the computational model is viable so long as no other theory is proven true that would exclude computation. If I read him correctly, this difference in our outlooks has enormous consequences for where we place the burden of proof.

[4] Rapaport does include a discussion of why he thinks natural-language understanding

is sufficient for passing the Turing test, but I am interested in whether it is necessary. On this latter subject, Rapaport provides no argument, but merely claims that it is.

[5] Rapaport points out that this is Gleik's characterization, not his own; yet I have argued in Note 1 that Rapaport implicitly adopts a similar stance in his metaphysics.

[6] Cole has criticized Searle's *Gedankenexperimente* because to imagine what it would be like to run a computer program by hand does not tell us what it would be like for a computer. For example, it might be tedious, boring, or confusing, but we cannot conclude that the computer would be bored or confused. I think this can be cleared up if we clean up some imprecision in Searle's formulation. I do not think the important part of the *Gedankenexperiment* is to find out 'what it would be like if one's own mind actually worked' on computational principles so much as it is to find out whether syntactic computations could possibly account for the information contained in cognitive activity, such as semantic content.

Cole has also objected that, since Searle's *Gedankenexperimente* give us no behavioral criterion to decide whether a system really is a mind or merely a computational system, it could be that there are 'computer-people' among us now, passing for minded human beings. I accept this consequence for the same reason I accept the proposal that there might be a substance called 'xater' that we are not able to distinguish from water: both are logical possibilities. But his objection misses a deeper point: the human mind has not been fully defined as yet, but the properties of computers were rigorously defined by Turing in 1938. Thus we can set firm logical limits on what computers can do and compare those limits to a minimum acceptable standard for cognition. If computers come up wanting, we are justified in saying that computation cannot account for the functioning of the mind.

[7] Rapaport has objected that the grammar and syntax of the symbols that Searle-in-the-room works with would 'give away' their relationships and hence their meanings. He has also stated that Searle-in-the-room's instructions would contain a lexicon and grammar. The problem would be how to translate such a grammar and lexicon into machine language for a computer. If the Chinese Room is to be a true computational simulation, the instructions could only say that the symbol that bears such-and-such a (syntactic) relation to the other symbols in the input string should correspond to such-and-such a (syntactic) relation in the record book. To say more than that would violate the limits of what can be specified in a computer program.

REFERENCES

Carnap, R.: 1967, *The Logical Structure of the World: Pseudoproblems in Philosophy*, University of California Press, Berkeley, California.

Cole, D. J.: 1984, 'Thought and Thought Experiments', *Philosophical Studies* **45**, 431–44.

Fetzer, J. H.: 1988, 'Signs and Minds: An Introduction to the Theory of Semiotic Systems', in J. H. Fetzer, *Aspects of Artificial Intelligence*, Kluwer, Dordrecht, pp. 133–61.

Fetzer, J. H.: 1989, 'Language and Mentality: Computational, Representational, and Dispositional Conceptions', *Behaviorism* **17**, 21–39.

Flanagan, O. J.: 1984, *The Science of the Mind*, MIT Press, Cambridge, Massachusetts.

Gleick, J.: 1985, 'They're Getting Better at Predicting the Weather (Even Though You Don't Believe It)', *New York Times Magazine*, 27 January, pp. 30+.

Moor, J. H.: 1988, 'The Pseudorealization Fallacy and the Chinese Room Argument', in J. H. Fetzer (ed.), *Aspects of Artificial Intelligence*, Kluwer, Dordrecht, pp. 35–53.

Rapaport, W. J.: 1981, 'How to Make the World Fit Our Language: An Essay in Meinongian Semantics', *Grazer Philosophische Studien* 14, 1–21.

Rapaport, W. J.: 1985a, 'Machine Understanding and Data Abstraction in Searle's Chinese Room', in *Proc. 7th Annual Conf. Cognitive Science Soc.*, *University of California at Irvine*, 1985, Lawerence Erlbaum, Hilldale, New Jersey, pp. 341–45.

Rapaport, W. J.: 1985b, 'Meinongian Semantics for Propositional Semantic Networks', in *Proc. 23rd Annual Meeting Assoc. for Computational Linguistics*, *University of Chicago*, 1985, Association for Computational Linguistics, Morristown, New Jersey, pp. 43–48.

Rapaport, W. J.: 1986a, 'Discussion: Searle's Experiments with Thought', *Philosophy of Science* 53, 271–79.

Rapaport, W. J.: 1986b, 'Philosophy, Artificial Intelligence, and the Chinese-Room Argument', *Abacus* 3, 7–17.

Rapaport, W. J.: 1986c, 'Logical Foundations for Belief Representation', *Cognitive Science* 10, 371–422.

Rapaport, W. J.: 1988a, 'Syntactic Semantics: Foundations of Computational Natural-Language Understanding', in J. H. Fetzer (ed.), *Aspects of Artificial Intelligence*, Kluwer, Dordrecht, pp. 81–131.

Rapaport, W. J.: 1988b, 'To Think or Not to Think', *Nous* 22, 585–609.

Rapaport, W. J.: forthcoming, 'Meinongian Semantics and Artificial Intelligence', in P. Simons (ed.), *Essays on Meinong*, Philosophia Verlag, Munich. (A later version of Rapaport 1985b.)

Searle, J. R.: 1980, 'Minds, Brains, and Programs', reprinted in John Haugeland (ed.), *Mind Design: Philosophy, Psychology, Artificial Intelligence*, MIT Press/Bradford Books, Cambridge, Massachusetts, pp. 282–306.

Searle, J. R.: 1982, 'The Myth of the Computer', *New York Review of Books* 29, 29 April, pp. 3–6. See also correspondence in *ibid.*, 24 June, pp. 56–57 .

Searle, J. R.: 1984, *Minds, Brains and Science*, Harvard University Press, Cambridge, Massachusetts.

Shakespeare, W.: 1601, *Twelfth Night, or What You Will*, in G. Blakemore Evans (ed.), *The Riverside Shakespeare*, Houghton Mifflin, Boston, Massachusetts, pp. 404–42.

Turing, A. M.: 1964, 'Computing Machinery and Intelligence', reprinted in Alan Ross Anderson (ed.), *Minds and Machines*, Prentice-Hall, Englewood Cliffs, New Jersey, pp. 4–30.

Venit, S. and W. Bishop: 1985, *Elementary Linear Algebra*, Prindle, Weber and Schmidt, Boston, Massachusetts.

Department of Physics
University of Minnesota
Duluth, MN 55812
U.S.A.

YORICK WILKS

FORM AND CONTENT IN SEMANTICS

ABSTRACT. This paper continues a strain of intellectual complaint against the presumptions of certain kinds of formal semantics (the qualification is important) and their
bad effects on those areas of artificial intelligence concerned with machine understanding
of human language. After some discussion of the use of the term 'epistemology' in
artificial intelligence, the paper takes as a case study the various positions held by
McDermott on these issues and concludes, reluctantly, that, although he has reversed
himself on the issue, there was no time at which he was right.

1. INTRODUCTION

This paper is written from the point of view of one who works in
artificial intelligence (AI): the attempt to reproduce interesting and
distinctive aspects of human behavior with a computer, which, in my
own case, means an interest in human language use.

There may seem little of immediate relevance to cognition or epistemology in that activity. And yet it hardly needs demonstration that
AI, as an aspiration and in practice, has always been of interest to
philosophers, even to those who may not accept the view that AI is,
essentially, the pursuit of metaphysical goals by nontraditional means.

As to cognition in particular, it is also a commonplace nowadays,
and at the basis of cognitive science, that the structures underlying AI
programs are a guide to psychologists in their empirical investigations
of cognition. That does not mean that AI researchers are in the business
of cognition, nor that there is any direct inference from how a machine
does a task, say, translating a sentence from English to Chinese, to
how a human does it. It is, however, suggestive, and may be the best
intellectual model we currently have of how the task is done. So far,
so well known and much discussed in the various literatures that make
up cognitive science.

My first task in this paper concerns epistemology but in a rather
narrow way and does not directly address the large topics I have named
above. It is to observe and criticise the fact that one school of AI
researchers has, in effect, hijacked the word 'epistemology' and used

J. H. Fetzer (ed.), Epistemology and Cognition, 175–197.

it to mean something quite unrelated to its traditional meaning: the study of what we know and how we know it. The term has been used within the ongoing dispute in AI about how we represent knowledge (facts, generalizations, performances, etc.) in AI programs so that machines can be said to know things, or rather, how they can be programmed so as to perform as if they know things, such as telling you about the trains to Washington at a station where you type a question to a publicly available computer.

The AI researchers who use the word 'epistemology' (e.g., Lifschitz 1987) are part of what is frequently called the 'Logic Approach to AI': the claim that the representations required by the task just mentioned are those of first-order predicate logic and its associated model theoretic semantics. My overall task in this paper is to present a criticism of that whole tradition of logic-based representation in AI. My own view is that we do need representations as opposed to the current trend of connectionism (e.g., Smolensky 1988, Waltz and Pollack 1985, who deny that), but that their form, if interpretable, is largely arbitrary, and we may be confident it has little relationship to logic. I shall restate the view that the key contribution of AI in unravelling how such complex tasks as 'understanding' might be simulated by a machine lies not in representations at all but in particular kinds of procedures (that much, at least, my view shares with connectionism). It would be the most extraordinary coincidence, culturally, evolutionary, and intellectually, if what was needed for the computational task should turn out to be formal logic, a structure derived for something else entirely. Although, it must be admitted, strange coincidences have been known in the history of science.

The view under criticism here, then, the 'Logic Approach to AI', is not merely being accused of misusing a word ('epistemology'), nor of getting its representations wrong. Its whole larger dream is under attack: that concentrating on the deductive relations of propositions can yield a theory of mind or even machine performance.

There is a well-known tradition, going back to Plato at least, that what we can be said to know includes the deductive consequences of other things we know. But that inquiry alone has never been thought to yield a theory of mind, or an epistemology. If anything in AI were ever to bear on, or contribute to, the study normally indicated by that tired old word, it would surely come when a computer not only behaved as if it knew things (and in a complex, coherent way, not as a recitation of facts) but could also relate them directly to its own physical manipulations, as we can. Moreover, it might (so as to qualify) also have to come to know new things under roughly the conditions we do, and, I suggest, *not* know things that we cannot in principle know, such as aspects of our internal functioning at the level of the brain (see Wilks 1984a).

All these possibilities for a serious 'electronic metaphysics' are a long way off. My task here is not to advance such endeavors but is merely domestic, perhaps only housecleaning, by suggesting that the AI uses of 'epistemology' and the 'Logic Approach to AI' have nothing to do with that task. The particular way in which I shall use the limited space available here to make that general point will be to undertake a criticism of McDermott's views on this central issue. His more recent views have enjoyed a wide criticism, and I do not intend here merely to add to that literature but to undertake a review of the very different positions he has adopted at different times. That will, I think, be an interesting way of highlighting the general points I want to make. It is in no way a vendetta against McDermott's writings, which I much admire, but rather a tribute to their range and influence.

2. EPISTEMOLOGICAL ADEQUACY AND THE LOGIC-BASED APPROACH TO AI AND NATURAL LANGUAGE PROCESSING

Let us advance scholarship in a video age by hunting our intellectual quarry on videotapes, rather than in journals, though serious scholars will find the distinctions discussed here also in McCarthy (1977). In setting out what he calls the Logic Approach to AI, Lifschitz (1987) distinguishes epistemological and heuristic adequacy as follows:

An epistemologically adequate model is one such that a solution to a given problem follows from the model.

A heuristically adequate model is one which provides, in addition, a method for finding that solution.

This he explains best in terms of chess, where the rules of chess give a solution to a board problem, and hence form an epistemologically adequate model; but only additional heuristics yield an effective solution, if one is available.

The last phrase is crucial, since Lifschitz's illustration ignores a crucial fact about chess: that the game is decidable only from a certain range of positions, usually known as 'saddle points' (Botvinnik 1971) and, hence, in no serious sense are the rules of chess an epistemologically adequate model on Lifschitz's own definition. But let us treat that point as mere carping, even though its flavor will continue to permeate our discussion of those key notions and their impact and significance for the representation of knowledge in AI.

Lifschitz's distinction, under various names and guises, has been central to the 'Logic Approach to AI' since the publication of McCarthy and Hayes (1969). My concern in this paper will be with its impact on the area of processing in AI that I know best, namely, natural language processing. But that will not be merely an arbitrary focusing of this paper, within the general area of epistemology and cognition, for two reasons.

First, the areas of natural language representation and processing have been major ones in recent years for developments of formal representations (under influence from the McCarthy and Hayes work and its successors in AI, and from the work of Montague (1974) and its successors in formal linguistic semantics). Secondly, much of the work in the philosophy of language in this century has been to recapitulate, if not absorb, other areas of philosophy, such as the philosophy of mind. So to discuss the issue of epistemology from a language-oriented viewpoint is in no way revolutionary.

Lifschitz quotes Bundy approvingly to the effect that AI abounds in formalisms that are plausible but lack a proper semantics. This has been a familiar line in the McCarthy and Hayes tradition in AI: Hayes himself (1985) applied this stern medicine to a range of AI formalisms, including that of the present author.

That, says, Lifschitz is what happens when you have only a heuristics, but do not have the epistemological part properly worked out. As we shall see, this last means no more or less than having a classic model-theoretic semantics, which has no natural relation to any normal meaning of 'epistemological' or to 'knowledge' at all.

Mere appeal to logic is not enough, he then warns us, since even some users of logic are guilty of insufficient attention to epistemological adequacy, and he cites negation-by-failure in logic programming as an example (one to which we shall return below).

Let us at this point pause and ask again what is this epistemological adequacy? It is still a fair question since, as we saw, the chess example, which was intended to explain the notion, actually raised more doubts that it assuaged. Certainly, the notion has little to do with traditional epistemology: the part of metaphysics that deals with human knowledge, with what we know and how we come to know it and, in the British tradition at least, the intimate relation of those two. Lifschitz's epistemological adequacy (let us call it EA) has nothing to do with that; he never considers or displays any interest in what we know, its degree of certainty, its possible limitations, its contents, or how we come to know anything. If EA has philosophical antecedents – and its proponents usually assume this without any evidence – it is probably Plato, with his view that we know all consequences of what we know innately. But, again, Plato, unlike our AI colleagues, gave a great deal of thought to what and how we know innately, and it was that which made him an epistemologist.

Nor has EA anything to do with cognition, in the sense of the psychology of what we know or how we come to know it; in the chess example, a psychologist would focus almost entirely on what Lifschitz dismisses as the heuristics of the game: the abstract sense in which the rules condition possible moves would probably be of very little interest to a cognitive psychologist. Unlike Chomsky in a similar dilemma over cognition and universal grammar, it will be difficult for Lifschitz to separate himself from these cognitive problems, since he clearly does believe that, in some magical way and independently of any evidence, logic is at the basis of cognition. I suppose this, even if false, is clearer than Chomsky's (1965) resort to an inscrutable competence-performance distinction. .

So what is EA about? It is simply another way of putting clothes on the thin skeleton of model theoretic semantics, applied to areas that are not prima facie appropriate for its attentions: common sense knowledge, natural language, even chess. We need logic, says Lifschitz, because the facts are logically complex. But that is precisely the point at issue: in natural language representation it is not agreed what the facts are, although it is agreed that, whatever they are, they are complex. But why logically complex? What possible evidence is there for that, given that it would be very foolish to deny, at this stage of AI research, that the 'facts of language' can be represented on a (connectionist, nonlogical) network of arbitary complexity (cf. Smolensky 1988). That is a representational claim; as to the corresponding cognitive claim, the disarray is even greater.

But let us stick to man-made domains that might seem to suit Lifschitz's case: chess, above all. EA for chess, as stated by him, establishes the opposite of what he intended, in that it cannot lead to a chess player, artificial or human. That must require heuristics, as practical research has amply shown. And, as I noted, chess does not even support the abstract claim about derivability of positions by formal methods. What can the content of EA then be? I suggest, nothing: it is no more than a disguised statement of faith that a set of logical statements capture a situation and that a semantics will be made available at some point to give computational decidability to any putative consequence of the axioms and rules of inference. To know that some model is EA is to know just that; and yet can we be given some nontrivial domain for which that can be known of a model? If not, then all this may be magnificent, but it is not knowledge representation, let alone AI.

Let us stay, for a moment longer, with another of Lifschitz's chosen domains: the one of negation-by-failure, as implemented in standard Prolog. It is especially revealing for our efforts to find out the real content of EA.

Lifschitz maintains that negation as failure (which we shall refer to as NAF) is not EA, which might seem plausible if NAF meant something like an unsound method of reasoning in general, given that it is not always right to take something as true because we cannot prove it false. I cannot prove it false, on the basis of what I know right now, that it is raining in Sydney. But I feel no urge at all to assert that therefore it is raining in Sydney. I simply lack evidence: both the facts and plausible meteorological generalizations and statistics.

But alas, it seems that Lifschitz means nothing so reasonable in his dismissal of NAF. NAF he says has no classical semantics; its semantics are in the form of a procedure, and we all know that procedural semantics is wrong. Let us go slowly here: this point of Lifschitz's, even if true, has nothing whatever to do with epistemology in any standard sense nor, interestingly, has it anything to do with EA as he defines it, as it might if a solution to a problem would not follow in general from the facts of a model and a logical program using NAF, simply because NAF is a perfectly effective procedure within logic programming. It just does not (always) fit commonsense intuitions.

The mask is off: the only argument Lifschitz has against NAF is its lack of a classical semantics, and having that feature is all that EA means for him. EA models cover simply and only what can be known by (semantically justified) deduction from assumptions with whose knowledge-status one is not concerned. Here we note again that even the very deductively-oriented metaphysicians, like Descartes, did also worry a great deal about the status of the assumptions or first principles.

Lifschitz also concedes that a semantics has in fact been given for NAF (at least for 'stratified' systems, though one can be provided for virtually any effective procedure, given the nature of human ingenuity). Now he has a real problem, in that he wants to reject NAF, presumably on the commonsense grounds given above, but cannot because now it meets the only criterion he has: having a classical semantics. For the moment I rest my case that EA, even if it has content, has nothing to do with epistemology, cognition, problem solving, or knowledge representation.

3. AN INTERESTING CASE STUDY: MCDERMOTT

Let us turn now to examine McDermott's various positions on the logicist approach to AI. My aim will be to show that maintaining proposition p at one time (that formal semantics is the proper basis of AI) and Not-p at another is not, in itself, any guarantee of being right at least once.

All well-brought-up children know that there is more joy in heaven over one sinner that repenteth, etc. But this is not heaven, so I shall push ahead, uncharitable though it may be to do so. The plan will be as follows: first, a discussion of McDermott (1976), which has been reprinted many times and contains the germ of his logicism; second, we examine McDermott (1978) where the espousal of Tarskian semantics became explicit; and, finally, McDermott (1987) where his recantation was announced.

3.1. *AI Meets Natural Stupidity* (1976)

Any writer in this field who has ever used the phrase 'natural language' in a paper must have felt acute pain while reading McDermott's inspired "Artificial Intelligence meets" where he targeted "Natural Stupidity" (AINS for short). The quick and easy use of 'epistemology' was also savaged, as was a whole mass of pretentious usage in AI and linguistics, particularly wishfulfillment programming: the naming of flowchart modules with terms like UNDERSTAND. However, we should, in honesty, concede that that is very much the same point that Dreyfus made about

AI for years, in particular about Bobrow's use of 'understand' (1972, p. 46).

But McDermott overstated his case at one point when he attempts to determine what he calls the 'intrinsic description' of a link in a semantic net, and thereby commits what I shall call the Gensym Fallacy. McDermott takes the IS-A link between FIDO and DOG in a semantic network (of the sort that is standard in AI) and says that its intrinsic description is 'indicator value pair inheritance link' (AINS, p. 5). He argues that it is begging the question to call it 'IS-A' because one sense of 'is a' is what it is supposed to explicate. In the same vein, he asks those who would use a node labelled 'STATE-OF-MIND' to rename it 'G1073' and see if they still admire their system as much.

McDermott is clearly right that such systems have never, as yet, done much in practice and that the inflated naming of nodes gives a spurious satisfaction to the researcher involved. But the essence of the error is the failure to deliver and the ability to fool oneself that one has delivered: it is certainly not node naming as such. If the system is bad then naming the node 'G1073' doesn't make it better, but is irrelevant. McDermott is slipping into the Gensym Fallacy: that everything is logically all right if names are all (arbitrary) number names. Shakespeare might not have been so pleased with one of his sonnets if the words had been named, in order, 'G1' to 'G140', but that proves nothing, nor does the disillusion of the researcher who is forced to write 'G1073' instead of the more fulsome 'STATE-OF-MIND'. He could still produce just as silly a program and make just as silly claims.

I think McDermott's error is to believe that there really are 'intrinsic descriptions' and that we could use these innocently in a way that wishful descriptions are not innocent. This is an error, because our high level program items are not, and cannot be, purpose-free if we are to understand and communicate what we are doing. Suppose someone said that to call the truth table mapping that we could write by the vector (1 0 1 1) "material implication" was begging the question, and it should always be called "truth table mapping type 4" until shown to explicate implication. But "truth" begs the question too, so let's be even purer and say it should be called "TF table mapping type 4". Communication would be impeded, would it not, and no one would have any idea of the purpose of such descriptions and the papers containing them? One could make just such a remark about material implication itself: Schapiro (1976, p. 5) quotes the great phrase of

Anderson and Belnap, when they write that "(material implication) is no more a kind of implication than a blunderbuss is a kind of bus".

McDermott has not followed the logic of his own arguments and, were he to do so, he would, in my view, be forced to choose one of the following more radical positions (where in AINS his own general position is never explicitly stated, for the soft target shooting is so much more fun):

(1) There should be no perspicuous (meaning: easily interpretable with respect to some natural language, such as English) representation in AI natural language processing.

This is consistent with his view that "It seems much smarter to put knowledge about translation from natural language to internal representation in the natural language processor and not in the internal representation" (1976, p. 6). On that view, the representation could be largely or wholly arbitrary. If he means *largely*, I agree with him for the reasons stated earlier; but if he means *wholly* arbitrary – and his use of Gensyms suggests this – then either he commits the Gensym Fallacy or he is a closet connectionist, where implementation procedures are everything and representations are totally unperspicuous, as their critics have claimed (Charniak 1989). My intuition is that McDermott is no connectionist and that he believes symbolic but arbitrary representation can still be defended.

(2) The interpretation of a representation, however arbitrary its symbols, can be provided by scientific procedures in some direct relation to the arbitrary items. No natural language need creep into this process.

I am sure that McDermott would be strongly tempted by that possibility, and it is, of course, no more or less than the grand design of the Vienna Circle: the Unified Science grounded in Protokolsaetze (Neurath 1932). That project, incorporating Carnap's Logical Syntax of Language, was a clear precursor of both AI and Chomskyan linguistics.

But alas, it was all a magnificent mistake: there are no protocol, or basic, sentences and no scientist now believes such things, any more than he or anyone else should believe McDermott when he writes that "Eventually, though, we all trick ourselves into thinking that the statement of a problem in natural language is natural". Yes, we do, but it is not a trick, and the collapse of Unified Science showed just that.

(3) There is a representation with some degree of (non-arbitrary) interpretation, which can be provided by logic, properly conceived.

McDermott never states this view explicitly, but it is the ground of his later views and implicit in "Clearly, there must be some other notation, different in principle from natural language". This is an essential plank in the logicist case, and one for which there is no evidence. There is of course mathematics, but we are here discussing commonsense subject matter (love, life, chairs, tables, smart weapons, cars and intentions) and not the domains of which mathematics treats.

My argument is that this choice is not really available, at least if that means an interpretation wholly unconnected to, and independent of, natural languages. A language of Gensyms without interpretation is as vacuous as any other calculus, logical or otherwise, without interpretation. Nor can "Unified Science" provide interpretations and thereby bypass natural language considerations. Weighted networks might do so, but no one is very clear about that issue yet.

I am sure that (3) would have been McDermott's choice at the time he wrote AINS. He was led into confusion by his own assertion that "Many researchers tend to talk as if an internal knowledge representation ought to be closely tied to the structure of native language." He gave no references at that point to AI researchers, and it would be hard to do so. To the best of my knowledge, I am the only person who has argued this within AI – and then only very surreptitiously, because it is so unacceptable (even if true).

When he wrote those words, McDermott probably believed that Schank and the Yale School did accept that proposition, but he was simply confusing two things if he did. Schank always strongly denied that his representations were related, in their representational structure and primitive alphabet, to natural language, specifically to English. Unkind critics like myself repeatedly pointed out (e.g., Wilks in Charniak and Wilks 1976) that Yale representations did in fact have many residues of surface English, both in form and in content.

But none of that is what McDermott claimed: that the researchers wanted such a similarity. This is not mere nit-picking, but evidence of radical confusion in McDermott's thought. He fails to distinguish:

(i) claiming that one's representation is based on natural language, from

(ii) having one's representation interpretable only in terms of natural language.

If I am right, this last charge (ii) tells as much against McDermott as anyone, because there are no viable alternatives: a language of uninterpreted Gensyms or a logic of uninterpreted predicates is just gibberish, unless and until connectionism saves the day for us all. McDermott is as guilty as those he criticises: if there is a "natural language fallacy", he too must be commiting it, unless he can show us a clear way out, as AINS certainly does not.

3.2. *McDermott on Tarskian Semantics* (1978)

In a later paper (1978 abbreviated as NSWD: "No Semantics without Denotation"), McDermott brings out more forcefully the assumptions of his earlier AINS and ties them to the denotational semantic theories associated with Tarski. And yet, the doubts that overcome him later are already present, as when he writes "the application of SD (systematic denotational semantics) in an informal way can still be valuable" (p. 278), a remark that only has sense on the assumption that the full rigorous application of the method is not possible, as is indeed the case within AI and programming in general.

The bulk of NSWD is an informal examination of a small number of wellknown AI systems such as Schank's and the observation that some of the rules proposed for it are not generally true. Two most important points must be made here, one polemical and one substantial. First, even if it is of value to show that a rule in an AI system is not generally true or is inconsistent with other rules, that can always be established simply by argument and .careful observation: it does not call for the tools McDermott uses in NSWD. There is no sense in which the application of denotational semantics, formally or informally, helps one to see this. Indeed, it is known that there can be no such proof of inconsistency for any system of interesting richness, so this defect is more than practical. There is no clear relation between the disease (false rules, if that is a disease) and the remedy proposed.

Although NSWD is intended as a robust defense of denotational semantics in Artificial Intelligence, it does contain an argument against its use:

It would perhaps be surprising for an outsider to learn that computer scientists, in spite of the fact that they study purely formal objects like programs and data structures, have a pronounced 'anti-formalist' streak. This arose initially from the painful discovery that even the most formal objects have to be debugged. (p. 8)

He is right about many of his colleagues, but, as ever, the reason given is the wrong one. This anti-formal "streak", insofar as there is one, is not about formalisms as such at all: programs must be totally formal or they do not run. The opposition – from papers like the present one – is to the application of a particular methodology – model theoretic semantics – and has nothing to do with debugging, which is a pure red herring. It has to do with the application of computational methods to areas of AI like natural language processing, where the formal structure of the area to be explicated does not support those methods.

This fact was touched on earlier and the argument appeared in fuller form in Wilks (1971), but it can be set out again here in simple form. The argument is that the meaningful sentences of a natural language like English do not form a recursive or decidable set, where this fact makes any strong application of model theoretic semantics to, say, a natural language understanding system, inappropriate.

The argument that natural language sentences are not such a set goes as follows: given any string of English words, it can be rendered meaningful, and given an established use, by successive explanations in the way Wittgenstein (1953) constantly illustrated. It is merely a question of ingenuity and determination.

If that is the case, then there is no prior survey of the "theorems of English" in the way that there is for, say, the Propositional Calculus. In that formalism, we knew – in advance of the production of a decision procedure (the truth tables in 1919) – what was and was not a theorem of the Propositional Calculus. There were firm intuitions as to the truth of certain well-formed formulas, and well-established deduction procedures to establish others. The semantics associated with the calculus – the truth tables – then underpinned that "syntactically based" deduction with a decision procedure.

None of this is available for a natural language, and it is an essential feature that it is not. If it were, we would not be dealing with a natural language. Any fragment of, say, English, that could be axiomatised, would then not be a natural language precisely because the freedom to extend it, as we all do every day, would be gone.

What does it mean to claim that the prior survey of English sentences is not available? It is simply that we cannot construct lists of definite sentences and definite non-sentences in the way that we can for formal languages, whch we must be able to do if the Tarskian techniques devised to underpin theoremhood and deduction are to grip. Tarski himself, as we all know, did not believe natural languages were suscep-tible to these techniques, though that fact is in no way decisive.

Such a claim does not mean anything in particular about the intuition of what a meaningful sentence in English is about or how it is related to the meanings of its parts. There is nothing compositional about the point I am making. It does follow from this claim that an axiomatisation of English, if it were conceivable, could not be a good way to enumerate English sentences, for there would always be a denumerable infinity of English sentences it could not produce.

The above position, if true, has consequences for the semantics of internal representations, too, in spite of McDermott when he writes:

> The objection has been made that denotational semantics cnnot be the semantics of natural language in all its glory. This may or may not be true . . . but has nothing to do with its use as a semantics of internal knowledge structures. (NSWD, p. 281)

But this is simply not so, and the consequence is fatal to McDermott's whole case, given the non-recursive property of sets of sentences of a natural language, for this property will also be true of the formulas of the internal representation if there is any straightforward mapping between them. Human beings provide that mapping (on any "internal representation" theory of mental processing) as do parsers between computer representations and sentences. So McDermott's point fails unless the natural language and the internal knowledge structure are independent. But they are not, and McDermott has never suggested for a moment that they are.

This point can even be strengthened in the following way: let us make the fairly sensible assumption (to all except adherents to "fuzzy logic") that quantification is a discrete phenomenon as regards any semantics to be given for its appearance in a natural language or in an internal representation language. Now, if the semantics given for quantified formulas of an internal representation language is a Scott–Strachey semantics for programs (and in AI that might seem a natural additional assumption), then that semantics requires the phenomena to be continuous overall (Scott and Strachey 1971). This fact can be interpreted in a number of ways with respect to the discussion so far, but the most rational is to take it as evidence that a program semantics cannot be given for internal representations of at least one basic aspect of natural language.

This conclusion may be too facile, however, given the possible inter-actions of the assumptions required to reach it. But on any manipu-lations of those, the conclusion tends to tell against McDermott's as-sertion in the last passage quoted, namely, that we might reasonably expect a more rigorous semantics for an internal representation than for a "decoupled" and less rigorous natural language, one that corre-sponded to internal expressions in some one-to-one or many-to-one manner (over sets of sentences or formulas).

3.3. *The Critique of Pure Reason* (1987)

In his most recent work (abbreviated CPR), McDermott has seized on a Kantian title to withdraw much of the content of AINS and NSWD, although he does it not by withdrawing earlier arguments, but by attack-ing other logicist positions and drawing new conclusions inconsistent with those of the earlier two papers. The burden of the paper is that

(i)   in understanding, including the understanding of natural lan-guage, many or most inferences are non-deductive.

(ii) deductive techniques (and hence the formal semantics machinery that underlie them) have no role in assessing confirmation of belief, which is a quantitative matter.

As the author of a paper in 1973 called "Understanding without Proofs" (which drew attention to Hume's point that the proofs of non-mathematical conclusions are short and non-deductive, a claim McDermott attributes to Pat Hayes!), I can only welcome his conver-sion, while trying to keep at bay the slightly sour response of the lifelong tee-totaller welcoming recently reformed drunks.

The second point carries a strong flavor of discussions of connectionist computation (prevalent everywhere in artificial intelligence at the mo-ment) and might yet lead to a further radical shift in McDermott's position, one also hinted at in his remark that "What we now conclude is that content theories are of limited usefulness in the case where the contemplated inferences are non-deductive" (CPR, p. 14).

Connectionism is, of course, almost by definition, a non-content theory, as all its critics have pointed out in their different ways. What McDermott means by this last quotation is to be understood in oppo-sition to a clear case of a content theory: logic programming, and the belief associated with it – that the content of our knowledge would be simply written down in an appropriate formalism – a position McDermott himself held at one time, which is close to what we earlier called the classic logicist position of McCarthy and Hayes (1969).

There is a small but crucial difference here between the content-theory (in the sense of procedure-free logic programming), on the one hand, and the older logicist program in AI, on the other. The logicists, like McCarthy and Hayes, never thought that what they were advocating was procedure free: it naturally required some set of trusty machine logic procedures. So, too, of course, does logic programming, even though they are hidden tidily away in the Prolog interpreter itself.

McDermott draws on this very distinction between logic and logic programming for a different purpose, but he fails to see that it undermines his discovery (appearing just before the last quotation) that "there is no way to develop a 'content theory' without a 'process model'" (CPR, p. 14).

But this is as true of classical machine logic as of any other part of AI, and the logicists knew it. In itself, it constitutes no reason at all to flirt with procedural (as opposed to denotational) semantics for knowledge representations. I write as one who firmly believes (Wilks 1981) in a procedural semantics, whatever it may turn out to be. My point here is that McDermott's reasons for shifting from a wrong view to a right one are bad ones.

This is equally true of his discovery of (i) above, construed as a claim about human psychology. It may be true, as Russell once said, that no one has ever performed a useful or practical deduction on any serious topic, but he did not allow that to interfere with his technical work. Even if true, it says nothing about how research in machine logic should proceed, nor about whether formal deductions can be produced to cover the inferences humans make. It has always been an assumption in traditional logic that any enthymeme (inference or truncated deduction) can be made deductive by the addition of suitable additional premises, where logicians could always provide these, as it were, by inspection.

It is an open question whether a machine logic can locate non-trivial assumptions, in general, so as to produce a consequence that is deductive. By "nontrivial" there, I mean: other than an assumption of the form $p \rightarrow q$, where p is a conjunction of the existing assumptions and q the consequent. The logicists continue with their program in the belief that it can be done but, whatever is the case there, observations by McDermott like the following do nothing to throw doubt on that program:

> But many inferences are not deductive. If I come upon an empty cup of soda pop that was full a while ago, I may infer that my wife drank it, and that's not a deduction . . . but an inference to the best explanation. (The only way to mistake this for a deduction is to mistake logic programming for logic . . . .) (p. 8)

But logicists know all this, and that such inferences can be made deductive, by trivial methods if necessary. One of these would be to have an assumption equivalent to "if this cup, situated in my house, which was full at t_0, is empty at t_1 (where t_0 precedes t_1), and if my wife was in the house at some time between t_0 and t_1, then she drank it." It might well be argued at this point that the discovery and justification of such an assumption is what is traditionally called induction, rather than deduction. Logicists in the AI tradition normally make no distinction between those unless they also chose to call their work "machine learning", which is an area that seeks to show that perfectly formal accounts can be given of non-deductive inferences (e.g., Michalski 1976). If that is what McDermott is drawing attention to with his nice remark about logic versus logic programming, then so be it; but I suspect he is not, since induction is not a notion that figures in his work. Unless he is prepared to offer some alternative account under such a heading – and I suspect he is not – nothing follows from these observations that logicists are not already fully aware of, and they do not of themselves create any general doubt about the logicist program for AI (as opposed to, say, one for psychology).

The bulk of McDermott's CPR consists of technical criticisms of devices in recent AI logic (non-monotonicity, circumscription, etc.) that have been advanced to support, and develop, the logicist case. The criticisms are admirable in themselves, interesting largely because of the past views of the author, and I have no wish here to dispute either their detail or their general thrust. They are in fact unimportant for the purpose of this paper – other than their intense biographical interest, of course – since those criticisms do not bear directly on the general issues of principle raised in this paper. As I just noted above, any logicist can say of these criticisms that they are merely technical details being fixed, just as he can say that diagnosing most human inferences as enthymemes, or incomplete deductions, in no way bears on the logicist program or on the general viability of machine deduction.

There are, I believe two casual remarks in CPR where McDermott moves close to the real problems for the logicist program in principle rather than in detail. They are:

(a) when he notes "The notation we use must be understandable to those using it and reading it" (p. 2); and,
(b) when writing of non-monotonic logic: "Either theories like this don't have theorems, in which case they can't serve as the idealized inference engines we are seeking; or we are stuck with a weak notion of theorem, . . ." (p. 6).

The first remark is interesting because, although implicit, it is one of the few direct withdrawals of a claim in one of the earlier papers: It clearly withdraws the whole line of argument in AINS that terms in the knowledge representation should be replaced by (inscrutable) Gensyms, so as to give moral health to a program description by removing the overtones imported from natural language.

It is obvious to anyone with experience in writing programs in high-level languages that this cannot be done or, if it can, that it removes the point of using such languages in the first place. McDermott does not note the significance of this retraction but, in the light of the previous discussion of the present paper, it should be clear that insofar as such notations for knowledge representation are understandable, they are to that degree dependent on some natural language and therefore cannot have a semantics independent of it. From that point, ignored by McDermott, most of the arguments offered here directly follow.

Point (b) simply notes a possibility and is passed over immediately, but it is of course a possibility that is taken here to be a fact concerning the status of natural languages for axiomatisation (as regards their meaningfulness, at least), and is the issue of principle on which, in my estimation, the logicist enterprise hangs.

In view of the nature of the arguments in CPR – and the virtual ignoring of issues of principle, while concentrating on ones that give the logicist no more than passing problems – it will not be surprising that I conclude that, although McDermott has apparently reversed his position, he remains wrong on the core issues. There need be no formal problem in saying this: one can perfectly well maintain P and Not-P at different moments, while retaining some false q throughout, where q

is in the chain of inference to both P and Not-P. It is such q's that I have sought to isolate here, particularly with regard to the non-independence of the representation language and natural language(s) and the status of statements of meaningfulness for natural languages as constituting a formal language whose meta-logical properties are to be investigated.

4. CONCLUSION: ARE THERE EMPIRICAL DIFFERENCES BETWEEN THESE RESEARCH PROGRAMS?

If we stand back from McDermott's intellectual struggles now and return to the general fray, the obvious general question to ask is whether there are, or can be, genuine testable differences between the logicist program for AI and any discernible alternatives, such as something we might call "commonsense" semantics. I shall make no attempt here to define the term in opposition to formal semantics. Commentators on the distinction as different as Israel (1989) and Sparck-Jones (1989), however, broadly agree on where the line is to be drawn.

All this is to say, will programs inspired by one of these classes of formalism be capable of performing some indisputably AI task, which the other cannot? All parties should agree to such a test and probably would. But does this allow us to sit back comfortably, taking an optimistic view of scientific progress and await the outcome? I fear the matter is not so simple.

Let us consider an empirical task in natural language processing, which is often tackled by AI techniques and sometimes by those of formal semantics: machine translation (MT) from one natural language to another. This is not a task chosen at random, of course; it is the original, founding task of computational linguistics, a task rather like that of playing the piano sonatas of Mozart, according to Rubenstein: too easy for the amateur, too hard for the master.

There is no doubt that MT is now possible with some degree of success, (see, e.g., Lawson 1982), but that the very hard problems required for its proper solution are nowhere near at hand. A relevant and concrete example of such a problem would be the following: the choice between generating "a" and "the" is notoriously difficult in English, one that non-native speakers continually get wrong. Examples are sometimes hard to grasp in one's own language, and the choice between "des" and "les" in French is similarly crucial and notorious. Though it is not the same distinction as the English one, yet it rests on the same kind of semantic criteria. It is not a problem with an arbitrary solution: French grammar books claim to offer the principles that underlie the choice.

It might also seem, on the surface, to be a problem that formal semantics, or any logicist approach to language structure, ought to help with: it is certainly some form of idiosyncratic quantification. Those particles are exactly the kind for which Montague grammar, say, offers large, complex structures, just as (as Sparck–Jones [1989] notes) those systems offer such minimal, vacuous, understanding.

Much of the recent success of MT, it must be said, gives no comfort to either kind of semantics, formal or "commonsense", referred to in this paper. It has often been a matter of very crude theories, whose performance has been improved over anything thought possible twenty years ago simply by the use of software engineering techniques. One might risk the following principle:

> There is no theory of language structure so ill-founded that it cannot be the basis for some successful MT.

Those who doubt this should study the history of the SYSTRAN system (Hutchins 1979). The point of the principle, if true, is that it makes any prospect of an empirical test or decision – as between formal semantics and any other type – applied to a concrete empirical task like MT very improbable indeed. And that is exacerbated by another principle that lurks behind much of the discussion of this paper:

> AI programs in general (including MT programs) do not always work by means of the formalisms that decorate them.

This is an important issue, and one which serves to separate the issue under discussion (of finding some empirical programming task to settle the issue between types of AI representations and their associated semantics) from what might be an illuminating historical parallel – that of rival theoretical descriptions of physical phenomena between which a crucial experiment was sought: ether-waves versus relativity, say, or particle versus wave accounts of subatomic phenomena.

Programming, alas, is not like that in the following sense: it is perfectly possible to write a program to perform some task (MT will still serve) using a descriptive theory or language even though, in fact – and sometimes hardly perceived by the programmer – the results are achieved by part of a program that functions in such a way that it cannot be appropriately described by the upper-level theory at all, but requires some quite different form of description. Sometimes this happens for totally banausic reasons, ones which involve an element of deceit or flattery: a student programs a system for his supervisor, describing what he is doing in terms consistent with the cherished theory of that supervisor, who does not himself write programs. In order to make the system function, the student is forced to reconceive the task at another level, and it is there that he develops the "real" theory, one which never emerges in any published description.

Cases like this are not as unusual as one might hope. But a more common situation is what happened to the SYSTRAN Russian-to-English MT itself: it had and has a very elementary system of linguistic description in terms of grammar rules. After nearly thirty years of operation a very large number of lexical "patches" have been added to the system (of the order of half a million (see Wilks 1979)) which deal with particular input strings in Russian, rather as if one had a special dictionary of syntagms, such that the grammar was only accessed where the syntagms failed to "match" the input.

Now, consider the situation where, as I believe to be the case, SYSTRAN is described by the simple grammatical theory, although in fact the system's success is largely attributable to the dictionary of "semi-sentences" that does not appear in the top-level description. It should be clear that, whatever the details of this particular system, the situation is not at all one of rival theoretical descriptions of phenomena, as in physics, but of determining what are the real, operational principles by which a program works, as opposed to its apparent, sometimes merely decorative, ones.

This problem is well known in the field, but has no obvious solution: in one sense it is precisely the problem of finding a proper semantics for programs, in the Scott and Strachey sense (1971), one that is close in methodology to formal semantics in the sense in which we have discussed it here. Unfortunately, and whatever the claims of its devotees, the semantics of programs cannot provide this service, even in principle, since that technique requires only the specification of objects and relations so that input is reliably transformed to output, as in a deduction. There is no requirement whatever that the objects chosen have any relationship to the "natural" objects of the theory with which the program works: they could be as remote as were the loyal student's principles from those of his advisor. They can be simply incommensurable in just the way that the semantics of a program at different levels of internal programming language translation are incommensurable (Scott and Strachey).

The conclusion may seem pessimistic but, even in a situation of no reliable test or outcome, the social and psychological forces at work in an empirical and formal discipline like AI continue to function, nonetheless. Machine understanders and translators will continue to appear, and we shall be able to judge to some degree whether they benefit from formal semantics techniques or not. For those cases where there are reasonable doubts about that, there is coming into being a battery of techniques for reimplementing systems with somewhat changed and controlled principles and structures (see Ritchie and Hanna 1990), which can do much to help us decide what are and are not the formal principles underlying AI programs. So, as Leibniz would write at this point in an argument: come, let us compute together!

REFERENCES

Botvinnik, M.: 1971, *Computers, Chess and Long-Range Planning*, Longman, London.
Charniak, E. and Y. Wilks (eds.): 1976, *Computational Semantics*, North Holland, Amsterdam.
Charniak, E.: 1989, 'Connectionism and Explanation', in Y. Wilks (ed.), *Theoretical Issues in Natural Language Processing*, Erlbaum, Hillsdale, New Jersey.
Chomsky, N.: 1965, *Aspects of the Theory of Syntax*, MIT Press, Cambridge, Massachusetts.
Dreyfus, H.: 1979, *What Computers Can't Do*, 2nd ed., Harper & Row, New York.
Hayes, P.: 1985, 'Some Problems and Non-Problems in Representation Theory', in R. Brachman and H. Levesque (eds.), *Readings in Knowledge Representation*, Morgan Kaufmann, Los Altos, California.
Hutchins, J.: 1979, 'Linguistic Models in Machine Translation', in *UEA Papers in Linguistics*, Norwich, England.
Israel, D.: 1989, 'On Formal versus Commonsense Semantics', in Y. Wilks (ed.), *Theoretical Issues in Natural Language Processing*, Erlbaum, Hillsdale, New Jersey.
Lawson, V. (ed.): 1982, *Practical Experience of Machine Translation*, North Holland, Amsterdam.

Lifschitz, V.: 1987, 'The Logic Approach to AI', *Stanford Computer Science Video Journal*, Morgan Kaufmann, Los Altos, California.

McCarthy, J.: 1977, 'Epistemological Problems of Artificial Intelligence', in *Proc. IJCAI77*, pp. 1038–44.

McCarthy, J. and P. Hayes: 1969, 'Some Philosophical Problems from the Standpoint of Artificial Intelligence', in B. Meltzer and D. Mitchie (eds.), *Machine Intelligence 4*, Edinburgh University Press, Edinburgh.

McDermott, D.: 1976, 'Artificial Intelligence Meets Natural Stupidity', in *SIGART Newsletter No. 57*, pp. 4–9. Reprinted in J. Haugheland, *Mind Design*, MIT Press, Cambridge, Massachusetts, pp. 143–60.

McDermott, D.: 1978, 'Tarskian Semantics, or No Notation without Denotation', *Cognitive Science* **2**, 277–82.

McDermott, D. and commentators: 1987, 'A Critique of Pure Reason', *Computational Intelligence* **3**, 1–24.

Michalski, R.: 1976, 'Learning by Inductive Inference', in J.-C. Simon (ed.), *Computer Oriented Learning Processes*, Noordhof, Amsterdam.

Montague, R.: 1974, *Formal Philosophy: Selected Papers of Richard Montague*, R. Thomason (ed.), Yale University Press, New Haven, Connecticut.

Neurath, O.: 1932, 'Protocol Sentences', *Erkenntnis* **3**.

Ritchie, G. and K. Hanna: 1990, 'AM: A Case Study in AI Methodology', in D. Partridge and Y. Wilks (eds.), *The Foundations of Artificial Intelligence*, Cambridge University Press, Cambridge.

Schapiro, S.: 1976, 'The Relevance of Relevance', *Indiana University Computer Science Department*, March 1976.

Schiffer, S.: 1987, *Remnants of Meaning*, MIT Press, Cambridge, Massachusetts.

Scott, D. and C. Strachey: 1971, 'Toward a Mathematical Semantics for Computer Languages', *Proceedings of the Symposium on Computers and Automata*, Polytechnic Institute of Brooklyn.

Smolensky, P.: 1988, 'On the Proper Treatment of Connectionism', *Behavioral and Brain Sciences* **11**, 1–23.

Sparck-Jones, K.: 1989, 'They say It's a New Engine but It's Still the Same SUMP', in Y. Wilks (ed.), *Theoretical Issues in Natural Language Processing*, Erlbaum, Hillsdale, New Jersey.

Waltz, D. and J. Pollack: 1985, 'Massively Parallel Parsing: A Strongly Interactive Model of Natural Language Interpretation', *Cognitive Science* **9**.

Wilks, Y.: 1971, 'Decidability and Natural Language', *Mind* **70**.

Wilks, Y.: 1973, 'Understanding without Proofs', *Proceeding of the International Joint Conference on AI*, Stanford, California.

Wilks, Y.: 1979, 'Comparative Translation Quality Analysis', *Report to AFOSR*, F33657-77-C-0695.

Wilks, Y.: 1981, 'Some Thoughts on Procedural Semantics', in M. Ringle and W. Lehnert (eds.), *Strategies for Natural Language Processing*, Erlbaum, Hillsdale, New Jersey.

Wilks, Y.: 1984a, 'Consciousness and Machines', in C. Hookway (ed.), *Minds, Machines & Evolution*, Cambridge University Press, Cambridge.

Wilks, Y.: 1984b, 'Is Frege's Principle Trivial or False?', *Proc. Linguistic Assn. of GB*, Annual Conference, University of Essex.

Wilks, Y.: 1989, *Theoretical Issues in Natural Language Processing*, Erlbaum, Hillsdale, New Jersey.
Wittgenstein, L.: 1953, *Philosophical Investigations*, Blackwells, Oxford.

Computing Research Laboratory
Box 30001
New Mexico State University
Las Cruces, NM 88003
U.S.A.

WILLIAM EDWARD MORRIS

KNOWLEDGE AND THE REGULARITY THEORY
OF INFORMATION

ABSTRACT. Fred Dretske's *Knowledge and the Flow of Information* is an extended attempt to develop a philosophically useful theory of information. Dretske adapts central ideas from Shannon and Weaver's mathematical theory of communication, and applies them to some traditional problems in epistemology. In doing so, he succeeds in building for philosophers a much-needed bridge to important work in cognitive science. The pay-off for epistemologists is that Dretske promises a way out of a long-standing impasse – the Gettier problem. He offers an alternative model of knowledge as *information-based belief*, which purports to avoid the problems justificatory accounts face. This essay looks closely at Dretske's theory. I argue that while the information-theoretic framework is attractive, it does not provide an adequate account of knowledge. And there seems to be no way of tightening the theory without introducing some version of a theory of justification – the very notion Dretske's theory was designed to avoid.

Fred Dretske describes *Knowledge and the Flow of Information*[1] as an "attempt to develop a philosophically useful theory of information".[2] He offers a naturalistic yet "genuinely *semantic*" conception of information, one which he believes yields "a plausible, and theoretically powerful, analysis of a signal's information content . . . that can be used in cognitive and semantic studies (KFI, p. x). As such, his book is an extended exercise in building a bridge for philosophers to important work in the cognitive sciences.

Dretske launches his project by adapting and extending some central ideas in the mathematical theory of communication which Claude Shannon and Warren Weaver developed in the late forties.[3] He uses the "underlying structure" of their theory to "provide the key" for the development of his own account of information as "an objective commodity, defined in terms of the network of lawful relationships holding between distinct events and structures" (Precis, p. 170).

There is a pay-off for epistemologists. Dretske claims his theory avoids a remarkably persistent impasse in contemporary theory of knowledge – the Gettier problem. Gettier's notorious counterexamples show that the traditional analysis of knowledge as justified true belief is too weak; it permits accidentally true beliefs for which one has some support to qualify as knowledge.[4] The traditional account needs to be strengthened, but how?

J. H. Fetzer (ed.), Epistemology and Cognition, 199–222.

After 25 years, we still don't know. Though we have "a plethora of epistemological theories",[5] no one theory holds sway. No account of the concept of knowledge has yet provided anything like a satisfactory theory of justification. We need a measure which specifies how much evidential support is required for knowledge, but there is no consensus about what that measure should be, or how it might be obtained.

Dretske promises a way around the issues the Gettier problem poses for the theory of justification. While he is not the first to attempt to avoid the demand for an adequate account of justification, his view is in some ways the most developed. Dretske offers an alternative model of knowledge as *information-produced belief* – belief that is caused, or causally sustained, by information, so that

K knows that s is $F =_{df} K$'s belief that s is F is caused (or causally sustained) by the information that s is F.[6]

Dretske believes that "this characterization of knowledge is a version of what has come to be called the 'regularity analysis' of knowledge. It is an attempt to get away from the philosopher's usual bag of tricks (justification, reasons, evidence, etc.) in order to give a more realistic picture of what . . . knowledge is" (Precis, p. 177).

Dretske's claim that his account is a version of "the regularity analysis of knowledge" is somewhat misleading. It is information, not knowledge, that is characterized in terms of regularity in his theory. What Dretske offers is not, strictly speaking, a regularity account of knowledge, but a theory which explains knowledge in terms of a regularity account of information. This is important. It is both the distinctive feature of Dretske's theory and the source of its strength.

Dretske's view is unusual in its emphasis that features formerly thought exclusive to knowledge turn out to be transmitted to it from features peculiar to information. This tight connection between information and knowledge, prominently displayed in Dretske's definition, is the basis of his strategy for responding to objections and counterexamples. It is the key to the way his theory sidesteps the Gettier problem:

Gettier-like difficulties . . . arise for any account of knowledge that makes knowledge a product of some justificatory relationship . . . that *could* relate one to something false. The problem is evaded in the information-theoretic model, because one can get into an appropriate justificational relationship to something false, but one cannot get into an appropriate informational relationship to something false (Precis, p. 179).

This is an attractive prospect, but it is one we must examine carefully. If Dretske's use of the information-theoretic framework successfully avoids appeal to justificatory concepts, it is important to understand just *how* it manages this. To find out, we must look closely at the ways in which he adapts and extends Shannon and Weaver's mathematical theory of communication. A good place to start is with Dretske's claim that his account of information is both ordinary and objective.

1. ORDINARY INFORMATION

Dretske maintains that his conception of information is essentially our ordinary one, characterized systematically by "a suitably relaxed set of information-theoretic notions" (AR, p. 82). Communication theory, he emphasizes, "was developed for quite different purposes": it "has its attention elsewhere" (Precis, p. 171). But "the ideas clothed in this mathematical dress . . . have an application far beyond the restricted set of conditions required for application of the mathematical theory" (Precis, p. 179).

To apply these theoretical notions outside their intended context, Dretske had to alter them considerably. This is because communication theory, among other things, "does not tell us what information is. It ignores questions having to do with the content of signals, what specific information they carry, in order to describe how much information they carry". It is "preoccupied with average amounts of information," while Dretske's concern is with "what is conveyed in particular messages or acts of communication" (Precis, p. 171).

Dretske adapted the mathematical theory to deal with the information a given signal carries. To do so, he had to "relax" the concepts of the theory so they would apply, in a way they don't in their original setting, "to systems (gauges, speech, sensory processes) that, in some ordinary sense, transmit information". This allowed him to extend the "wealth of epistemologically suggestive terminology" incorporated in the "underlying structure" of the mathematical theory to produce "a genuine theory of information" (AR, p. 83).

Dretske stresses that to be philosophically useful the "theory should . . . preserve enough of our common understanding of information to justify calling it a theory of information" (Precis, p. 169). He argues that his account does just this. It captures much of "what we normally or ordinarily mean by talking of some event, signal, or structure as carrying (or embodying) information about another state of affairs" (KFI, pp. 41–42). But he warns that his characterization of information shouldn't be confused with a slavish attempt to codify pretheoretical intuitions about "information". "The theory", Dretske says, "is not a candidate for *Webster's Dictionary*" (KFI, p. 46). The explanatory power of the theory should warrant some regimentation of cases or uses if necessary. Dretske regards this as nothing more than good scientific practice. After all, one of the central things information theory tells us about information is that it is *"an objective* commodity" (Precis, p. 69).

2. INFORMATION AS AN OBJECTIVE COMMODITY

Information is objective in the sense that it is

something whose generation, transmission, and reception do not require or in any way presuppose interpretive processes. As such, it is the sort of thing that can be delivered to, processed by and transmitted from instruments, gauges, computers, and neurons. It is something that can be *in* the optic array, on the printed page, carried by a temporal configuration of electrical pulses, and stored on a magnetic disk, and it exists there *whether or not anyone appreciates this fact or knows how to extract it.* (Precis. p. 174)

The way in which information is largely independent of interpretation is like the way in which certain systems of representation are largely independent, in what they represent, of the interpretations of conscious agents. For Dretske, there are "deep connections between representational systems and information-processing models of human cognition".[7]

There are several distinct types of representation systems. The relevant ones are those which indicate something in themselves. We exploit the natural powers of indication (what H. P. Grice called "natural meaning"[8]) in such systems for our own particular purposes. In the sense that we assign them a function or purpose, their status as a representational system is partly conventional. But the conventional character of how they represent always rests ultimately on their natural powers of indication or representation. We make signs work as symbols in systems of this kind.

So though the calibrations on a thermometer or a gas gauge are in a sense conventional, the natural laws or regularities we exploit in constructing the device are not. It is these powers of natural indication that ensure that the device represents what it represents, whether any-one knows how to read the dial or gauge, or is even aware that the device is functioning. What the instrument represents is in this sense an "objective commodity."

Information is objective in a precisely parallel sense. According to Dretske, "talking about information is . . . a . . . way of talking about the fundamentally important relation of individuation or natural mean-ing." It is a

commodity . . . which, though we speak of it as being *in* a signal or *at* a receiver, is constituted by the network of relationships existing between a signal and a source. This is objective in the sense that the amount of information transmitted is independent of its potential use, interpretation, or even recognition (AR, p. 82).

These remarks about the way in which information is objective involve several new ideas which are central components of Dretske's theoretical apparatus. We may best understand them by looking at how they function in a structural account of the communication situation.

3. INFORMATIONAL CONTENT AND THE COMMUNICATION SITUATION

In Dretske's theory, communication occurs when someone receives a signal, or message, which tells that person something about the environment. The signal is carried along a channel. The person who receives the signal is the subject, or the receiver. The state of affairs in the environment about which the subject receives the signal is the source. On this view, the source need not be the cause of the signal.

A person can receive a signal without thereby receiving information. A message carries information about a source to the extent that some-one could learn something about the source from the message. Equivo-cation – "noise" – can reduce, or even eradicate entirely, the amount of information a signal carries. A message carries information only when it unequivocally carries truth about its source. There is no equivo-cation when "the message has whatever reliable connections with the source are required to enable a suitably equipped, but otherwise igno-rant, receiver to learn from it that message" (Precis, p. 179).

These reliable connections are taken to be lawlike regularities be-tween a source and a signal. They determine the signal's informational content:

The amount of information at r about s is a function of the degree of lawful (nomic) dependence between conditions at these two points. When there is a lawful regularity between two events, statistical or otherwise . . . we can speak of one event's carrying information about the other (Precis, p. 172).

Then the nature of the required nomic regularity or reliable connection is spelled out in terms of the conditional probability that, given a signal, the source has the property attributed to it by the signal. Dretske explains:

Communication theory only makes sense if it makes sense to talk about the probability of certain specific conditions given certain specific signals. This is so because the quantities of interest to communication theory are statistical functions of these probabilities. It is this *presupposed* idea that I exploit to develop an account of the signal's content. These conditional probabilities determine how much, and indirectly *what*, information a particular signal carries about a remote source. One needs only to stipulate that the content of the signal, the information it carries, be expressed by a sentence describing the condition (at the source) on which the signal depends in some regular, lawful way (Precis, pp. 172–73).

Dretske attempts to capture all of this in his definition of informational content. Though the definition mentions a signal (r) as carrying information about a source (s), this is shorthand for the more complex claim that r can be any event, condition, or state of affairs, the existence or occurrence of which may depend on s's (an indexical or demonstrative expression referring to some item at the source) being F. The definition also assumes that s's being F always carries with it some positive amount of information:

Informational Content: A signal r carries the information that s is $F =_{df}$ the conditional probability of s's being F, given r (and k) is 1 (but given k alone, less than 1) (KFI, p. 65).

Dretske adds this important qualification: "whether a signal carries the information that s is F does depend, along with other things, on what the speaker already knows about the objects" (Precis, p. 174). This qualification is encapsulated in the only new element in this crucial definition – the mysterious 'k'. Dretske explains that "it relativizes information to what (if anything) the receiver already knows about the possibilities at the source." But he insists that "this relativization does not undermine the essential objectivity of the commodity so relativized" (Precis, p. 174).

Dretske stresses that for the most part, the relativization will not matter. Most subjects, in most instances, will share a common background of knowledge about the possibilities existing at the source.

Dretske offers no argument for this claim. He regards it as a "harmless" simplifying assumption which allows us to avoid "distracting complications," analogous to the way we treat the observer's situation in physical theory. He says:

> ...we have indulged in the harmless fiction that the number of possibilities existing at the source ... was fixed *independently* of what anyone happened to know ... the fiction is often rendered harmless by the fact that the assessment of the information contained in a signal ... is carried out against a background of communally shared knowledge in which individual differences are submerged. That is, what is known about the various possibilities at the source ... is the same for all relevant receivers, and the discussion can proceed (for all practical purposes) as though the commodity in question was *absolute* and fixed. We do the same sort of thing when discussing such relative magnitudes as weight, velocity, and simultaneity. Only when there is a shift of reference systems does the need arise to make explicit the relative nature of the quantity under consideration. Information is no different (KFI, p. 80).

In the physical theory case, the observer's frame of reference determines what information she can receive. This is objective, though observer-relative: any observer similarly placed could receive similar information. At a concert, for example, I may be able to see more from my seat than you can from yours. So I may learn that Flo is singing in the chorus, while you can't tell. But if you were in my place, you would see what I'm seeing. You would learn what I learn if you were suitably placed.

But this analogy with physical theory doesn't seem to capture what Dretske has in mind. For Dretske, what information one receives depends upon what one already knows about the possibilities that exist at the source. This is a different and additional source of "relativization". It says that I bring background information or a "framework" of knowledge to my position. This background affects what information I get from the observations I make at that position. Not everyone, then, in the same (or relevantly similar positions) will receive similar information unless their background information or "frameworks" are relevantly similar.

To follow my concert analogy, I may be able to identify the members of the chorus from my seat, while your seat is too far away for you to pick them out. But if I don't know who Flo is, then I don't get the information that she is singing in the chorus from what I observe from my seat. Since you do know who she is, you would get that information if you traded seats with me.

This additional source of relativization is also harmless. It doesn't affect the objectivity of the information received. But it does suggest a problem for the way Dretske describes this relativization.

Dretske describes the cases as ones where "a receiver's background knowledge is relevant to the information he receives" (KFI, p. 81). This sounds like the physical theory analogy. There is information to be had at a location, but only those with the proper background knowledge can receive it. But this is not what Dretske means. For he also says: "Whether a signal carries the information that s is F does depend, among other things, on what the speaker knows about the object s" (AR, p. 84). This makes a stronger claim. It says that whether the signal carries the information at all depends on the subject's background knowledge. It raises two related questions about Dretske's theory.

The first question concerns whether we need to describe the cases this way. Why not describe them as cases where you and I receive relevantly similar information when we are situated in relevantly similar locations, but where you, knowing who Flo is, are able to do more with the information than I am? You can couple the information you receive with your background information, and infer something that I can't.

Dretske might try to rule this out by saying that you don't infer that Flo is singing from your background information and your present observations, you just see that Flo is singing. This makes it difficult to see how we might settle this issue. Both descriptions arguably fit the facts.

But if we modify the case a bit, Dretske's position looks less plausible. Suppose Flo and Jo are identical twins. Both are in the chorus. If I know Jo is in Europe, then I can identify Flo by her characteristic features, even though I couldn't have distinguished Flo from Jo at that distance. If you don't know that Jo is in Europe, then you can't. Here it seems more plausible to say that we get the same signal, but I can do more with it than you can. Why I can do more with it is due to my background knowledge. It allows me to draw the conclusion that it is Flo, not Jo, on stage.

Or compare the case where you tell me that either Flo or Jo was on stage, but you couldn't tell which at that distance. Since I know Jo is in Europe, I also know that it was Flo on stage. If we're in adjacent seats, we get relevantly similar signals. At that distance, it isn't possible to tell by looking alone whether it is Flo or Jo on stage. I can do more to tell by looking alone whether it is Flo or Jo on stage. I can do more with the information I get from what I see than you can with the information you get from what you see. I know that it was Flo on stage. It is reasonable to think that I inferred this from what I saw, together with what I already knew. After all, it seems that we saw relevantly similar things.

While I think that my reading of these cases is more plausible than Dretske's, I admit a conclusive resolution of this issue may be difficult, if not impossible. But we are certainly not forced to Dretske's conclusion that, in cases like the above, "I must have received *more information* from this single observation than you" (KFI, p. 78). That does not follow from anything Dretske has shown.

Dretske does have a reason, internal to his theory, for preferring his reading of these cases to mine. If inference is involved in these cases, then we can raise questions about what kind of inference is involved. We can also raise questions about the quality of the inferences. These evaluative questions strongly suggest answers which would involve a notion of justification, and this is just what Dretske wants to avoid. Whether he can ultimately avoid such notions remains to be seen. For the present, however, we can leave the issue moot. As Dretske says, "intuitions may differ on how best to characterize such a situation in informational terms" (KFI, p. 78).

On either account of these cases, however, information remains objective. But one may raise another question about Dretske's definition of informational content. The account may seem intolerably strong in its requirement that the conditional probability be 1. It may seem to demand too much for the transmission of ordinary information. It may be objected that, in most practical situations, there will surely be some amount of equivocation. The amount may be quite small, but any equivocation is enough to make the conditional probability less than 1.

4. CHANNEL CONDITIONS AND RELEVANT ALTERNATIVES

Dretske anticipates this objection. He traces its source to sceptical worries about the transmission of information. A sceptic about information might demand that a signal be self-authenticating. Such a demand requires that a signal, in addition to carrying the information that *s* is *F, also* carry the information that the channel is not in a state where the signal can be received without *s*'s being *F*. The information sceptic holds that this requirement is rarely, if ever, satisfied. There are always possible alternatives which are potential sources of equivocation.

Dretske rejects these sceptical arguments. He holds that one has to give up the view that all possibilities must be ruled out, "if possibilities are identified with what is consistently imaginable". No signal can do that:

No signal, for instance, can eliminate the possibility that it was generated, not by the normal means, but by some freak cosmic accident, by a deceptive demon, or by supernatural intervention. If such contingencies are counted as genuine possibilities, then every signal is equivocal (KFI, p. 30).

But if every signal were equivocal, we would never be able to receive information. Dretske thinks this sceptical conclusion is outrageous. We are not only able to receive information, we frequently do. Information is sometimes conveyed; communication sometimes succeeds. The sceptic's possibilities, then, must be irrelevant to whether a signal is equivocal. Dretske concludes that "sceptical irregularities don't count as such for purposes of communication" (KFI, p. 127).

This information-theoretic version of the paradigm-case argument attempts to shift "the burden of proof" to the sceptic. Merely citing a logical possibility is not enough to challenge the noiselessness of a communication channel. To be taken seriously, the sceptic "must show that these imagined circumstances can obtain, that these imagined possibilities do occur".

Dretske grants that the information sceptic's position is, in a sense, based on a genuine discovery. The sceptic has discovered that "a signal bearing information about a source typically depends, not only on the source, but on a variety of other circumstances of which we are (normally) ignorant" (KFI, p. 114). But the sceptic errs in drawing from this discovery the conclusion that information is not conveyed in such cases. This overlooks the fact that "some existing conditions (on which the signal depends) generate no information, or no new information, for the signal to carry". When these conditions generate no new information, the fact that they could generate information is, for the purposes of communication, an irrelevant possibility.

So the sceptic was right to demand that the channel be "noiseless" if information is to be conveyed along it. His mistake was to suppose "that a signal's dependence on a source is less than optimal insofar as it is conditioned by factors about which the signal carries no information".

Dretske diagnoses the sceptic's mistake as ultimately resting "on a confusion between: (1) the information (about a source) a signal carries, and (2) the channel on which the delivery of this information depends" (KFI, p. 111).

This distinction between source and channel is perhaps the most important feature of Dretske's characterization of the communication situation. It allows him to distinguish relevant and irrelevant alternative possibilities:

the distinction between a relevant and an irrelevant alternative . . . is just the distinction between a *source* (about which information is received) and a channel (over which information is received). The source, as a generator of information, is the locus of relevant alternative possibilities, since it is these possibilities that the signal is called upon to eliminate. The channel, being that set of conditions (on which the signal depends) that have no relevant alternative states – thus generating no new information – constitutes the fixed framework within which dependency relations between source and receiver are determined (KFI, p. 129).

While any signal depends on conditions both at the source and along the channel, only the source can generate new information. The signal only carries information about the source. But without a channel, there can be no source. The channel is constituted by those conditions that, in the communication situation, are stable or permanent enough to count as fixed for the purposes of communication. These conditions make up "the framework within which communication takes place". They are "not a source about which communication takes place". This is why they generate no new information about the source. Dretske incorporates these features of the distinction between source and channel in his definition of the communication channel:

The channel of communication $=_{df}$ the set of existing conditions (on which the signal depends) that either (1) generate no (relevant) information, or (2) generate only redundant information (from the point of view of the receiver). (KFI, p. 115)

It is important that the requirement that the channel conditions generate no new information does not mean that we must know that they generate no new information. Their conditions constitute a channel if they are in fact stable, if in fact they have no relevant alternative states. For Dretske:

Whether the receiver is ignorant of these particular conditions or not is beside the point. As long as the conditions of which he or she is ignorant (holds no beliefs about) are conditions which in fact have no relevant alternative states – or, if they do, have alternative states that have been excluded (whether this is known or not) by prior test and calibration – then these conditions function as the fixed framework (channel) within which equivocation (and hence information) is reckoned. They are not a source of equivocation (information). Information (and therefore knowledge) depends on a reliable system of communication between source and receiver – not on whether it is *known* to be reliable. (KFI, p. 123)

The sceptic may retort that a given channel may be equivocal, even if we have checked it and monitor it regularly. There may be a genuine possibility that the channel is noisy. We may, through ignorance or carelessness, have overlooked, ignored, or failed to recognize that fact.

Dretske agrees that such genuinely possible states do generate new information. Then there is equivocation; the channel is noisy. In such circumstances, we simply don't receive the information. Dretske grants that such cases can't always be ruled out. Further monitoring of the channel, past a certain point, is not only impracticable, it eventually becomes impossible. But he suggests that worry about them reflects a demand, not for the information itself, but for information about the information, not unlike the demand of some sceptics that to know, we must know that we know. Dretske regards this as another sceptical confusion. Though "there is a limit to our ability to monitor the channels over which we receive information . . . this limit does not represent an obstacle to our receiving information over these channels. Rather, it represents an obstacle to receiving that higher-order information that the signals being received do indeed carry information about the source" (KFI, p. 121).

We may, with Dretske, set this sceptical worry aside. But there remains a question, which need not be sceptical, as to when a given possibility is a "relevant" one. Dretske has so far given us no clear criteria for what counts as "genuine" or "relevant" alternative possibilities. But he thinks the answer to this question about criteria is in large part an empirical matter:

To qualify as a relevant possibility, one that actually affects the equivocation of (and therefore information in) a signal, the possibility envisaged must actually be realizable in the nuts and bolts of the particular system in question. If, in the past, signals of kind *R* have arrived when *s* was not *F* (whether or not this is known is immaterial), that settles the matter. Signals of kind *R* are equivocal with respect to *s*'s being *F*, and they are equivocal whether or not, on *this* occasion, *s* happens to be *F*. (KFI, p. 131)

Though he admits that the result is fallible, and sometimes inconclusive, Dretske argues that "the way communication theory" assesses whether a possibility is relevant "is by taking what does (and does not) happen (over a sufficiently long run) as an index to what can (and cannot) happen". The theory lets long-run frequency be our guide to what counts as a relevant alternative. He does not, however, explain just how we are supposed to use the data observed regularities provide.

Dretske is aware that consulting past regularities may not give us all the genuinely relevant alternatives. There may be relevant possibilities which just didn't happen to occur in our past experience, even though they might well have occurred. There is nothing to insure that these possibilities won't occur in the immediate future. One can worry about this aspect of Dretske's account without raising sceptical objections.

This approach also leaves room for non-sceptical worries that in many ordinary situations where we take ourselves to know, there will in fact be relevant alternatives of which we're unaware. If such alternatives introduce equivocation and make the resulting conditional probabilities less than 1, then we in fact receive much less information than we usually take ourselves to have. This raises another source of worry that Dretske's account of information is too strong in its demand that the conditional probability be 1.

Dretske seems aware of this problem, but his response to it is puzzling. He says, in effect, that the requirement that the probability be 1 only appears to be too strong. The concept of information is indeed absolute. But when we look at the criteria for determining, in an actual case, what the probability is, there is considerable flexibility. This is because information has a "social" or "pragmatic" aspect·

whether an existing condition is stable or permanent enough to qualify as part of the channel . . . is a question that may not have an objectively correct answer. When a possibility becomes a *relevant* possibility is an issue that is, in part at least, responsive to the interests, purposes, and, yes, values of those with a stake in the communication process. (KFI, pp. 132–33)

This seems to introduce not just flexibility, but genuine relativity as well. Dretske admits this, but insists that this "relativization" does not conflict with the absolute character of information:

. . . to have received information, is to have eliminated all relevant alternative possibilities. These concepts are absolute. What is not 'absolute is the way we apply them to concrete situations – the way we determine what will qualify as a relevant alternative. (KFI, p. 133)

Dretske's position is unclear. He may mean either that our judgments that a possibility is relevant are relative to our interests and purposes, or that we determine constitutively what possibilities are relevant in light of our interests and purposes.

Neither alternative is attractive for Dretske's theory. On the first reading, we (the epistemic community, that is) might make a decision about what the relevant possibilities were in a given situation – and be wrong. If it came to light that we were wrong, however, we should revise our views about whether information was transmitted in that situation. This allows us to hold that information is absolute, while our judgments about when information is transmitted or received are relative to our interests and purposes.

Unfortunately, this answer, which seems attractive and sensible in its own right, is far too "realistic" to square with the passage I just quoted, to the effect that questions about relevant alternatives may not always have objectively correct answers. For this alternative makes the decision a function of our interests and purposes. If we obtain further evidence that our decision is wrong, we will, if we are reasonable, modify our decision in the light of that evidence. But this seems to imply that while there is an objectively correct answer to questions about relevant possibilities, it may just be that we don't know what the answer is, and our decisions about those answers, shaped in part at least by our interests and purposes, do not always square with what we find after further investigation.

Accordingly, this reply seems too weak to be a satisfactory interpretation of what Dretske means. For one might agree, without thereby becoming a sceptic, that while this reading may provide an accurate description of our actual behavior – that is, our decisions about what are the relevant possibilities in a given case are at least partially determined by our interests and purposes – it may also be the case that our judgments in general poorly reflect the way things really are. Whatever we may find convenient, natural, satisfying, important, or even right to decide, given our interests and purposes, it may be that most if not all of the conditional probabilities in such cases are less than 1. There may be relevant alternatives we simply (and perhaps, systematically) overlook because they do not square or mesh in the right ways with our interests and purposes. Since there is no guarantee that our interests and purposes invariably steer us toward correct decisions in epistemic or any other matters, if we are reasonable we will be fallibilistic about any decisions we reach about relevant possibilities. But this very real possibility of error should make us equally fallibilistic about any claim we make to have received information in a given situation. And this does not seem to square with Dretske's interests and purposes in introducing the relativization provided by decisions of this sort.

This pushes our interpretation toward the alternative reading, where our decisions actually constitute what the conditional probabilities are, where there is "no objectively correct answer" apart from appeal to our interests, purposes, and values. This is genuinely relativistic.

Other things Dretske says suggest, however, that this is indeed what he has in mind. In AR, he considers whether a scale – calibrated to the usual standards of precision – can tell us that something weighs exactly seven pounds. It may seem that it can't, with a probability of 1, at least, if there is even a very small margin of error. For then there will be an equally small but nonetheless real chance that the object doesn't weigh exactly seven pounds. To do so is to rule out certain possibilities of error as irrelevant.

We certainly can do this, and probably do so in fact more than many epistemologists would care to admit. But it opens Dretske's regularity theory of information to objections that parallel those Richard Feldman and others have raised as the "the problem of generality" for reliability theories of knowledge.[9] The generality problem charges that the reliability theory provides no independent standards for determining the reference class for a reliability claim. Reliability is primarily a property of types of process. But the process that results in a particular belief may be described in a variety of ways, to which different process types will correspond. These types may differ considerably as to their reliability. To which of these types should we refer in deciding whether the particular belief was arrived at in a reliable manner?

The relativistic reading of Dretske's view accentuates the problem for the reliability theory of information. For it says that the reference class is determined by our interests and purposes, which leaves any decision made on this basis open to the charge of being arbitrary and ad hoc.

Dretske frequently overlooks this non-sceptical difficulty in his haste to show that the requirement that the conditional probability be 1 doesn't encourage sceptical doubts. Replying to his critics in the BBS symposium, he says:

Do we ever get information from a newspaper about the events of which it purports to inform us? We all know that newspapers aren't infallible; they sometimes publish falsehoods . . . . The point is that the relevant reference class is not "stories appearing in newspapers" but "stories on *this* topic appearing in *this* newspaper". We are entitled to this more restricted reference class when the reader knows the paper is the *Wall Street Journal* (not the *National Enquirer*), and the topic is the performance of the Dow Jones average (not the secret sex life of Nancy Kissinger). (AR, p. 85)

There is perhaps something to what Dretske says here as a device for ruling out idle sceptical doubts. But it hardly helps with the non-sceptical doubts raised by the exposure of the fraud involved in the recent Pulitzer Prize-winning articles by a *Washington Post* journalist about a pre-adolescent heroin addict. If any paper is reliable, the *Post* is. This doesn't mean that I have to take the astrology column or "Capitol Gossip" seriously. To argue that I should is to give in to sceptical doubts of the sort Dretske rightly rejects. But how do I decide whether, given the fraud, I get information from a series of articles about the circumstances surrounding Len Bias's death? Is it sufficient that it is a different topic, a different author?

What Dretske says provides little concrete advice as to when restricting or expanding the reference class is appropriate, let alone when it is correct. Nor is it clear how – and why – interests and purposes are relevant here. And if the correctness of the reference class is determined by our interests and purposes, what happens when our interest and purpose is to arrive at the most likely account of what happened?

Dretske's remarks do little to help him avoid the charge that decisions about what possibilities are relevant may well be arbitrary and ad hoc. But they do, for better or worse, complete his picture of the regularity theory of information.

5. KNOWLEDGE AS INFORMATION-CAUSED BELIEF

It is a short step from Dretske's account of information to his account of knowledge. If Karen believes that s is F as the result of receiving the appropriate information about s, then she knows, "If the belief is caused by the appropriate information, it qualifies as knowledge whatever *else* may be capable of causing it" (Precis, p. 179). Dretske "characterizes" knowledge accordingly:

> K knows that s is $F =_{df} K$'s belief that s is F is caused (or causally sustained) by the information that s is F (KFI, p. 86).

This looks like a definition. But Dretske warns against this natural interpretation:

> ... this is not intended to be a *definition* of knowledge, something that might be established by conceptual analysis or by an inquiry into the meanings of the terms "knowledge", "information", "belief", and "cause". It represents a coordination between our ordinary concept of knowledge ... and the technical idea of information ... It attempts to describe, with the conceptual resources of information theory, the state that is ordinarily described with the verb "to know". In this respect the equation is analogous to a thermodynamic redescription of hot objects in terms of their heat capacity, conductivity, and temperature. (KFI, pp. 91–92)

In other words, the formula represents the theoretical reconstruction of our conception of knowledge in terms of the theory of information. Dretske is correct to describe the formula as a "bridge principle" rather than as a definition. The formula, however, does specify what knowledge is.

Dretske thinks that this principle has some obvious advantages. It allows us, he thinks, to retain the traditional conception that knowledge is absolute. It also allows us to explain why knowledge has that property; it inherits its absolute character directly from the absoluteness of the concept of information. And it seems to avoid the central problem that plagued justificatory analyses of knowledge, because "one cannot get into an appropriate informational relationship to something false" (Precis, p. 179). The Gettier cases all involve belief that is not information-based in this sense. Given the definition, that feature of information is immediately transmitted to knowledge.

The substantial addition the definition provides is the requirement that knowledge that s is F be caused by the information that s is F. Information must not only be transmitted by a signal and received by a subject, the subject's belief must be caused by that information as well. This is an important addition to Dretske's theory. It is intended to quell lingering doubts that the information-theoretic account of knowledge leaves out an important element central to traditional analyses of knowledge: the basing relation. In these accounts, knowledge is belief based on adequate justification. Dretske's theory replaces the basing relation with a causal condition, as his definition makes explicit. Dretske explains:

> The idea of information causing (or causally sustaining) belief is intended to capture what is worth capturing in the doctrine that for a person's belief to qualify as knowledge, there must not only *be* evidence to support it, the belief must be *based on* that evidence.

Insofar as the information that s is F causes K's belief that s is F, we can say that the belief is based on the information that s is F. (KFI, p. 91)

Understanding Dretske's principle requires that we distinguish cases where information is conveyed and received, and where the subject forms a belief about p, but where the subject's belief is not caused by that information, from cases where it is so caused:

When, therefore, a signal carries the information that s is F *in virtue* of having the property F', when it is the signal's *being F'* that carries the information, then (and only then) will we say that the information that s is F *causes* whatever the signal's being F' causes. (KFI, p. 87)

Dretske both explains and motivates this idea of a belief's being caused by "the appropriate information" in this sense with an effective illustration. A spy is waiting for a courier to arrive. The courier is to use a special knock to signal her arrival. She is to knock three times in rapid succession, pause, and then give the same sequence of three rapid knocks again.

It is this sequence that signals the spy that the courier has arrived. The time of day, the volume or pitch of the knocks is irrelevant. If the spy hears the knocks, and if hearing the sequence of knocks causes the spy to believe that the courier has arrived, then his belief has been caused by the appropriate information. He knows. If on the other hand, the spy has dozed off, the courier uses her pistol handle to give the sequence of knocks, and the spy, awakened by the loud noise is caused by the noise to believe that the courier has arrived, then his belief hasn't been caused by the appropriate information. His belief was caused by the volume of the knocks and not their sequence. The spy doesn't know.

For Dretske, this notion of a belief's being caused by the appropriate information takes the place of the basing relation in traditional accounts of knowledge:

The idea of information causing (or causally sustaining) belief is intended to capture what is worth capturing in the doctrine that for a person's belief to qualify as knowledge, there must not only *be* evidence to support it, the belief must be *based on* that evidence. Insofar as the information that s is F causes K's belief that s is F, we can say that the belief is *based on* the information that s is F. (KFI, p. 91)

This completes Dretske's account of knowledge as belief caused by information.

6. CONCLUSION

Though Dretske is most concerned with answering objections which charge that his account of knowledge is too strong, the real question for his theory is whether it is too weak. Is his theory able to handle examples that seem to satisfy his definition of knowledge, but which, "because of defective background beliefs (compensating false beliefs, etc.) appear not to be genuine cases of knowledge" (AR, p. 86)?

Dretske responded to several counterexamples of this kind in the BBS symposium by reminding his critics that he "attempted to answer such cases in my discussion of the technician consulting a pressure gauge in Chapter 5" (AR, p. 86). That example involves an engineer who doubts the accuracy of a gauge which indicates water pressure in a boiler. If his doubts concern genuine possibilities of which we are unaware, then the gauge doesn't convey information. But if there are no such relevant possibilities, then the engineer's doubts are, in Dretske's view, "immaterial". If the gauge is "perfectly reliable, then it carries information about the boiler pressure whatever people may happen to believe . . . about the operation of the instrument" (AR, p. 86). The engineer's doubts cannot create equivocation.

Of course, the engineer's doubts may make us aware of sources of equivocation which might not have otherwise occurred to us. Still, Dretske is correct to say that the gauge is registering information about the pressure in the boiler (in the circumstances imagined) whether anyone credits it, pays attention to it, or forms a belief on the basis of what the gauge registers.

The problem for Dretske arises with how he uses this point. Though "the engineer's doubts may induce others to mistrust the gauge", if reading the gauge causes someone to believe, then he also knows. The engineer's doubts may influence an attendant in the power station. As a result, the attendant may not accept the gauge's reading. But if he does come to believe what the gauge says – however dogmatic, unreasonable, or even irrational this may be in the circumstances – then he knows. "When suspicions affect neither the cause (information) nor the effect (belief), they are powerless to destroy the resulting knowledge" (KFI, p. 128).

Dretske doesn't acknowledge the possibility of slack between the receipt of information and knowledge that he can't account for by the subject's failure to believe. "One *does* know if one's belief is caused by the relevant piece of information *no matter* how one might have acquired the disposition to believe on that basis. I bite the bullet" (AR, p. 86).

Dretske needs an argument to back up his claim that the only alternatives in such a case are either knowledge or else no belief at all. For cases like the following suggest that information based belief is insufficient for knowledge.

Wayne believes his neighbor is a spy, and wishes to monitor his activities. He has noticed that sometimes, late at night, his telephone rings three times and then stops. At some of these times, he rushed to pick up the phone but only heard a great deal of line noise. Wayne believes that these rings are caused by his neighbor's modem, which he thinks his neighbor is using to send messages to his fellow agents. And he knows that the neighbor has had a separate phone line installed for the modem.

Suppose further that, although Wayne's neighbor isn't a spy, he does use his modem to communicate with various electronic bulletin board services. He always calls at night in order to get the cheapest rates. When he uses his modem, Wayne's phone is caused to ring three times and then stop. This is the result of a crossing of wires in the apartment building's telephone switchbox. The crossing occurred when the telephone company installed the special line for Wayne's neighbor's modem. Because of the crossing, Wayne never gets any other calls. When he randomly picks up the receiver, he hears a normal dial tone. None of this surprises Wayne. He only recently moved to the city, and knows no one except business associates who call him only at work.

In these circumstances, the telephone's ringing three times late at night and then stopping is a reliable indicator that Wayne's neighbor is using his modem. When Wayne hears the sequence of rings late at night, he believes that his neighbor is using his modem. But does this case meet the rest of Dretske's requirements for knowledge as information-based belief?

To determine whether the case does meet Dretkse's requirements, we need to answer two questions: Does Wayne receive the information that his neighbor is using his modem? And if he does receive the information, is his belief that his neighbor is using his modem caused or produced by that information?

Wayne does receive the information that his neighbor is using his modem. The phone's ringing is due to nomic regularities for which there are no relevant alternatives. In the circumstances described, there is a conditional probability of 1 that the neighbor is using his modem when Wayne's phone rings three times and then stops. On Dretske's account, it should be a case where the signal conveys the information that the neighbor is using his modem, information that is received by Wayne when he hears the phone ring.

Dretske could object that there are relevant alternatives which my description omits. They introduce equivocation, so there is no information conveyed for Wayne to receive.

The supposed equivocation must have its source in the unusual way in which the neighbor's modem causes Wayne's phone to ring. Since Wayne knows nothing of the way in which his phone has become a reliable indicator of the neighbor's modem use, it might be said that he doesn't know enough about either the conditions at the source or about the genuinely relevant alterative possibilities that obtain to count as knowing. While a phone company electrician might receive the information that the neighbor's modem was in use, Wayne cannot.

There are two ways in which Dretske might press the charge of equivocation here. The first concentrates on Wayne's inability to rule out alternative possibilities. The second centers around what we must attribute to Wayne. Wayne presumably must have the false belief that it is the interference from the modem that causes his phone to ring. In the circumstances, Wayne cannot get this information. There is no such information to be had.

The first line of reply shouldn't be open to Dretske. For it must use the notion of Wayne's ruling out alternative possibilities, and this is too strong for Dretske, who even suggests, in replying to his critics, that this confuses knowing with knowing that you know (AR, p. 86). Dretske also claims (about slightly different cases) that to require that we know how the mechanisms which cause us to believe actually work is too strong. What really matters is whether the conditional probability is in fact 1, not whether I know this, believe it, or even have any reason to believe it. This way out, then, should be unacceptable to Dretske. It makes ordinary knowledge too hard to come by to suit the conception he is trying to develop.

The second line of argument shouldn't be acceptable to Dretske, either. It also requires more than he thinks is necessary for knowledge. In this case, it is Wayne's false beliefs about how the connection works that supposedly keep him from knowing. Dretske did admit, replying to Rundle, that this kind of case is harder to accept than the case where one simply has no beliefs at all about the mechanism (AR, p. 86). But he once again bites the bullet. For he says about a case where someone predicts the weather from examining the woolly bear caterpillar's hair, where that turns out to be a reliable indicator of what the weather will be:

> ... there seems to be a strong case for saying that these prognosticators really *did* know that we were in for a bad winter, and they knew this *however* they may have acquired their confidence in caterpillar fur as a meteorologically significant indicator. If they got it at their mother's knee, or from some crazy notions about divine intervention, I can accuse them of having been unreasonable, both in believing their own predictions and in thinking they knew what was going to happen, but this, remember, isn't the issue. The question is whether they know, not whether they were reasonable in thinking they knew, or whether their knowing was a piece of luck. (AR, p. 86)

While Dretske doesn't directly answer "the question", he seems committed to the claim that the weather predictors know. In these cases, and more so in Wayne's case, the requirement that we know the mechanisms that are operative is too strong. The question is whether appropriate mechanisms are operative, and whether they produce reliable connections which yield a conditional probability of 1. When these conditions are fulfilled, information is transmitted. Dretske is committed to the view that any stronger requirement would be too strong. Few of us have more than vague beliefs about how our own phone systems, or most of the complicated devices we use every day, operate. To require that we know that they are working in the appropriate manner is to require too much. So the second line of argument also fails.

On Dretske's theory, then, information is transmitted by the phone's ringing. Wayne receives it when he hears the phone ringing. When Wayne comes to believe that his neighbor is using his modem, does the information that the modem is in use cause his belief?

It is implausible in these circumstances to deny that the information that the neighbor's modem is in use is the cause of Wayne's belief. While it is true that Wayne can't get the information that the modem's use interferes with his phone in the ways he thinks this works, because there is no such information, he can get the information that the modem is in use from the phone's ringing, as well as the information that the modem's use is causing the phone to ring. This at least causally sustains Wayne's belief, and so meets Dretske's conditions for knowledge. But it is also the most reasonable candidate for what causes Wayne's belief. On Dretske's theory, then, Wayne knows.

Dretske, of course, could "bite the bullet" and count this case as knowledge. But this is as implausible as it is unattractive. Wayne clearly has a felicitously true belief which fails to qualify as knowledge. Yet it is a belief that is based on a nomic regularity, one for which there are, in the circumstances, no relevant alternatives. So the conditional probability that the signal carries truth about the source is 1. By Dretske's account it should be a case of knowledge.

Wayne's case is not an isolated counterexample. It represents a range of cases where there is a gap between information-caused belief and knowledge. This is devastating for Dretske's account of knowledge. For there seems to be no way of tightening his definition to avoid cases like these without introducing some version of a theory of justification. But justification was the very notion Dretske's regularity theory of information was introduced to avoid.[10]

NOTES

[1] Dretske (1981), referred to hereafter as 'KFI'.

[2] Dretske (1983, p. 170), referred to hereafter as 'Precis'.

[3] See Shannon (1948) and Shannon and Weaver (1949).

[4] Gettier (1961).

[5] The phrase is John Pollock's; see Pollock (1979).

[6] KFI, p. 86. Dretske restricts his account to "what might be called perceptual knowledge, knowledge about an item s that is picked out or determined by factors other than what K happens to know (believe) about it". His main intent seems to be to rule out problems concerning knowledge of necessary propositions. See Dretske's 'Author's Response' (1983a, p. 87), referred to hereafter as 'AR'. Dretske also is aware of the difficulties surrounding the notion of a piece of information causally sustaining a belief. See the disclaimer (KFI, pp 88–90) about his discussion of that notion.

[7] Dretske (1988, p. 58).

[8] See H. P. Grice (1957).

[9] Feldman (1985). See also Goldman (1978) and (1986).

[10] Initial work on this paper was done at the 1986 NEH Summer Institute in Epistemology, directed by Alvin Goldman and Keith Lehrer. I am grateful for the stimulation and encouragement the participants – especially Fred Dretske and Jonathan Vogel – and directors provided. Grants from the Taft Faculty Committee and the Provostial Support Program of the University of Cincinnati made my attendance at the Institute possible.

Earlier versions of this paper were given to the Ohio Philosophical Association and at the Eastern Division Meetings of the APA. I thank my commentators on those occasions, Jane MacIntyre and Michael Hand, for their helpful remarks. Revisions of the paper were helped by the comments of Jack Bender, Charles Dunlop, Mylan Engel, Christopher Gauker, John Heil, Gene Mills, Kirk Robinson, Miriam Solomon, and Linda Weiner.

REFERENCES

Dretske, Fred I.: 1981, *Knowledge and the Flow of Information*, MIT Press/Bradford Books, Cambridge, Massachusetts.
Dretske, Fred I.: 1983, 'Precis of *Knowledge and the Flow of Information*', *Brain and Behavioral Sciences* **6**, 55–63. Page references to the reprint in Hilary Kornblith (ed.): 1985, *Naturalizing Epistemology*, MIT Press/Bradford Books, Cambridge, Massachusetts, pp. 169–87.
Dretske, Fred I.: 1983a, 'Author's Response', *Brain and Behavioral Sciences* **6**, 82–89.
Dretske, Fred I.: 1988, *Explaining Behavior*, MIT Press/Bradford Books, Cambridge, Massachusetts.
Feldman, Richard: 1985, 'Reliability and Justification', *The Monist* **68**, 159–74.
Gettier, Edmund L.: 1963, 'Is Justified True Belief Knowledge?', *Analysis* **23**, 121–23.
Goldman, Alvin 1.: 1979, 'What Is Justified Belief?' in Pappas (1979), pp. 1–24.
Goldman, Alvin I.: 1986, *Epistemology and Cognition*, Harvard University Press, Cambridge, Massachusetts.
Grice, H. P.: 1957, 'Meaning', *Philosophical Review* **66**, 377–88.
Pappas, George S. (ed.): 1979, *Justification and Knowledge*, D. Reidel, Dordrecht.
Pollock, John L.: 1979, 'A Plethora of Epistemological Theories' in Pappas (1979).
Shannon, Claude: 1948, 'A Mathematical Theory of Communication', *Bell System Technical Journal* **27**, 379–423; 623–56 .
Shannon, Claude and Warren Weaver: 1949, *The Mathematical Theory of Communication*, University of Illinois Press, Urbana, Illinois.

Department of Philosophy
University of Cincinnati
Cincinnati, Ohio, OH 45221-0374
U.S.A.

GEORGE GRAHAM

MELANCHOLIC EPISTEMOLOGY*

> I wake and feel the fell of dark, not day.
> What hours, O what black hours we have spent
> This night! what sights you, heart, saw; ways you went!
> And more must, in yet longer light's delay.

Gerard Manley Hopkins, *Poems*

ABSTRACT. Too little attention has been paid by philosophers to the cognitive and epistemic dimensions of emotional disturbances such as depression, grief, and anxiety and to the possibility of justification or warrant for such conditions. The chief aim of the present paper is to help to remedy that deficiency with respect to depression. Taxonomy of depression reveals two distinct forms: depression (1) with intentionality and (2) without intentionality. Depression with intentionality can be justified or unjustified, warranted or unwarranted. I argue that the effort of Aaron Beck to show that depressive reasoning is necessarily illogical and distorted is flawed. I identify an essential characteristic of that depression which is a mental illness. Finally, I describe the potential of depression to provide credal contact with important truths.

Hopkins has a knack for finding just the right descriptions – not the dulling prose of textbook clinical psychology, but the revealing metaphors of telling poetry. Depression, he says, is dark, and my purpose in this paper is to illuminate it. Specifically, I shall try to illuminate depression from an epistemic point of view. I shall be concerned with whether a person has good reasons for being depressed, or, as I put it in the paper, whether depression can be warranted or justified. By 'depression' I refer to the depressed state of mind or emotional condition rather than the character trait, the experience of depression rather than the melancholic temperament. I am interested in whether a person can be justified for the state or condition.

INTRODUCTION

In *The Varieties of Religious Experience* William James observes that "the normal process of life contains moments as bad as any of those

223

J. H. Fetzer (ed.), Epistemology and Cognition, 223–246.
© 1991 *Kluwer Academic Publishers. Printed in the Netherlands.*

which insane melancholy is filled with, moments in which radical evil gets its innings and takes its solid turn" (1958, p. 138). In this paper I go one huge step further than James. I argue that when life is bad, very bad, a person can actually be *justified* or *warranted* for melancholy or depression.[1] James recognizes that life may depress, because "evil facts . . . are a genuine portion of reality" (p. 137). I argue that life, or bad experience, can also *justify* depression. When life is bad or deeply unfortunate, it can be warranted, appropriate, or reasonable to be depressed.[2]

How can a person be justified for depression? This is a difficult and serious question. Later I shall attempt to answer it at length. First, I briefly describe why I as a philosopher am interested in depression.

The Main Issues

One frequently hears it charged that depressed attitudes are unjustified and distorted and that depressed people are virtually or actually mentally ill. Thus, for example, David Burns (1980, p. 205) writes:

Depression is an illness that *always* results from thoughts that are distorted in some way.

Admittedly, given the popularity of the picture of depression as bad and distorted, it may sound strange to claim that depression can be justified. The view I shall develop is not without antecedent however. In his *Spiritual Exercises*, St. Ignatius Loyola writes of the

Darkness of soul, disturbance in it, movement to things low and earthly, the disquiet of different agitations and temptations, moving to want or confidence, without hope, without love, when one finds oneself lazy, tepid, sad, and as if separated from his Creator and Lord.[3]

For the medieval and early Renaissance Christian – Loyola included – evaluation of depression oscillated between viewing the condition as a legitimate form of sorrow and dejection for sin versus as an expression of laziness and sloth which is itself sinful. As laziness, it was 'acedia', movement to things low and earthly; as sorrow over sin, it was positive 'tristitia', longing to be closer to the Creator and Lord. As sin, depression made a person bitter, unable to praise God, and slothful. As positive sorrow, it made a person penitent, desirous of moral perfection and avoidance of evil (Jackson, 1985, 1986; Lyons 1971).

The authors of the following statement speak of another culture

(Iran), but their remarks presuppose that a person can be justifiably depressed in any culture:

> The experience of ... melancholy and depression is rooted in two primary meaning contexts in Iranian culture: one associated with an understanding of the person or self, the other with a deep Iranian vision of the tragic, expressed in religion, romance, and passion, and in interpretations of history and social reality (Good, Good, and Moradi, 1985, p. 385).

If life is tragic, shouldn't those with 'deep vision' be depressed? Brown and Harris (1978, p. 83) comment:

> Depression may ... come from entirely accurate conceptualization, the 'fault' lying in the environment rather than the person.

If depression can be justified or appropriate, issues are raised for the philosopher. When is depression justified, appropriate, and when not? What are the boundaries between depression as deep vision or insight and depression as sickness or illness? As suggested in the quote from Good, perhaps there are 'melancholic truths' whose comprehension depresses. If so shouldn't there be 'melancholic epistemology' to evaluate credal contact with those truths? These are the sorts of questions – philosophical questions – which explain why I, a philosopher, am interested in depression.

When is a person justified for depression? It would be premature to answer this question without first describing what it means to be depressed. An equally important preliminary is to explain uses of 'justified' and 'appropriate' in statements like:

(1)   A person can be justified for depression.
(2)   In certain circumstances depression is appropriate.

I begin by providing a provisional sketch of how I believe we can and should use such terms. This sketch helps to guide the discussion of justification in Part 2.

I consider a state of mind or emotional condition like depression to be justified (warranted, reasonable, or appropriate) just in case it contains:

1. *Reasonable Beliefs*. Some states of mind (e.g., depression, fear) contain beliefs. When such a state is justified, it contains reasonable beliefs. Take, for example, a person who fears dying of cancer. A

person who fears dying of cancer believes that she may or is likely to die of cancer. If the fear is justified, the belief is reasonable.

To call a belief 'reasonable' means that the believer has good evidence or reasons for it and believes it because of those reasons. Thus, a person who reasonably believes that she may die of cancer has good evidence or reasons for this belief, and believes for those reasons.

2. *Appropriate Emotions.* Some states of mind (such as depression and fear) are or contain emotions or emotional feelings. When such a state is justified, the emotions or feelings are appropriate.

The notion of appropriate emotion is conveyed by such statements as 'You ought to feel that way' or 'Her feelings about her colleagues were amply warranted.' We sometimes criticize people for feeling inappropriately. 'You should not be elated over the death of your sister. You should grieve.' 'His anger towards me was unreasonable. I never intended to hurt him.'

A variety of approaches could be taken to whether emotions or emotional feelings are appropriate. I favor an approach which seems natural and intuitive, although perhaps unavoidably vague. An emotion is appropriate just when it *fits the person's circumstances.* A person afraid of removing his clothes experiences an appropriate emotion on the street, but not in his bedroom. While feeling or experiencing the fear on the street is suited to the street (for example, it prompts him to remain clothed and he avoids arrest for indecent exposure), it does not fit the privacy of his bedroom (where foolishly he sleeps in pants and shoes). A person who feels embarrassed for cursing may experience an appropriate emotion if he has cursed in church, but an inappropriate emotion if he cursed only while asleep.

3. *Appropriate Desires or Motivation.* Some states of mind are or contain desires or motivations. When states with desires are justified, the desires are appropriate.

Again a variety of approaches could be taken to the appropriateness of desires. Again, I favor an approach which seems natural and intuitive, although again this may be unavoidably vague. A desire is appropriate if and only if it derives from, or is consistent with, a person's better judgment about how he should be motivated. An example is desiring to diet for someone who wants to lose weight. Suppose in desiring to lose weight a person forms the desire to diet. The desire is appropriate if it derives from his better judgment about how he should be motivated. Presumably, such a desire would derive from such a judgment.

Of course, more could be said about the concepts of reasonable beliefs, appropriate emotions or emotional feelings and appropriate desires. But, since I do not have time here to offer accounts of these concepts, I rely in what follows on intuitive understanding and clear examples. I focus on cases of depression in which the reasonableness (unreasonableness) of beliefs, appropriateness (inappropriateness) of emotions and appropriateness (inappropriateness) of desires are or hopefully should be obvious or evident. I return, briefly, later in the paper to the topic of standards or norms for assessing beliefs, emotions, and desires.

The implications for justification of depression of the above are as follows. Given depression includes beliefs, emotions, and desires, a justified depression means that its beliefs are reasonable and its emotions and desires are appropriate. If depression is not justified, then either the beliefs are unreasonable, the emotions are inappropriate, or depressive desires are inappropriate.

The essay falls into three major parts. Part 1 describes features of depression which are present in prototypical cases.[4] The description of those features is used throughout the rest of the paper. Part 2 argues that depression can be justified. Part 3 offers a necessary condition of that depression which is a mental illness suggested by the considerations in Part 2 and offers a sketch of the potential epistemic utility of depression.

1. WHAT IS DEPRESSION?

CASE A. Alice K. is a forty-year-old housewife hospitalized because of strong suicidal impulses. During hospitalization, she makes two unsuccessful suicide attempts, and in addition, engages in a painful form of self-abuse: she claws at her face. These actions and impulses seem warranted to her because she wishes to atone for acts of adultery. She thinks of herself as guilty and blameworthy for extra-marital affairs. 'I'm going to burn in hell', she tells the doctors. 'God knows how terrible I am'. Two months prior to admission Alice lost all interest in sex and her personal appearance. Her daily behavior consisted of sleeping and 'doing all the housework neglected when I was in bed with other men.'

CASE B. Brian L., a twenty year old college student, learns that his 'best girl' has become engaged to a former high school classmate. The week that follows passes dreadfully. His romantic future looks hopeless since he believes that he will never love again. He blames himself for losing his girlfriend. 'I'm no good.' 'I don't deserve having her or anyone for a friend.' He skips classes, oversleeps, fails to concentrate on school work, and shrinks from phone calls for fear they are about his ex-girlfriend's engagement. He cannot visualize improving his lot.

CASE C. In 1943 Carl M., a forty year old Polish Jew, has been imprisoned in a Nazi concentration camp, where he has just recently lost his wife and children to the gas chamber. When he considers his present circumstances, he pictures a terrible and terrifying world. He feels spiritually bankrupt, miserable, impotent, and helpless. 'My family meant everything to me.' 'Without them I am nothing.' 'I am incapable of living.' Carl spends his days, immediately prior to his own execution, lying on a cold board in a bunkhouse, refusing to eat the meager, tasteless rations he used to share with another inmate when his wife and children – though separated from him in the camp – had been alive. He had kept himself alive for them. Now he wants to die.

The above three cases illustrate typical features of depression. Five in all: First, the person feels miserable, sad, or hopeless. Second, the person believes he or she has failed or lost something or someone important. Third, the person is severely self-critical over the failure or loss. Fourth, the person interprets events in a pessimistic manner or with a negative reasoning style; and finally, fifth, he or she desires to withdraw from the responsibilities and demands of living – to retreat from life.

These features individually and collectively have wide ranging, diverse causal effects on attitude and behavior, which include everything from not answering the phone to trying to commit suicide, from listlessness to self-abuse. Certain consequences of the five features are common enough to perhaps be included as features of depression. Listlessness, for example, is a typical consequence, and could be posited as a feature. Further, other cases can occur in which all of the above features are not present but to which the word 'depression' still applies. For example:

CASE D. David N. is eighty-three years old. David phones his brother and complains of feeling sad and not wanting to get up in the morning. When his brother visits him he sees that David has not prepared meals for himself nor changed his clothes in three days.

David's case differs from the case of Alice, Brian, and Carl because he does not believe he has failed or suffered a loss, does not pessimistically interpret events and is not self-critical. David's brother still might describe David as depressed, however, because his case exhibits the first and fifth features.

CASE E. Elizabeth O. had been a popular and successful professional ballet dancer in her mid-twenties when she is paralyzed from the neck down in an automobile accident. For several days in the hospital, she weeps uncontrollably. She concludes 'My career is over'. 'There's no dancing left for me.' 'I need to be able to move my limbs and can't.' She interprets her doctor's well intended but obviously forced efforts at optimism and enthusiasm as an indication that he, too, has given up hope. She feels helpless and hopeless.

Elizabeth also fails to exhibit all five features, but she can be described as depressed, since her condition is characterized by the first, second, and fourth features. As mentioned, features could be added to the five features consistent with depression. For example, the expression 'manic depression' (also 'bipolar depression') is commonly used to refer to cases in which a person experiences periodic euphoria or elation alternating with sadness and other features mentioned above. A manic depressive might also be intrusive or domineering.

In addition to the distinction between depression and manic depression, there is a difference between depression *with intentionality* and *without intentionality*. Depression with intentionality occurs whenever someone is depressed about something; his depression is directed at some event or experience. Figuratively, it points to something that depresses the person. The cases of Alice, Brian, Carl, and Elizabeth are examples of depression with intentionality, since these people are depressed about something. Alice is depressed over her promiscuity; Elizabeth is depressed over paralysis; Brian is depressed about his romantic loss; Carl is depressed about losing his family and being in the camp. Depression without intentionality occurs when a person is depressed in a manner which is not directed at something; it is depression which, figuratively, does not point to something that depresses the person. David's case is an example of depression without intentionality.

Depression with intentionality has a peculiar logical feature. If you are depressed about something *that* about which you are depressed might not exist. Merely believing it exists can suffice for depression. For instance, suppose Brian has not lost his girlfriend but only believes he has. She has broken off her engagement and wishes to return to him. Still Brian is depressed. It's his conceiving of or believing in the loss which depresses. He is depressed over the loss *as conceived* rather than as genuine actuality.

Clinicians may recognize the labels 'with intentionality' and 'without intentionality' do not occur in the clinical literature on depression. They are philosophers' locutions.[5] Intentionality depression is not idle semantics, however. The distinction between depression with and without intentionality underlies, in part, a number of concepts popularly used in the literature to distinguish between depression types: concepts such as exogenous/endogenous, reactive/biochemical, psychogenic/biogenic, and stress related/hormonal. For example, the distinction between reactive and biochemical is a distinction between depression with and without intentionality. In general, these categories raise sticky taxonomic and ontological issues which I shall bypass in the present discussion.[6] The philosophers' labels are involved in each pair of concepts, however, and they are also more pertinent for philosophic evaluation of depression, because they delineate depression subject to justification.[7] Depression must contain intentionality if it is to possess justificational virtues or vices. It makes no sense to ask whether depression without intentionality is justified. Suppose, for example, David's depression is produced by kidney toxins, independent of his beliefs. There is no more point asking if David's depression is appropriate than asking this of a flu or virus. But, it makes sense to pose such questions of depressions of Alice, Brian, Carl, and Elizabeth, as I plan to demonstrate.

Finally, *normal* should be distinguished from *severe* depression, and within the category of severe depression, *mental illness* must be distinguished from depression which, though severe, does not mean a person is mentally ill. Quickly put, normal depression is temporary and not intense. Severe depression is chronic and intense (or simply intense). As for the mental illness, I reserve this topic for Part 3.

In the rest of this paper, I am concerned with normal, severe, and mental illness depression. Also, I am concerned with depression with, rather than without, intentionality, and depression without, rather than with, mania.

2. JUSTIFIED DEPRESSION

When is depression justified? My answer is when the following conditions are met: Beliefs in depression are reasonable and desires and emotions are appropriate. Thus, is it appropriate to feel miserable or hopeless? Is it reasonable to believe that something important has been lost? Is it consistent with better judgment to want to withdraw from the demands of living? If the answers to these and related questions are affirmative, depression is justified or warranted. If the answers are negative, depression is unjustified or inappropriate.

A great deal depends on how the above conditions are understood. While other writers have said or implied that depression can be justified or reasonable, there has been no systematic argument for the position. James does not argue that depression can be justified. He argues only that life contains depressing evils.

Before clarifying and defending my answer, I should note a crucial ambiguity within it.[8] Saying that depression is justified may mean that depression (the state of mind or emotional condition) itself is justified, that is, warranted or appropriate under circumstances of, e.g., paralysis or incarceration in death camp. It can also mean that the person is warranted in how he reacts once depressed, that is, he is reasonable or prudent in the manner in which he allows depression to affect his life. There is, moreover, a danger of overestimating the strength or purport of the justification of depression. Does justification mean that a justifiably depressed person is entitled to act in whatever way he does? If I am warranted for depression, am I warranted in commiting suicide? Of course not. Suicide is an obvious case. A person who commits suicide might unreasonably end his life, though he was not unreasonable for being depressed. Again, although a person may be unjustified for depression, he may appropriately control the condition. A person can reasonably control an inappropriate condition.

CASE F. Fred P. is a forty-two year old college professor. He gets depressed each and every time one of his papers is rejected by an important professional journal. He believes that he is a good scholar, however, that he has enough publications to confirm this, and that he should not be depressed – disappointed or frustrated perhaps, but not depressed. So, when rejection depresses him, he invites a gregarious, good natured colleague to his home for dinner. After the visit he regains self-esteem, stops feeling sad, and enjoys life. He exercises his better judgment over depression. He resists allowing depression to undermine his career.

Of course, Fred is not severely depressed. His case does not illustrate the sorts of cases which confront psychologists and psychiatrists, in which people are overwhelmingly depressed and harm themselves unless they receive professional help. Alice, for example, is suicidal. My point, however, is that depression may be rationally controlled *by* a person with or without depression being justified *in* him. If we think depression is justified, we need not believe that responses in depression are reasonable.

The possibility of distinguishing between justification of (i) depression and (ii) reaction in depression raises different sorts of questions from whether depressive beliefs are reasonable, emotions suitable, and desires appropriate. I turn to these questions later in the paper. First, I show that depression can be justified. How am I going to show that? I argue that there is good reason to believe that depression is sometimes justified whereas, by contrast, there is no good reason for believing that it cannot be justified.

Depression is Sometimes Justified

Depressed people sometimes suffer in circumstances so bad or terrible that it is beyond belief that they are not justified for depression; to see their depression as unwarranted is to see it in opposition to human intelligence and sensitivity. Consider Carl. First, consider Carl's beliefs: that he has lost his family, that he lives now in a terrible and terrifying world, that he is going to be killed soon anyway, that he is weak, unable to control his plight. Each belief is reasonable, eminently reasonable. Carl has powerful evidence for these convictions. Second, consider his feelings and emotions. He feels emotionally bankrupt and miserable.

Could these be inappropriate? His misery, helplessly watching his family suffer, must have been unbearable. It certainly is appropriate to feel this way under those circumstances. The deeper one's love, the more miserable a person should feel. Finally, third, consider his desires not to eat and to die – to withdraw. These desires are appropriate. He is going to be brutally killed soon anyway; death is his best assurance of relief. If there is no good reason to stay alive, and food is without taste or nourishment, then there is also no good reason to eat. Such desires are consistent with Carl's better judgment about how he should be motivated.

The case of Elizabeth argues for the same point. Elizabeth identifies with her dancing career. She believes paralysis totally undermines that career. What helps to justify her depression is that her beliefs about the impact of paralysis on the career are reasonable and emotions on losing use of her limbs are also appropriate. All her life she has lived for the dance.

Such examples show that depression is sometimes justified. Just in case there are lingering doubts about whether depression can be justified, however, I shall now argue that there is no good reason for claiming it cannot be justified. There are in fact three arguments which I have received (in conversation and correspondence[9]) which purport to show that depression cannot be justified. I think these exhaust the opposition. None should produce conviction. Later I also introduce an important gloss on my argument for the justification of depression.

The Feeling Bad Argument

> The emotions or emotional feelings in depression (feeling miserable, sad, or hopeless) feel bad. It can never be appropriate to feel bad. Depression is justified only if its feelings are appropriate. So, depression cannot be justified.

The argument is correct in claiming that depressed feelings feel bad. Indeed, misery feels awful. Just because a feeling feels bad does not mean it cannot be appropriate, however. The sense of 'bad' in which something feels bad is that it is aversive; people try to avoid it, perhaps because it's painful. But, it can be appropriate to feel bad. For example, suppose I commit a terrible misdeed (e.g., I wantonly kill the Pope) and I feel guilty, which feels bad. Far from avoiding guilt, I appreciate my wrongdoing. Feeling bad is, ultimately, suited to the wrongdoing. Or suppose I do something to lower my self-esteem. For example, I am ungrateful for a genuine and generous gift received from a neighbor. I am ashamed, which feels bad. Feeling bad is appropriate, however, for it's part of suitably experienced shame. So, feeling bad can be appropriate.

The Argument from Direct Control

> Depression is not under a person's direct voluntary control. A person, that is, cannot decide to be depressed. However, only if something is under direct voluntary control can it be justified/unjustified. So, depression cannot be justified because it cannot be justified or unjustified; it's not the sort of state about which the question of justification can arise.

The second argument is correct to insist that depression is not directly voluntary. Presumably, people cannot become depressed at will.[10] Just because a state is not directly voluntary does not mean it cannot be justified, however. In many cases, beliefs are not under direct volitional control and yet beliefs can be justified (although they are not justified in the same manner as depression).[11] Also, there are things we can do to control (indirectly) states of mind that are not directly under voluntary control. If you make mistakes on exams, you can hire a tutor. If you have offensive moral views, you can read moral treatises. Exam mistakes, offensive moral views are all nonvoluntary, but we don't hesitate criticizing people for them, or judging them as unreasonable mistakes, unjustified views. The mere fact that depression is not directly voluntary does not mean it cannot be justified.

The Argument from Illogicality

> The thinking or reasoning of a depressed person (the fourth feature of depression mentioned above) is illogical. But no state of mind is justified if it includes illogical reasoning; instead it is unjustified. So, depression cannot be justified. It actually is unjustified.

Again, the above argument correctly insists that justified states cannot involve illogical thinking. We should, however, question the premise that depressed thinking is illogical.

The most systematic defense of the thesis that depressed thinking is illogical or distorted is by the psychiatrist Aaron Beck (1967, 1974). According to Beck, depressed thinking is illogical because it is composed of logical errors. Beck claims that there are several types (not mutually exclusive) of logical errors committed by depressed people: arbitrary inference (e.g., if Elizabeth believes that her husband no longer loves her because he does not smile at her); overgeneralization (e.g., Brian believes that because he has lost his best girlfriend he will never find another); magnification and minimization (e.g., when Alice exaggerates the moral effects of her adultery or a depressed person minimizes the impact of a positive event); and personalization (when a person holds himself responsible for bad things despite his not being responsible).

Beck's view, which in its own way is humane and compassionate, deserves to be discussed in detail, but here I simply wish to make two points about it. The first is that we should not accept his characterization of logical error uncritically. Concerning overgeneralization, for example, it is surely not clear whether depressives overgeneralize. Perhaps on the basis of available evidence they may have legitimate reasons for generalizing from negative events. Carl believes that like his family he will be gassed. Is this overgeneralization? Does his failure to consider the possibility that the camp will be liberated by the Allies mean he has made a logical error, and render his belief unreasonable? But, isn't there good reason behind the belief? He sincerely and certainly reasonably believes that he is living in a death camp and that his family and many inmates once around him have been gassed. He seeks to connect these facts to an expectation for the future. What is more reasonable to expect? That he will be gassed? Or that he will not? Clearly, given his experience, and evidence available to him, he will be gassed. Beck is inclined towards blanket statements about depressive belief formation, without complete consideration of individual variation and the strength of people's evidence. So we can, without opposing the facts, argue that the mere fact that a person is depressed and reasons depressively or negatively does not mean he commits logical errors.

In addition, there is a second point about depressed reasoning that I need to make. I speculated earlier that there may be 'melancholic truths', facts which depress people in credal contact with them. Blanket

characterization of depressed thinking as illogical and laced with distor-
tion is a dangerous attitude to take towards people's epistemic capacities, if contact with important truths depresses. It dampens appreciation
for and discourages that contact. For example, if you became severely
paralyzed in an accident, the fact that you are paralyzed might be a
melancholic truth, an important even if depressing reality, which you
must appreciate if you are to make intelligent decisions about the
future. How sympathetic could we be to your plight if we described
your reasoning as illogical? Should we dissuade you from believing you
are paralyzed? Should we deny your future is bleak? Should we abstract
from the terrible event which has happened to you, and argue that
logical errors keep your reasoning from being sound?

James Rachels (1986) has persuasively argued that terminally ill people should be mercifully killed if their better judgment is that active
euthanasia is in their best interest and various other conditions are
met. Should we decline to honor this right if a terminally ill person
is depressed? 'Depressed people's judgments are not up to rational
standards; they are laced with logical error.' The maintenance of such
a person's life would be tragically pointless and morally indefensible if
terminal illness gave him justification for depression while, behind a
Beckian epistemological veil, we mistakenly believe that his thinking is
infected with logical error.

Beck's analysis is an incorrect epistemic assessment. We may agree
with Beck that depressed people can and do commit logical errors,
which might make their troubled condition worse. But a person can be
depressed *without* making such errors.

Two Kinds of Justification – A Gloss

Although I reject Beck's charge that depressed thinking is illogical,
depressed people of course may make mistakes. Earlier I mentioned
that one possible mistake is reaction in depression. A depressed person
may mistakenly believe that he will always be depressed, or that he
should commit suicide, etc. Such attitudes and the behaviors which
stem from them can be unjustified even when depression is justified.

The contrast between the justifiability of depression and reaction
suggests that there is a difference between two quite different perspectives from which depression may be evaluated. These perspectives are

grounded in the ambiguity, noted earlier, in referring to justification for depression *qua* state of mind and *qua* reaction to the state.

Justification of depression – the state of mind – is based, in part, on the depressive's subjective, internal situation, his current beliefs, desires, evidence. By contrast, the justification of reaction rests, in part, on the external or objective life chances or prospects of the depressed person. Thus, Brian is perhaps justified for depression, or at least for mild depression, if he believes that his girlfriend has left him, and has good evidence for this. He would be unjustified, however, if he allowed himself to become chronically depressed and withdrew from contact with women. We might, for example, say of Brian later in his life that he lived an unreasonably or inappropriately unhappy life because he allowed himself to become chronically depressed. Had he dated he would have fallen in love again. The justified response in depression, according to this perspective, must not worsen or harm the person, whether or not the person knows or has good evidence for this. In brief, it must be prudent. The unjustified response is any response that would in fact turn out harmful or bad. It is imprudent.

Suppose Elizabeth expects to remain paralyzed. She has no idea, however, of whether she might discover sources of enjoyment consistent with paralysis. It is not clear how long she should wait before she decides if she can develop such interests, and whether such interests would improve her life, but clearly it is possible. There could then be a case, for example, which argues that although Elizabeth is justified for depression, she would be unjustified if during the initial months of paralysis – prior to making recuperative effort – she refuses medical treatment and asks to be killed. By contrast, Carl is justified for both depression and reaction, e.g., continuing to refuse food and persisting in wanting to die. For, he will be gassed to death. Given his future, tasteless food will not go well for him, refusing tasteless crumbs will not worsen his life. The deterioration he anticipates is forthcoming. His persistent refusal pays off by bracing him for impending misfortune.

There is a substantial clinical literature on the manner in which depression tends to cause people to make imprudent decisions or to react unreasonably once depressed.[12] For example, depressed persons are prone to underestimate the probabilities of good or positive events happening because they too vividly imagine the worst. Call this *The Depressed Probability Heuristic*. Predictions about the future when depressed are more likely to be false when good events happen than bad.

The Depressed Probability Heuristic is valid when the future will be bad and useful when negative expectations actually help a depressed person brace or prepare for difficulties which lie ahead (e.g., in the case of Carl). Such a predictive style, however, is self-defeating when the future holds genuine positive possibilities and a more optimistic attitude would induce a person to make things better than he pessimistically expects. The heuristic runs the risk of self-confirmation through demotivation. Expecting bad, a person might not attempt anything useful or good. Bad events may occur by default.

Confusing the two evaluative perspectives – of depression, of reaction – can produce incorrect assessments of justifiability. I believe that Beck, for example, imposes a prudentialist/externalist view of the justifiability of depression, and because he notes that depressed people reason according to negative heuristics, and that this may worsen them, he concludes that depressed thinking is essentially illogical. By contrast, appeal to how a person's life will or would go is germane to the justifiability of reaction. It is irrelevant to the appropriateness of depression. For example, if I allow depression to harm me, this does not mean depression is unwarranted. It means only that I react unreasonably or imprudently once depressed. As to why I am depressed, this may be perfectly reasonable: I lost my family in an avalanche, business in a fire, right arm in a battle, left eye on a branch.

3. ILLNESS AND INSIGHT

When is depression a mental illness? How might the concept of justified depression and reaction be used to determine when depression is an illness?

There is an intuition which says that if a state of mind is justified the *person* in the state is not mentally ill. However, nothing in the mere proposition that a person is justified in a state entails that she is healthy or not ill. For example, the beliefs, emotions, and desires germane to depression may be warranted, although the person is otherwise psychologically sick.

CASE G. Geraldine Q. is clinically paranoid. She is filled with excessive anxiety about other people, including grotesque plans to kidnap her. Geraldine locks herself in the trunk of her car to avoid (imaginary) kidnappers, but quickly realizes she cannot escape from the trunk.

Blaming herself for her predicament, feeling miserable about her fate, etc., she becomes depressed.

There is no contradiction in classifying Geraldine as mentally ill while arguing that her depression is justified. It must be allowed that sick people can 'enjoy' justified states. Such states may be beacons of rationality in a sea of sickness. If a person is justified in a state, however, her general mental condition can still be ill.

Another intuition claims that regardless of whether *depression* is justified, depression is mental illness only if the person is harmed or worsened by the condition.[13] I take that intuition to mean that depression is mental illness only if reaction in depression is unjustified or imprudent. The intuition strikes me as basically sound or correct, though, as noted below, we must properly and expansively understand reaction.

The manner in which reaction can be unjustified covers broad classes of harmful or worsening behavior, and needs to be defined relative to a person's situation and actual life chances. For example, suicide may be a blessing if it means avoiding a terribly painful or humiliating death, though for someone in normal circumstances it is seriously self-defeating. Many events or conditions which normally worsen are instrumentally helpful in depressing situations and thus not really harmful to a depressed person. For example, normally people should eat, but Carl ought to refuse food. He will fare better (less awfully) in the gas chamber (feel less fright or pain) numbed by self-imposed starvation than after having eaten tasteless, insubstantial rations.

Carl is not mentally ill; albeit sadly, his reaction is justified. Alice is mentally ill, however. Also, her attempted suicides, we may presume, are unjustified. They harm her. Depression over scarlet letters is no good reason to terminate life.

Further, I do not necessarily mean to promote this precise depression/reaction distinction. It would be a mistake to think that reaction in depression can or must always be clearly distinguished from reaction to the source or cause of depression. It may be that Carl wishes to die because he is depressed or has lost his family in a concentration camp or both. The crucial point behind the depression/reaction distinction is to ask whether a person is harmed or worsened by depression. As long as we distinguish whether a person has reasonable beliefs, suitable emotions, and appropriate desires sufficient to constitute justification of depression from whether he worsens or is harmed, the point of the distinction is preserved. One could, I suppose, say that the *onset* of depression may be justified, but that the *upshot* (e.g., persistent demotivation, suicide) may not. Also, perhaps one could say that certain features of depression may be justified or appropriate (the beliefs, say) while others (such as acute emotional severity) may not be justified. These other manners of speaking may be more perspicuous in certain cases than referring specifically to depression, reaction, and their justification.

I also do not mean to presuppose that knowing whether a person is worsened or harmed is clear or straightforward. We might debate what makes for being worsened. Alice would be worse off dead than alive, but what about Elizabeth? Also, sensitive souls may feel worse than they are. Insensitive persons may be harmed without knowing it. Senseless people may lead lives so self-destructive and self-defeating that negative reaction does not diminish them. There is nothing left to subtract. Despite these problematic cases, however, many depressed people, I believe, are worsened or harmed in depression, and the harmful character of their response is obvious on inspection.

Of course one can react prudently or appropriately when depressed. Much more should be said about appropriate response, but I want at least to say something about it. I had a little to say about appropriate response in the case of Carl. His response involves remaining depressed. It is also possible to respond appropriately by not remaining depressed, as in the case of Fred.

One interesting philosophical point about reaction concerns the role of depression as a spring or source of insight. A number of important philosophers have claimed that depression can be epistemically virtuous, a vehicle for capturing or conveying important truths. William James proposed that life's evil facts, though they depress, "may after all be the best key to life's significance".[14] Kierkegaard believed that the proper fulfillment of man is God, and in *The Sickness Unto Death* he argued that the recognition that such fulfillment is possible and proper only comes through a kind of depression or existential despair.[15] In despair one discovers the need for God. The epistemic utility of depression also has been pointed out in recent psychology. In a paper subtitled 'Sadder But Wiser' (1979), Alloy and Abramson propose that depressed people are less likely to overestimate their personal powers and abilities than nondepressed people. According to these authors, depressives tend to perceive personal causality for what it really is, namely seriously limited. Nondepressed people tend to have an inflated view of their own powers.

Given the potential epistemic utility of depression one appropriate reaction, then, can consist in drawing valuable insights from depression and using such insights to build a better life. Something like this is reported in John Stuart Mill's *Autobiography* (1969), in which he describes a depression he experienced as a young man, during which he seemed "to have nothing left to live for" (p. 94).

Mill reports that at first he hoped depression would lift itself, but it did not. It persisted. Then he tried to delve into his condition, to notice what it might reveal, and the results astonished him. He discovered things which he had 'previously disbelieved or disregarded' and these discoveries became 'cardinal points' in his 'philosophical creed' (pp. 118, 101). They included recognition of the necessity of aesthetic experience (enjoyment of poetry, of Nature, etc.) for a happy life and hope in the practical possibility of rebuilding a person's own character, which heretofore Mill had denied; indeed Mill's disbelief in the possibility of rebuilding character was an 'operative force' in his depression (p. 119). He had felt he was a 'helpless slave of antecedent circumstances', the conviction of which depressed him (p. 118). But through experiencing depression he came to believe people are not causal slaves and that a person could rebuild his character. How did Mill come to these insights or beliefs? What role did depression play? Very briefly, first, Mill surmised that his depression was caused in part by his being over-analytical, too detached and intellectual, and that his life lacked sufficient aesthetic pleasure. When depressed he felt the absence and thus grasped the necessity of aesthetic pleasure. Second, he was inspired by his ability to manage and domesticate depression by reading poetry and enjoying nature. He lifted himself out of depression. By using poetry and natural beauty he believed he had discovered the power to rebuild himself.

Mill's case is a possibility proof for appropriate, prudent reaction. For him depression served as a recognitional epiphany in which he discovered certain truths and used those discoveries to reshape his life. Remove depression and he had no reason to miss aesthetic experience. Nor may he have uncovered certain personal powers.

Though there is no limit to how bad depression can be, at a certain level, though depressed, a person can react appropriately and be made better; and, one interesting reaction is epistemic, in which a person acquires life-shaping insights. I am not prepared here to propose a complete theory of the conditions under which depression offers life-shaping insights. But James, Kierkegaard, and Mill each believe such offerings are possible. The proposed insights are wide ranging, and include self-knowledge as well as more general insights into the human condition. Nordentoft (1972, p. 300) makes the point nicely (if a bit ironically) in connection with Kierkegaard's personal melancholy, that depression may perform an important insight-bearing service:

It is not important to be healthy and sound at all costs, because sickliness contains the possibility of knowledge . . . a possibility from which the healthy and conflict-free person is cut off.

CONCLUSION

In this paper I have defended the thesis that depression can be justified. This thesis, while not absent from the contemporary literature, nonetheless is unpopular and has never been systematically defended. One source of unpopularity is the immense popularity of the contrasting so-called 'medical model' of depression. The medical model rejects or blurs focus on depression as justified or warranted, and concentrates on depression as primarily an unwelcome neurochemical condition, suitable to medical management or pharmacological elimination.[16] One reason that the thesis has never been systematically defended is that standards of reasonable belief, suitable emotion, and appropriate desire are difficult to articulate and plausibly define. Some standards or norms must be built into the notion of justified depression in order to distinguish it from unjustified cases. This normativeness is the most striking feature of the depressions of Carl and Elizabeth as opposed to, say, Alice.

Although I have stopped short of distinguishing sharply or fully between justified and unjustified depression, the analysis I have offered is meant to be a step in the right direction. We need to first appreciate intuitively the difference between these conditions before we choose a set of criteria to more precisely, if possible or desirable, distinguish them. And, I believe that I have captured certain appropriate normative intuitions about depression.

My intent in arguing that depression can be justified is not, of course, to advocate the need for more depression. Some people experience too much of it. Nor do I mean to imply that persons with subjective states similar to justifiably depressed people are obligated to be depressed; there may be legitimate excuses for failing to be depressed. But, were a person immune to depression in justifiably depressed circumstances, I think we should be inclined to think of him as psychologically deficient. Such an individual would either be self-deceived about his situation ('It's not a death camp, but a training center'), or expressing some emotional confusion, or in some other way impaired.

Another result of this paper is that it shows that there is not the slightest warrant for neglecting depression from the scope of philosophy and epistemology. Too little attention has been paid by philosophers to epistemic dimensions of depression – to its types, components, and appropriateness in certain circumstances.

Finally, what I find unsettling, even depressing, about the way in which the medical model of depression disowns questions of reason and justification (discussion of which I do not have space for here, but which is called to mind by the well-known and much lamented overprescription in American society of anti-depressive drugs in response to the genuine problems people face with their lives) is that it fails to recognize the potential of depression to capture truths which a person may need to reshape her life, truths which people should grasp although they may depress or require experience of depression. Suppose Kierkegaard is correct, and we ought to recognize that the proper fulfillment of man is God, and this recognition requires experiencing depression. Presumably such a fact should not be hedged or avoided.[17] So long, however, as we believe depression cannot be reasonable or justified, so long as we picture it as, say, an unwelcome neurochemical condition, we will try to avoid it. But, we should not curtail contact with important truths; and, to avoid depression may be to avoid their recognition. We can retain a basically sympathetic picture of the potential of depression to produce credal contact with important truths if we recognize that depression – depression with intentionality – may be justified. In fact, to the extent that depression is infused with intentionality – as is so often the case – it should be viewed as an expression of human intelligence and emotional sensitivity, an expression with its own – melancholic – epistemology. Good reasons may warrant a person to be depressed, even while reason warns of its possibly harmful effects.

NOTES

* Many persons helped in writing this paper. Special thanks are owed to my wife, Patricia Sedgeman Graham, as well as to Richard Garrett and Hugh LaFollette.

[1] The word 'melancholy' and its relatives (e.g., 'melancholia', 'melancholic', etc.) sound dated to the contemporary ear. Since about the end of the nineteenth century 'depression' has been much more commonly used than 'melancholy'. I shall follow contemporary practice in this paper. See Jackson (1986) for discussion of change in terminology.

[2] I use the words 'justified', 'appropriate', 'reasonable', and 'warranted' more or less interchangeably in this paper. Although distinctions may be made in their use, such distinctions are too complex to be useful here. Broadly speaking, a person is justified (warranted, etc.) for depression if he is depressed for good reason: his depressive beliefs are reasonable and emotions and desires are appropriate. See later pages for more extensive discussion.

[3] Quoted in Rowe (1978), p. 8.

[4] Extracting descriptions of mental states and processes from prototypical cases is common practice in textbooks in abnormal psychology and related publications (e.g., Rosenhan and Seligman, 1984; Oltmanns, Neale and Davidson, 1986). The use of case descriptions to which I am most indebted is by Rachels (1986) in his illuminating discussion of euthanasia.

[5] I should mention, for non-philosophers, that to speak of depression possessing intentionality does not mean that it is intentional in the sense of voluntary (e.g., 'His laughter was intentional'). In philosophical jargon, intentionality is aboutness. Depression with intentionality is about things, states, events, etc. (e.g., adultery, paralysis).

[6] Among the taxonomic and ontological issues is, for example, whether depression with intentionality 'reduces to' or can be explained (away) in terms of depression without intentionality. For instance, is the psychogenic (depression with intentionality) really biogenic (depression without)? Compare Akiskal and McKinney (1973) with Willner (1985). I believe the answer is negative, but the issue is too complex to address in the present paper. See Graham and Horgan (1988) for related discussion.

[7] Of course there are also mixed type depressions, both with and without intentionality, and mixed justifications where one but not another element in the depression is warranted. I neglect such types and the subtleties they pose for questions of justification in this paper.

[8] See Murphy (1979) for a parallel ambiguity in the concept of rational fear. Murphy's essay deserves a wider audience that it has received to date; and, I have profited from reading it.

[9] A distant cousin of this paper was presented at the Society for Philosophy and Psychology at the University of San Diego in June 1987, as part of a symposium on depression, rationality, and cognition. The following three arguments stem mainly from discussions I had with participants at the conference.

[10] If, contrary to presumption, depression can be induced at will, then the objection stands defeated from the start.

An interesting related issue is whether depression can be reinforced or retained at will. For reasons of secondary gain, a person may wish to remain depressed. Depression may help him avoid present and future performance responsibilities. See Hill, Weary, and Williams (1986).

[11] Typically, beliefs are justified by other beliefs and by reasons and evidence. Depression, since it is a complex condition containing emotion, is justified through justification of the complex condition not just its component beliefs.

[12] E.g., Abramson, Seligman, and Teasdale, 1978; Seligman, 1981; Peterson and Seligman, 1984; Williams, 1984; Fosterling, 1986.
Depressed people are also prone to overevaluate the impact or purport of negative events. Call these Depressed Negative Utilities. The idea is that you are more disappointed when your shirts are late from the cleaners when you are (already) depressed, rather than content and happy.

[13] The thesis that a psychological condition is a mental illness only if it worsens or harms its subject is a recurrent theme in the philosophical literature on mental illness. See e.g., Brown (1977) for discussion.

[14] James (1902/58), p. 137.

[15] Kierkegaard's *The Sickness Unto Death* (1849/1980), while not the only source for the view I attribute to him, I believe is the best. See also, Nordentoft (1972).

[16] On the medicalization of depression and its negative effect on appreciating the epistemology of depression, see Ignatieff (1987).

[17] I use Kierkegaard's thesis simply as an example of a potentially significant yet melancholic truth. Nonreligious examples, from e.g., Alloy and Abramson or Mill, may be used.

REFERENCES

Abramson, L. Y., M. E. P. Seligman, and J. D. Teasdale: 1978, 'Learned Helplessness in Humans: Critique and Reformulation', *Journal of Abnormal Psychology* **87**, 49–74.

Akiskal, H. S. and W. T. McKinney: 1973, 'Depressive Disorders: Toward a Unified Hypothesis', *Science* **182**, 20–29.

Alloy, L. B. and L. Y. Abramson: 1979, 'Judgment of Contingency in Depressed and Nondepressed Students: Sadder but Wiser?', *Journal of Experimental Psychology*: *General* **108**, 441–485.

Beck, A. T.: 1967, *Depression: Causes and Treatment*, Philadelphia, University of Pennsylvania Press.

Beck, A. T.: 1974, 'The Development of Depression: a Cognitive Model' in R. Friedman and M. Katz (eds.), *The Psychology of Depression: Contemporary Theory and Research*, New York, Winston-Wiley, pp. 3–20.

Brown, G. W. and T. Harris: 1978, *Social Origins of Depression*, New York: Free Press.

Brown, R.: 1977, 'Physical Illness and Mental Health', *Philosophy and Public Affairs* **7**, 17–38.

Burns, D.: 1980, *Feeling Good*, New York, William Morrow.

Fosterling, F.: 1986, 'Attributional Conceptions in Clinical Psychology', *American Psychologist* **41**, 275–285.

Good, B., M. D. Good, and R. Moradi: 1985, 'The Interpretation of Iranian Depressive Illness and Dysphoric Effect', in A. Kleinman and B. Good (eds.), *Culture and Depression*, Berkeley, University of California Press, pp. 369–428.

Graham, G. and T. Horgan: 1988, 'How to Be Realistic about Folk Psychology', *Philosophical Psychology* **1**, 69–81.

Hill, M., G. Weary, and J. Williams: 1986, 'Depression: A Self-presentation Formation', in R. Baumeister (ed.), *Public Self and Private Self*, New York, Springer-Verlag, pp. 212–239.

Hopkins, G. M.: 1948, *Poems*, London, Oxford University Press.

Ignatieff, M.: 1987, 'Paradigm Lost', *Times Literary Supplement* **4**, 939–40.

Jackson, S. W.: 1985, 'Acedia the Sin and Its Relationship to Sorrow and Melancholia' in A. Kleinman and B. Good (eds.) *Culture and Depression*, Berkeley, University of California Press, pp. 43–62.

Jackson, S. W.: 1986, *Melancholia and Depression*, New Haven, Yale University Press.

James, W.: 1902/1958, *Varieties of Religious Experience*, New York, Modern Library.

Kierkegaard, S.: 1849/1980, *The Sickness Unto Death*, ed. and trans. by H. V. Hong and E. H. Hong, Princeton, Princeton University Press.

Lyons, B. G.: 1971, *Voices of Melancholy*, London, Routledge & Kegan Paul.

Murphy, J.: 1979, 'Rationality and the Fear of Death' in *Retribution, Justice, and Therapy*, Holland, Reidel.

Mill, J. S.: 1924, *Autobiography*, New York, Columbia University Press.

Nordentoft, K.: 1972, *Kierkegaard's Psychology*, Pittsburg, Duquesne University Press.

Oltmans, T. F., J. M. Neale, and G. C. Davison: 1986, *Case Studies in Abnormal Psychology*, New York, Wiley.

Peterson, C. and M. E. P. Seligman: 1984, 'Causal Explanations as Risk Factor for Depression: Theory and Evidence', *Psychological Review* **3**, 347–374.

Rachels, J.: 1986, 'Euthanasia' in T. Regan (ed.), *Matters of Life and Death*, New York, Random House, pp. 35–76.

Rosenhan, D. L. and M. E. P. Seligman: 1984, *Abnormal Psychology*, New York, Norton.

Rowe, D.: 1978, *The Experience of Depression*, New York, Wiley.

Seligman, M. E. P.: (1981), 'A Learned Helplessness Point of View' in L. P. Rehm (ed.) *Behavior Therapy for Depression: Present Status and Future Directions*, New York, Academic Press, pp. 123–141.

Williams, J. M. G.: 1984, *The Psychological Treatment of Depression*, New York, Free Press.

Willner, P.: 1985, *Depression: A Psychobiological Synthesis*, New York

EDDY M. ZEMACH

HUMAN UNDERSTANDING

ABSTRACT. Contemporary thinkers either hold that meanings cannot be mental states, or that they are patterns of brain functions. But patterns of social, or brain, interactions cannot *be* that which we understand. Wittgenstein had another answer (not the one attributed to him by writers who ignore his work in psychology): understanding, he said, is seeing an item *as* embodying a type Q, thus constraining what items will be seen as "the same". Those who cannot see things under an aspect are meaning-blind.

That idea is expanded in this article. Its ontology consists of types only: entities that recur in space, time, and possible worlds. Types (Socrates, Man, Red, On, etc.) overlap; Socrates = Bald at some index and not in another. The logic used is thus that of contingent identity. Now some possible worlds are mentally represented; the entities that occur in them are meanings. But such entities may also recur in the real world. Thus the entities we experience, the phenomena, which serve as our meanings, may be identical in the real world with real things. A correspondence theory of truth is thus developed: a sentence is true iff its meaning constitutes, in a specified way, a real situation.

1. INTRODUCTION

I say, "The cat is on the mat" and you understand me. What does your understanding consist in? Two kinds of answers are now in fashion. The internalist answer offered by Fodor, Dennett, and other functionalists is, roughly, that the sounds I make cause some bits of gadgetry in your brain to interact according to some flow chart; as a result you acquire a tendency to behave in a certain way. Now surely such things do happen when you understand what I say, but that cannot be all that your understanding consists in, or else your understanding what I say could be the reshuffling of some chips in your hat rather than in your cranium. Suppose that as a result of some chips being tossed about in your hat your limbs tend to move in a certain way; surely that is not understanding? In understanding you become aware of some specific content. But a pattern of brain activity, even if typically connected to certain stimuli, has no inherent content; it may be interpreted in any way you please: any content whatever can be mapped onto the internal states of any automaton. If you do understand what I say, there is a definite, unique content that you are aware of. But no internal structure

247

J. H. Fetzer (ed.), Epistemology and Cognition, 247–264.

implies awareness, nor can it single out one content, to the exclusion of all others (or even *any* others, as Putnam proves).[1]

Moreover, why should brain states be interpreted at all? Apart from their relation to consciousness, a structure of neuron-firings calls for a semantic value assignment no more than does the pattern of electron-flow in the copper wires on your wall. An internal syntactic (i.e., satisfying a node in a flow chart) state that makes you react in a typical way to given stimuli need not have a content. There are many nonsentient, noncomprehending mechanisms that manifest typical reaction patterns to some stimuli; any molecule is such a mechanism; yet internal modifications in a molecule are not understanding. Understanding 'The cat is on the mat' is connected to a capacity for consciousness (e.g., of the cat on the mat); hence a certain pattern of neuron-interaction cannot be all that there is to understanding even if it is linked to standard inputs and outputs. Quine states that, to the contrary, a tendency to react to cats (and cats only) in a specific way does not amount to having the concept of a cat, or else doormats could be congratulated for their good grasp of that concept.[2]

Externalists (Davidson, Burge, etc.), on the other hand, attribute the meaningfulness of sentences and the specific content of beliefs not to inner structure (brain pattern, they admit, may differ in different individuals) but to the external conditions in which language is learned. Davidson claims that "our simplest sentences are given their meanings by the situations that generally cause us to hold them true or false".[3] "A sentence which one has been conditioned by the learning process to hold true by the presence of fires will be true when there is a fire present; a word one has been conditioned to be caused to hold applicable by the presence of snakes will refer to snakes."[4] The meaning of my words has nothing to do with internal representations. Beliefs are "states that are identified by their causes, such as suffering from snow blindness or favism".[5] "Beliefs are true or false, but they represent nothing": the content of a given belief has no relation to the particular way in which the world is presented to us by our senses.[6] "The causal connections between thought and objects and events in the world could have been established in entirely different ways without this making any difference to the contents or veridicality of belief."[7]

If Davidson is right, the content a medieval person expresses by the simple sentence "It is getting hot" is uniquely determined by the nature of the external situation that he has been conditioned to react to by holding that sentence true. The said situation is a rise in the mean molecular energy of the substance in question, so the content of the said person's belief, as well as the meaning of the words that he holds true, is that the mean molecular energy of that substance rises. Thus what the medieval person believes, the content of his statements, is exactly the same as the content believed by a twentieth century physicist. That conclusion is truly remarkable: how redundant scientists' work must be, if medieval persons have already held beliefs about mean molecular energy!

Externalists make meaning free of the way in which an item presents itself to us. They divorce 'p' from the particular way in which a subject interprets and structures the situation P; rather, what one means by 'p' is what causes one to hold 'p' true. But which of the infinitely many aspects of that cause is conveyed by 'p'? "Words and thoughts are, in the most basic cases, necessarily about the sorts of objects and events that cause them", says Davidson.[8] Yet to understand a word or a thought is not to grasp some object, *simpliciter*; that is impossible. We think of objects in terms of features we believe them to have given our innate strategies of representing data. If what 'p' means has nothing to do with how I represent the state that causes me to accept 'p', then 'p' has for me no meaning and expresses no belief of mine. I cannot ever understand it.

The externalist's conception of meaning is self-refuting. If the content of the belief that p is the state that causes 'p' to be held true, then physicists and psychiatrists make semantic discoveries by finding new causes of our holding 'p' true. To understand what the externalist says, I must wait until latter-day science discovers what has really caused him to hold his beliefs! On the other hand, if 'p' means, 'whatever causes 'p' to be held true', then all basic sentences have the same content, and all basic beliefs are identical, i.e., "I am caused to hold this very belief". But that is either nonsense or false.

2. A WITTGENSTEINIAN MENTALISTIC SEMANTICS

"What?" I hear the reader say, "A theory that is both Wittgensteinian and mentalistic? Was not Wittgenstein the great foe of mentalism in semantics?" Wittgenstein is usually interpreted as saying that if meaning is what constrains the use of words, mental items cannot be meanings.

A cat-image, e.g., cannot constrain the use of the term 'cat' since it can be interpreted to sanction the application of 'cat' to cats, to noncats, to snakes, to undetached cat parts, or to anything else; thus it is irrelevant to meaning.

Many writers take Wittgenstein's view to be that a term is meaningful which has a specific role in a language game. But what is a role? How does having a certain role differ from lacking it, e.g., haphazardly occurring in all kinds of contexts with no role to play? Formally, anything that happens in the game constitutes a role. So what can distinguish a correct use of a word from an arbitrary, or wrong, use? Baker and Hacker, and Colin McGinn, hold that correct use is a practice that can be mastered. But that cannot be all. Wittgenstein's point was that neither past use nor mental images as such can determine which kind of behavior complies with a rule and which violates it. How can we say then that one kind of behavior manifests the practice (say, of riding a bicycle) while another is an example of having failed to master it? What makes a case of staying on the bicycle a success in the practice and falling off it a failure, rather than the other way around? A practice is not given, except by means of past examples and mental items (e.g., rules or images) concerning it; but the whole point was that these do not constrain new cases. To assume, without further ado, that it is simply given what action is a case of the practice, is to beg Wittgenstein's question.

Wittgenstein has faced that puzzle and offered a solution. Mental items are aspected. The word 'cat', or a mental image C, may indeed be interpreted in any way at all, but in fact they are given us in one specific way. There is a perceptual difference between seeing 'cat', or C, as representing cats or snakes. It is the difference between seeing a Necker cube as facing up or as facing down, or the difference between seeing the Jastrow drawing as a duck or as a rabbit. C is seen under an aspect, interpreted, and there is a palpable difference between seeing it as akin to cats (mandating the application of 'cat' to cats) and seeing it as akin to snakes. The difference is so great that one may not realize that one was given the same stimulus on both occasions: it looks so different. Wittgenstein calls that aspected mental representation 'impression' (*Eindruck*) or 'image' (*Vorstellung*), combining perception and interpretation. His later work is devoted to the notion of *seeing-as*, i.e., seeing an object to fit (*passen*) one kind of things and not another. To lack that ability of seeing-as is to be *meaning-blind*.

This is not the place to go into exegesis of Wittgenstein;[9] I shall therefore only give what I think was his conclusion. If you see the duck-rabbit as a duck, he argued, you see ducks as fitting it, and hence you can use it as the meaning of 'duck', constraining the use of that word in the future. Of course there are borderline cases, but usually you see the duck-rabbit as akin to some things and not to others. It is preposterous to hold that having the mental image C you still have no clue on whether it applies to cats or to snakes. To see C as a cat is to see it as fitting cats and not snakes. It is possible to see it otherwise, but *you* don't. Wittgenstein says that if you do not know that what you see can also be seen under another interpretation you will not say, "I see it now as an F"; but those who are aware of that possibility may say about you: "He sees it as an F" (say, as a cat) and thus predict how you would use the term 'cat'.

But what is it, to understand the term, 'cat'? It is not the *use* of the term 'cat'; understanding, says Wittgenstein, occurs *now*, at this *zeitpunkt*. It is, rather, a certain way of seeing the term 'cat' or the mental image C. If Jones sees C as a snake and Smith sees C as a cat, they see different foreground/background organizations, and group differently what is seen. Try to see C as a snake (Wittgenstein often urges us to try and see a familiar word as having a different meaning or a person as having a different name) and note how odd it looks! Which features of C are standard and which 'expressive'? If you see it as a domestic cat, it looks fairly large; but if you are not familiar with the species *felis domesticus* and see it as a tiger, it looks miserably small. If all the cats you know have tails, its having none (it is a Manx) has great perceptual salience, etc. Perception is interpretation. It is because things are seen as such and such that demonstrative definitions are possible. We can define 'cat' by presenting one with a cat because he will see it as a cat and not as anything else. Our life-styles, values, and interests make mental items interpreted where their external counterparts are not. We do not (although other creatures may) see things as, to mention but a few notorious philosophical monstrosities, Quine's undetached rabbit parts, Goodman's grue, or Kripke's quaddition.

Let me summarize. The question was, how can a mental item be the meaning of a word? How can C constrain the future use of the term 'cat' when it is possible to take C together with any item and apply 'cat' to, say, snakes or prime numbers? The answer is that C guides the use of the term 'cat' because we see it as a cat. Everything is potentially ambiguous and open to interpretation; everything is a duck-rabbit. Yet a duck-rabbit can constrain our use of the word 'duck' if we see it as a duck. We may know that the duck-rabbit can be interpreted as a rabbit, but we do not see it in that way. We see the duck-rabbit as right for some objects (ducks) and not for others (rabbits), just as a musical accord seems to 'request' a resolution, and certain tunes seem to fit funerals and not weddings. Thus, a duck-rabbit can be used to define 'duck'. Creatures who have no aesthetic preferences may fail to realize how an ambiguous figure can help us understand the term 'duck'. They may invent a behavioristic theory of meaning, saying that our use of words is regulated by social reenforcement only. But that is a caricature of human understanding.

3. MENTAL ENTITIES AND PHENOMENA

When mental entities are mentioned we usually think of pains, afterimages, mental pictures, thoughts, dreams, etc. But since the seventeenth century it has been known that color cannot be a nonrelational property of an object any more than the pain or pleasure it causes the observer can be such a property. Einstein taught us that the same is true of shape, mass, and motion, since simultaneity and identity of place are framework dependent relations. Quantum mechanics added all the rest of Locke's primary properties to the list. Naive Realism, i.e., Human-Sensory-Equipment Chauvinism, is not a viable position. Some form of Kantianism with respect to observables is inevitable: one must admit that we perceive phenomena, objects-for-us, in a framework constrained by our human sensory equipment. Now a phenomenon (e.g., this cat) is a mental entity in the same sense that an afterimage of a cat, a mental image of it, or a dream image of it, are mental phenomena: as Kant and Sellars say, objects in our common-sense world are mental phenomena. Thus C, the meaning of my term 'cat', need not be a cat-like mental picture that I have to conjure up in giving myself an ostensive definition of the meaning of the word 'cat'; what I may do instead is just look at my cat. As a phenomenon it, too, is given me under some aspect and not under others.

Kant's move disposes of one Lockean skeleton; another Lockean skeleton that must be laid to rest before any mentalistic theory of meaning can make sense is his notion of concepts. If 'cat' is a general term applying to many distinct cats, Locke and Berkeley asked, how can its meaning be a particular mental item such as *C*? A particular cat would not fit all cats. Hence mental items must be nonparticulars; Locke's idea was that what we have in mind are concepts, i.e., mental items that symbolically stand for all cats. But if what I have in mind are mere symbols, they may just be the electrical currents and chemical reactions in the brain. Thus the road from Locke to Dennett, Fodor, and Stich, i.e., to the view of the mind as a word processor, is very short. The problem of particular vs. general mental items cannot, however, be resolved without going into its origin, the most pernicious problem in philosophy, i.e., What is it to be a particular thing?

4. TURNING TO ONTOLOGY

A thing, a substance, is traditionally defined as that which can survive some changes. If this desk is a substance, then it may be brown at one time and white at another, be mine today and yours tomorrow, without jeopardizing its identity: it is the same thing that has different properties at different indices. To say that a is F at one index and G at another index is not to say that one part of a, b, is F and another part of a, c, is G. Those who adopt that manner of speaking (e.g., Quine) abandon the notion of a substance, for if 'a was F and is G' is replaced by 'Fb & Gc' then nothing survives change; there is nothing that is slightly different at different indices. If every change in a thing constitutes its becoming a new thing ('b' and 'c' replace 'a') then things are reduced to bundles of properties. For indeed with every change we have a new bundle of properties, but such a bundle is not a thing. A thing is what can be reidentified, be found again, albeit somewhat altered, at another index.

In other articles I have developed a strictly nominalistic system of logic and ontology that recognizes the existence of things only in the world.[10] The logic (called 'Substance Logic') uses no predicates, the ontology recognizes no universals. The basic notion of the system is that of a substance (an entity). An entity (such as Plato, Snow, or Red) occurs at various indices. The same entity, Plato, is present at more than one temporal point and at more than one possible world. Snow is present at more than one place, and so is Red. Plato can change: he is bald at one time and nonbald at another; so can Red: it is a shirt at one place and a flag at an other. A red shirt is an occurrence of the entity Red, and also an occurrence of the entity Shirt; hence, these two entities overlap. Since entities such as Red and Shirt, or Plato and Man, overlap, identity is relative to index: Red = (I) = Shirt; Plato = (I) = Man. Just as two routes are identical in one state but not in another, the two entities, Plato and Greek, are identical where Plato is: $P = (P) = G$. They are not identical where Greek is: $(P = (G) = G)$. The latter statement is true only if Plato is the only Greek. To say that Plato is Greek is therefore to say that, at Plato, Plato is identical with Greek; to say that all Greeks are men is to say that wherever you find Greek, you find Man: $G = (G) = M$; Greek and Man are identical at Man. To say that all men are Greek, i.e., $G = (M) = M$, is to say that at Man, Greek is identical with Man. In a domain, identity is transitive: if Plato is Man (at Plato), i.e., $P = (P) = M$ and Plato is Greek (at Plato), i.e., $P = (P) = G$, then (at Plato), Man is Greek: $M = (P) = G$ (hence, some men are Greek). But if Plato is Man at Plato, $P = (P) = M$, and Socrates is Man at Socrates, $S = (S) = M$, it does not follow that Plato = Socrates at any index. The sentence 'Jemima is a cat' says that two entities, Jemima and Cat, are identical at some index. Indices are entities; so entities overlap at entities. For example, Jemima and Cat are identical at Jemima. Those who understand the terms 'Jemima' and 'cat' can identify Jemima and Cat wherever they find them.

Once we have the entity Cat, we define particular occurrences of Cat, where Cat is identical with some spatiotemporal location. Requiring a certain kind of contiguity between those locations (I skip the details) the notion of an individual cat can be derived from that of the entity, Cat. I then use lowercase italicized letters as place holders substitutable for names of individual cats. Then we can assume that the domain is always the total one, and write 'Jemima is a cat' as 'Jemima = c', i.e., 'Jemima is identical with some cat (in the total domain)'.

Let us now distinguish between simple and complex substances. A simple substance is an item whose concept implies no particular privileged division into parts; thus Plato, Snow, and Red are all simple substances. On the other hand a kick, a love, a giving, etc., are conceived of in a way that implies a privileged division into parts. Where Platonists find the two-place relations Kicking and Loving, and the three-place relation Giving, I have the complex material things Kick, Love, and Giving. As we identify individual cats by tracing Cat, so we identify individual loves and kicks. These entities have a certain characteristic appearance; they are no less things, and no less material, than a house or a cat. A loving couple *is* Love: look at John and Mary; if you know what love is, you can see it there. The mereological whole John&Mary is a particular loving that has four hands, two heads, etc. John&Mary is a loving: $JM = l$, just as Plato is a man: $P = m$. 'Plato', 'Man', and 'Love' are all names of material things; the difference between the entities named by the first two terms and the entity named by the third is only that the latter has two privileged parts, i.e., a lover part and a loved part. Thus, 'John loves Mary' has the following form: 'some loving is such that John is its Lover-part, and Mary is its Loved-part'.[11]

We learn the term 'means' in just the way we learn the term 'cat'; it is no more difficult to recognize the entity, Means, than it is to recognize the entity, Kicks, or the entity, Cat. That entity, Means, is a complex substance consisting of two entities, its name part and its named part. If you see a pair of lovers as such, as a loving, you will recognize other instances of Love; if you see a name-named pair as the relation, Means, you will identify other instances of that entity. Human beings can reidentify an entity; you can reidentify Plato even if he grows older or shaves his beard; so, you can reidentify Cat at other locations even if there it is called 'Tabby' rather than 'Jemima' and is male rather than female. The same is true of 'means': you learn that word by learning to recognize, Means; if you see its instances as such, you can reidentify that entity wherever it is, and hence you can apply the term 'means' correctly. Locke's worry, how a particular cat-image can guide the application of 'cat' to all (and only) cats, is answered by Wittgenstein. I borrow his answer, and add that we can reidentify Cat and Means just as we reidentify Plato. If you see C as a cat you need no rule for its future applications; you will immediately see what fits it.

5. WORLDS IN THE HEAD

One of the most maligned and ridiculed notions of medieval philosophy is its distinction between the formal existence of an entity in the real world and the objective existence of that entity in the mind. That the same thing may exist both in reality and in the mind was considered a major blunder; modern thinkers argued that what is in the mind is a representation of the thing out there, a symbol for it, but not it, itself. It seems to me, however, that the said notion is perfectly sound; if the same entity recurs at many indices, why should some of them not be possible worlds that we mentally represent?

No possible world other than R, the real world, exists; yet we do not think it odd to say of some entity that exists in R that it is also found in some nonexistent possible worlds. Segments of possible worlds can be imagined, dreamed, or sensed by us. The psychological processes of imagining, sensing, projecting, occur in the real world, but their content, i.e., what is dreamed, imagined, or sensed, is a possible-world-segment. There is no reason why real entities cannot feature in fiction (most stories have some real entities – e.g., places – that occur in them). An entity is real iff it occurs in R, but it may also occur in other, nonreal worlds, and we can see it there when we visualize a possible world at which it occurs.

If Naive Realism is false, then the world of common sense is no more real than the world projected on a movie screen; it is a figment of our sensory apparatus. All that we are ever conscious of are segments of possible worlds projected by our senses. The difference between dreams and sense experiences lies in the nature of the cognitive faculty involved and in its method of processing data, but neither one is the real (the noumenal) world. Still, some entities found in those unreal worlds that we project may also exist in the real world, although there they probably are different from how they are in the worlds segments that we project. That is hardly surprising, for no entity stays the same (overlaps the same entities) at all the indices where it is found. You, too, are different at temporal indices that are fifty years apart.

For the schoolmen, the relation between the mental and the extra-mental entity was not conventional. Locke and Berkeley, who took it for granted that mental entities that stand for cats are not cats, concluded that mental items are conventional symbols. Fodor's Mentalese is a development of that line of thought, and so is functionalism and Quine's rejection of meanings. I have argued that this route has led us astray. Thus, strange as it may sound, I say with the schoolmen that we do have cats in mind, i.e., in the possible world segments mentally projectable by us. The real world is not the only possible world where Cat resides: nonreal cats are cats, but the word 'cat' is not a cat. One may learn what 'cat' means by seeing or by imagining cats; cats may appear in dreams, in movies, and in hallucinations; these are all modes of sensory presentation. On the other hand, one whose understanding of *all* words is limited to synonyms, having no sensory presentation of any item named, one who is unable to sense an item in a possible world, understands nothing. Meaning does not reside in syntax, for any structure can be mapped on any meaning. To be understood, definition must end in presentation.

A term's meaning is an intra-mental occurrence of the entity it names. Call the set of worlds that a person S can envisage at time T, $W(ST)$. If C is the trans-world entity named by 'c', then the meaning of 'c' for S at T, $M(ST)$'c' is an entity that is identical with C in $W(ST)$ and does not exist elsewhere. In other words, M'c' is the occurrence of C in $W(ST)$ for some S and T. The referent of 'red' (as used by S at T) is the trans-index entity Red; an item i in a possible world W is an occurrence of Red iff, had S inspected i at T, S would have applied 'red' to i. Thus $M(ST)$'red', the meaning of the term 'red' as used by S at T, is the occurrence of Red in $W(ST)$. The same holds for all terms.

What S sees $M(S)$'c' as determines what according to S is essential to C. What Mary takes to be essential to Plato, Witch, and even to Red, may differ from what Joe takes as essential to them; hence the extensions they will give these substances in some possible worlds will differ; Mary and Joe call somewhat different entities by the names 'Plato', 'Witch', and 'Red'. That fact need not bewilder us, since if Joe and Mary share a 'form of life', we can assume that the distinct entities called 'Plato', 'red', and 'witch' by them will overlap in the vast majority of indices. How one sees the meaning of a term determines what would disqualify a given item from being an occurrence of the entity denoted by that term. But that does not bring us anywhere near Relativism. If you are a right-to-lifer and I am not, then the entity denoted by your term 'Socrates' is somewhat different from the entity I refer to by this term, since the entity you talk about is a few months longer than the entity I talk about (yours includes a fetus stage, mine does not). But that does not hamper communication between us, nor does it jeopardize the independent ontological status of Socrates, since the two entities we talk about do exist and mostly (in a vast majority of the indices where they are found) overlap. People in the same culture tend to pick out similar entities, and hence have no difficulty in understanding each other.

An entity may overlap different entities at different indices (e.g., it may change) without compromising its self-identity. The entity Red can survive changes in chemical constitution (Red may be identical with a flag here and with an apple there) but not in color, while Aluminum may survive changes in color (it may be identical with White now and with Black then), but not in chemical constitution. The same considerations hold for the Possibility dimension too, where identity across possible worlds, rather than across times, is in question. What constraints the trans-world-heir-line of an entity depends on the kind of entity it is; what is essential for Red is inessential for Aluminum or for Plato. Thus if M'red' is the meaning of my term 'red', i.e., Red as I represent it in my $W(ST)$, I can also identify it in any other world W', for I know that anything which I would see as similar in color to my M'red' is an occurrence of Red. I also have M'Plato' in my $W(ST)$, and it is Plato as I represent him, but I do not expect Plato to have the same color in every possible world where he exists. An occurrence of Plato in another world W' has to satisfy some other identity criteria, e.g., having in W' roughly the same historical position that it has in the world as I represent it. Here the identity criteria stress similarity in provenance and causal dependence more than qualitative similarity. The special role of origin (rightly insisted on by Kripke) for the identification of individuals across possible worlds yields another strategy for identifying the same individual. Any representation-world, e.g., the world of my dream, or my sensory experience, or my beliefs, etc., is causally related to the real world R. My idea of Plato is somehow due to Plato; thus an entity in my belief-world is Plato, only if Plato in R has a special role in its provenance and would feature in an explanation of its existence in my belief-world. In R, Plato is that segment of R which accounts in some crucial way for my having M'Plato' in my belief-world. Had I been able to interpret my belief-world by inspecting the real world, R, and assign segments of it as interpretanda to segments of my belief-world, Plato is the entity that I would assign to my M'Plato'.

6. SENTENCES

I have partly explained how I can understand the sentence, 'The cat is on the mat': the entities Cat, Mat, and On also exist in worlds that I am acquainted with (where they are the meanings M'cat', M'mat', and M'on'). But the sentence alleges something else to be the case; it says that some *on* (a complex entity) is such that its *top* part is the cat and its *bottom* part is the mat. How can the sentence mean it? I answer, like Barwise and Perry,[12] that sentences name situations; but I take the situation, The-Cat-Being-On-The-Mat, named by the above sentence, to be a palpable thing that one may see and touch.

A complex entity is an entity whose identity depends on its having privileged parts, but these parts need not be distinct. A kicking must have a kicker part and a kicked part; but if one kicks oneself, the kicker is also the kickee. A giving must have a giver, a gift, and a receiver, but some of these parts may be identical (e.g., when one gives oneself to another). A situation is a degenerate complex entity. It includes three components: a domain, and two entities who, at that domain, are identical. The situation, Plato-Being-Wise, is an entity whose components are Plato and Wise, who are identical at Plato. One can see that situation: that is how one finds out that 'Plato is wise' is true. That situation is not identical with Plato, for Plato is a simple entity (having no privileged parts) while the situation, Plato-Being-Wise, is a complex entity. Even the situation Plato = Plato has privileged parts, and hence is not identical with Plato (who has no privileged parts). To specify a complex entity one must specify both the entity and its privileged parts.

Consider the following example: A has some parts that are bigger than others, but that does not make '$A = (A) =$ Bigger-Than' true. Bigger-Than is a complex substance, A is a simple substance, and hence they cannot be identical. Otherwise, A would have been identical (at A) with Heavier-Than, too, since A also has some parts that are heavier than others. That is true of all things; so it would follow that Bigger-Than is identical with Heavier-Than everywhere, i.e., there is no difference between being bigger than something and being heavier than something. Obviously, that is false. The error is in identifying a simple entity like A with a complex entity like Heavier-Than. The rule on the identity of complex entities is that an entity A whose components are $B_i \ldots B_n$ is identical with an entity C whose components are $D_i \ldots D_n$ iff $B_i = D_i \ldots B_n = D_n$, i.e., if their components are pairwise identical everywhere. In our example, B_i (the heavier part) is sometimes identical with D_i (the bigger part) and sometimes with D_n (the smaller part); hence Bigger-Than is not the same entity as Heavier-Than. Thus neither Plato nor Wise, who are simple entities, can be identical with the complex entity, the situation Plato-Being-Wise.

No situation is identical with a complex entity that is not a situation. The situation, Joe-Giving-Rover-to-Sue, is not the same as that giving,

for although both have three components, their components are different. The components of the situation are (1) the domain, Joe&Sue&-
Rover; (2) some giving; (3) Joe&Sue&Rover. The components of the
giving are (1) Joe, (2) Sue, and (3) Rover.

The situation, Someone-Being-Wise (call it 'B'), is a complex entity
one of whose components is the entity Wise, which, at some entity, x,
is identical with x. This entity x varies at various occurrences of B.
Situations are entities and thus they recur. At the situation, Plato-
Being-Wise (call it 'P'), $P = B$; i.e., every occurrence of Plato-Being-
Wise is an occurrence of Someone-Being-Wise. Yet these situations are
not identical; take the situation, Socrates-Being-Wise (call it 'S'): at S,
$B = S$, but $P = S$ is nowhere true. The same is true of the situation,
Plato-Being-Wise-Or-Socrates-Being-Wise (call it 'O'): wherever P is,
it is identical with O, but not vice versa; hence P and O are distinct
situations. Just as some man can be wise without Man being Wise
everywhere, and some loving can be some older-than without 'Loving =
Older-Than' being true everywhere, so can two situations, e.g., P and
O above, be identical at P, but not at O. Given an occurrence of P,
we also have an occurrence of O, but not vice versa. That is why 'p'
implies '$p \vee q$', but '$p \vee q$' does not imply 'p'.

7. BELIEF

I have argued that if you understand the sentence 'p', there is a certain
entity, the situation P, that exists in some possible world that you can
envisage. One of the possible worlds that you can envisage is the one
you take to be a correct replica of the real world, R. That is your
belief-world. For every person S at time T there is a world $B(ST)$, such
that a situation P is in $B(ST)$ iff S believes at T that p. Thus S understands the sentence 'p' at T iff P is in $W(ST)$, and S believes that p at
T iff P in $B(ST)$.

A major difficulty for this view is that we have impossible beliefs.
Indeed, some philosophers deny that; Barcan-Marcus is willing to deny
that people ever believed that water is not H_2O, or that the evening
star is not the morning star.[13] But that is counterintuitive. To solve the
problem, take metaphysically impossible beliefs first. If S does not
believe that Hesperus is Phospherus, I say, then in his belief world

these are two distinct planets. In R, Phospherus and Hesperus are identical, but, since identity is relative to index, there is no reason why they cannot be distinct in $B(ST)$. If Pierre believes (in Kripke's puzzle) that London is ugly and Londres is pretty, then in his $B(ST)$ London and Londres are distinct cities.[14] One of these cities is (there) ugly and the other pretty. The reverse is also true: the identity of Ford and Freud in Huxley's *Brave New World* does not make them identical in reality.

Take now logically impossible beliefs. Joe, a school boy, believes that 9 is a prime number. Is there a possible world where 9 is prime? I have said that $M(J)$'9', Joe's meaning of the term '9', has all and only those properties that Joe believes 9 has; hence MJ'9' is prime. But '$3 \times 3 = 9$' is analytically true; if it is also necessarily true, then 9 is nonprime in every possible world, including Joe's belief-world $B(JT)$. So either MJ'9' is not 9, in which case Joe does *not* believe that 9 is prime, or else analytic truths need not be necessary. The number MJ'9' has some of the features of 9, and lacks others. For example, if the notion of a square root is alien to Joe, the value of $\sqrt{MJ(q)}$ is undetermined. So again, if $\sqrt{9} = 3$ is true in all possible worlds, then it is true in $B(JT)$ too, and hence it is false that in $B(JT)$, MJ'9' = 9. But is it true that analytic truths are metaphysically necessary?

Consider the following example. Before Cardan and Bombelli introduced imaginary numbers into arithmetic, it was considered analytically true that -1 has no square root, since it followed from the axioms of arithmetic that the square of any two numbers is positive. Now we say otherwise. No one says, however, that the conflict is due to equivocation, for to introduce i, i^2, $-i$, etc., as multiplicands is to replace the original multiplication that took no such arguments by a new arithmetical function. No one says that the term 'multiplication', the symbol '-1', the minus sign, and the very word 'number', have different referents in texts predating and postdating the introduction of complex numbers. The rules of the game have been changed, yet we do say that '-1', e.g., denotes the same number in all these texts, despite the fact that different analytic propositions are true of it in these systems of arithmetic. For another example, consider the nondistributivity of multiplication in quantum logic. By Hanckel's universally accepted Principle of Permanence (1867), which defines the concept 'number', distributivity is a necessary condition for multiplicands to qualify as numbers. Yet no one doubts that in quantum logic we multiply numbers. Thus, the same numbers can appear in various arithmetical systems, which contain different analytic truths. In quantum, intuitionistic, and other nonstandard arithmetics, the number 9 has properties that are different from those analytically attributed to it in classical calculi; yet we do say just that: *it*, the number 9, is referred to in all these systems. I conclude that although an entity cannot survive a change in its necessary properties (that is what 'necessary' means), it can survive changes in the properties that it has by definition at a given index.

Kripke's example of the meter in Paris can also be used to make the same point. That this particular rod is one meter long is analytically true, for that is how 'meter' was defined; yet it is a contingent fact that the said rod is one meter long, for it might have been longer or shorter than it is. One more example: Every good encyclopedia will tell you that originally the Bishop in Chess could not move across the board; it was limited to moving two squares diagonally, like a knight. One could protest that this is an equivocation, since a Bishop is defined as a piece that moves in a certain way; one may even say that a game that has no such piece is not Chess, so the encyclopedia is wrong. But that is nonsense; although it is analytically true that a Bishop moves in a certain way, we say that *it*, the same piece, could move differently. Thus, analyticity does not imply necessity, and it may be true that in $B(JT)$, 9 has somewhat different properties than those that it (analytically) has in R. Therefore it is not impossible that in $B(JT)$, $M(J)'9' = 9$.

For the same reason, $B(JT)$ includes no contradictions (a world in which contradictory statements are true is impossible). A mathematician more skilled than Joe could find some contradictions between statements that Joe accepts as true, but Joe cannot, and what Joe does not believe at T does not exist in $B(JT)$. The logic and calculus he uses are limited, but there is nothing logically wrong or problematic in systems of inference whose rules are weaker than those of classical logic. If Joe does not see that a certain inference is permitted, that inference is *not* permitted in $B(JT)$. Such *ad hoc* blocks on inference and inference-patterns are typical to human psychology. They block the way to conclusions that for some reason we cannot or would not draw. Computational difficulty as well as psychological unacceptability constrain inference in belief-worlds. Such inference-rules make the logic of our belief-worlds inelegant, but that is a small price to pay, given their usefulness for our other needs.

8. CROSS-WORLD PUZZLES

We saw that in the case of ordinary individuals such as Plato or London, explanatory power and causal connections count toward cross-world identity more than similarity. The assumption that Pierre's 'London' and 'Londres' refer to cities that are identical in R and distinct in his belief-world explains his behavior and shows how he came to have his beliefs via various links to the real city of London. An interpretation assigning London in R to one of these terms only would fail to account for the provenance of Pierre's beliefs that involve the other. As Kripke points out, had Pierre never left France we could not deny that his term 'Londres' refers to London, and had he never been in France we could not deny that his term 'London' refers to London. So how (to echo Parfit in another context) can double success be tantamount to failure? In Joe's case, we must similarly say what entities in R *are* his meanings. Poor mathematician as he may be, we must interpret his beliefs by assigning to items in $B(JT)$ some items in R. That is how we understand each other: one interprets the other's world-segments as local values of transworld entities whose other occurrences one is familiar with. We identify what they talk about with things we know. In such interpretations the provenance of an item in a belief-world is crucially important; Freud's dream interpretations are good examples of how such considerations are used to assign a value, A, in the commonsense world to an entity B in a dream world, when B is only minimally similar to A. In assigning interpretanda, we ask how an item we know would appear in a world that has other inputing strategies (e.g., Primary Processes for dreams, or a *Weltanschauung* for a belief-world). The methodological principle which mandates, "identify cross-world entities" makes criticism possible; otherwise, one would just say, "I don't know what you are talking about". It is necessary for us to find such cross-world entities if we are to understand others; hence cross-world identification is fundamental to rationality.

We all make mistakes; but it is one thing to say that we err, i.e., have in our belief-worlds entities that are there unlike what they are in reality, and quite another thing to say that there is no reality in which our beliefs may be interpreted. The first claim is true; the second, not even coherent.[15]

NOTES

[1] In the appendix to *Reason, Truth, and History* (Cambridge, 1981) and in the appendix to *Representation and Reality* (MIT, 1988).

[2] W. V. O. Quine: 1983, 'Ontology and Ideology Revisited', *The Journal of Philosophy* **80**, 499–502: "If the subject is disposed to react to the presence of any and every cat in some manner in which he is not disposed to react to anything but cats, then I shall reckon the term 'cat' to his ideology".

[3] D. Davidson: 1989, 'The Myth of the Subjective', in M. Krausz (ed.), *Relativism: Interpretation and Confrontation*, University of Notre Dame Press, Notre Dame, Indiana, pp. 159–71. Quote is on p. 164.

[4] Ibid., p. 165.

[5] Ibid., p. 170.

[6] Ibid., p. 156.

[7] Ibid.

[8] Ibid., p. 164.

[9] I discuss this issue in my 1989: 'Wittgenstein on Meaning', *Grazer Philosophische Studien* **33–34**, 415–435.

[10] See my 1976: 'Substance Logic' (with E. Walther), *Boston Studies in the Philosophy of Science* **43**, 55–74 'A Plea for a New Nominalism', *Canadian Journal of Philosophy* **12**, 527–37 and my 1985 'Numbers', *Synthese* **64**, 225–39.

[11] The formalization of that statement involves a variable-binding operator, $x(\ldots x \ldots)$. It is, $l(J = l_1 \ \& \ M = l_2)$.

[12] J. Barwise and J. Perry: 1983, *Situations and Attitudes*, MIT, Cambridge, Massachusetts.

[13] See, e.g., 'Rationality and Believing the Impossible', *Journal of Philosophy* **80**, 321–38 (1983).

[14] See S. Kripke, 'A Puzzle about Belief', in A. Margalit (ed.): 1979, *Meaning and Use*, Kluwer, Dordrecht, pp. 239–83.

[15] I argued that point in my 1987: 'Truth and Some Relativists', *Grazer Philosophische Studien* **29**, 1–11.

The Hebrew University of Jerusalem
Jerusalem
Israel

EPILOGUE

ERIC LORMAND

FRAMING THE FRAME PROBLEM

ABSTRACT. The frame problem is widely reputed among philosophers to be one of the deepest and most difficult problems of cognitive science. This paper discusses three recent attempts to display this problem: Dennett's problem of ignoring obviously irrelevant knowledge, Haugeland's problem of efficiently keeping track of salient side effects, and Fodor's problem of avoiding the use of 'kooky' concepts. In a negative vein, it is argued that these problems bear nothing but a superficial similarity to the frame problem of AI, so that they do not provide reasons to disparage standard attempts to solve it. More positively, it is argued that these problems are easily solved by slight variations on familiar AI themes. Finally, some discussion is devoted to more difficult problems confronting AI.

Once upon a time there was a causation-computer named C2 by its creators. Its only task was to read about simple events and to report their likely effects in as much detail as it could. One day its designers arranged for it to learn that a bomb was in a room, resting on a wagon, and that the wagon was pulled through the doorway. C2 quickly reached the obvious conclusion that the bomb rode out of the room. "CONTRADICTION!" it printed, to the surprise of its teachers. "THE BOMB WAS BOTH IN AND OUT OF THE ROOM. CONTRADICTION! CONTRA" – they were forced to unplug it. Poor C2 could not understand that the time at which the bomb was out of the room was different from the time at which it was in the room.

Back to the drawing board. "The solution is obvious", said the designers. "Since states may change from one moment to the next, our next computer must represent the particular moments at which they obtain". They called their next model, the chronological-causation-computer, C3. C3 was told that the bomb was on the wagon at $t1$, and that the wagon was pulled a moment later, at $t2$. Then the programmers put it to the test:

"Tell us as much as you can about the effects at $t3$".
"THE WAGON WAS OUT OF THE ROOM AT $t3$".
"Anything else? Did anything happen to the bomb?"

267

J. H. Fetzer (ed.), Epistemology and Cognition, 267–288.
© 1991 Kluwer Academic Publishers. Printed in the Netherlands.

"I DON'T KNOW. WHERE WAS IT WHEN THE WAGON WAS PULLED?"
"We just told you it was on the wagon, you tin ninny!"
"SURE, IT WAS THERE AT $t1$, BUT MAYBE THAT CHANGED BY $t2$".

Further questioning confirmed the worst – they had neglected to teach C3 how to tell which changeable facts persisted from one time to the next. "What color is the wagon?" "I DON'T KNOW – MAYBE IT CHANGED BECAUSE THE WAGON WAS PULLED". "What is your name?" "I DON'T KNOW – IT WAS 'C3' BEFORE YOU TOLD ME ABOUT THE ROOM". After a few more questions, mercifully, someone pulled the plug.

Back to the drawing board. "We might try giving it 'frame axioms'", said the designers, "which put a border around the effects of an event". They soon realized that this was hopeless, however, since the number of frame axioms would mushroom. They would have to teach their next model that reading about a wagon does not change its color, that pulling a wagon does not change one's name or change the number of pink elephants in the world, and so on. This presented the 'frame problem': how to design a system which could, unlike C3, infer the persistence of nonchanges, but which could do so *automatically* – that is, without explicitly storing or processing frame axioms for them.

Before long, the programmers discovered various ways for a system to infer automatically the persistence of nonchanges. Their favorite was the suggestion that representations of facts should refer not to particular *moments* but to *intervals* of time. Thus was born a chronological-causation-computer-for-persistence, named C3P. C3P was given the same problem that had stumped C3. When C3P learned that the bomb was on the wagon at $t1$, it generated this internal representation:

R: THE BOMB IS ON THE WAGON FROM $t1$ ONWARD.

R did not need to be updated with each passing moment to handle persistence, since R itself meant that the bomb was on the wagon at $t2$, $t3$, and so on. This allowed C3P, unlike C3, to infer the bomb's motion, when it was told that the wagon was pulled at $t2$. The programmers also gave C3P the ability to 'snip' representations such as R, by representing finite intervals. For example, when C3P learned that the bomb was taken off the wagon at $t100$, it substituted 'TO $t99$' for

'ONWARD' in R. As a result of all of this, C3P was able genuinely to ignore facts that it understood to be unchanged by a given event, focusing only on purported changes. This feature, coupled with one or another way of automatically inferring the persistence of nonchanges, came to be known as the 'sleeping-dog strategy' – letting sleeping representations lie, unless there is some positive reason to wake them. Since the sleeping-dog strategy avoided the need for frame axioms, the designers of C3P were satisfied that they had solved the frame problem.

All was calm, all was bright, until one night three wise men arrived from the East. C3P received no homage from them, however, much less any expensive gifts. The first wise man deemed the frame problem "a new, deep epistemological problem" which "whatever it is, is certainly not solved yet". The second wise man intensified the point, suggesting that the frame problem is "foisted on unsuspecting epistemology by misguided presumptions underlying AI as a discipline". Needless to say, the programmers found this completely mystifying. "You may suppose that you have solved the frame problem", explained the third wise man, "but in fact you are begging it. How could the depth, beauty, and urgency of the frame problem have been so widely misperceived?" In answer to his own question, he pronounced, "It's like the ancient doctrine of the music of the spheres. If you can't hear it, that's because it's everywhere". Satisfied that their hosts were completely at a loss for words, the wise men bid them farewell. As they left, the first wise man turned and issued the ominous warning, "If there is ever to be a robot with the fabled perspicacity and real-time adroitness of C3P0, robot-designers must solve the frame problem".

I have transcribed the words of the three wise men from the reports of Daniel Dennett, John Haugeland, and Jerry Fodor, respectively (Dennett 1987, pp. 42–43; Haugeland 1987, p. 93; Fodor 1987, p. 142). The rest of this paper is devoted to criticism of their attempts to display the frame problem as a deep, difficult problem. In a negative vein, I will argue that their problems bear nothing but a superficial similarity to the original frame problem of AI (see McCarthy and Hayes 1969). Of course, it must be conceded that the terminological issue is unimportant. In order to emphasize this, and to minimize confusion, I adopt the more descriptive term 'persistence problem' for the frame problem as I have described it (see Shoham 1988). But the point is more than terminological, for it weighs against the philosophers' use of their frame problems to disparage the sleeping-dog strategy (the term, incidentally, is Haugeland's). The primary negative claim of this paper, then, is that the sleeping-dog strategy is not susceptible to criticism based on their new problems. More positively, I will argue that their problems are easily solved by slight variations on familiar AI themes.

1. RELEVANCE AND THE FRAME PROBLEM

The Relevance Problem

My introductory fable is a twist on a fable with which the first wise man, Daniel Dennett, introduces the frame problem of AI (Dennett 1987, pp. 41–42). I will first retell his tale, and then explain how it is misleading in this role. The robots in Dennett's fable are charged with the task of mentally testing a plan, given a goal to be reached and some idea of the initial conditions under which the plan is to be executed. Each of them comes complete with these three states:

G: the goal of saving its spare battery from a live bomb.
I: knowledge of the initial conditions that the battery and the bomb are on a wagon in a room.
P: the plan of pulling the wagon out of the room (to remove the battery).

Plan testing also requires a fourth element, a set R of 'inference rules'. To test a plan, one tries to find a sequence of rules in R which allows the goal to be inferred from the plan and the initial conditions. In other words, one searches for an 'inferential path' from the plan and the initial conditions to the goal, one for which each step along the way is sanctioned by an inference rule.[1] Very roughly, if such a path exists, the plan passes the test.

Dennett begins with a simple robot, R1, which can recognize 'the intended implications of its acts', but not 'the implications about their side effects'. In other words, in testing a plan, R1 uses only inference rules which correspond to intended effects of the plan. Since G is an intended effect of P, of course, P passes R1's test. So R1 proceeds to pull the wagon out of the room without recognizing the tragic side effect due to the fact that the bomb is also on the wagon. Back to the drawing board go the designers; out pops the robot-deducer, R1D1, which can test its plans for side effects. It does so by removing all restrictions on which inference rules and initial conditions it can consider in testing a plan. As a result, in searching for an inferential path from P to G it 'deduces' everything it can: that P '[does] not change the color of the room's walls', that P 'cause[s] [the wagon's] wheels to turn more revolutions than there [are] wheels on the wagon', and so on. Boom! Therefore, the designers install in their next robot a method for tagging implications as relevant or irrelevant to its goals. They call the new model R2D1, the robot-relevant-deducer. The relevance tags don't help, however, since not only does R2D1 waste time inferring all the same irrelevant implications, but it also generates more inferences to the effect that they are irrelevant. "All these robots suffer from the frame problem", Dennett concludes. "If there is ever to be a robot with the fabled perspicacity and real-time adroitness of R2D2, robot-designers must solve the frame problem".

R1D1 and R2D1 do seem to illustrate the original frame problem – the persistance problem – since they engage in explicit inferences about nonchanges such as the color of the walls. The persistence problem requires one not to use frame axioms to infer the persistence of nonchanges. My claim is that a good dose of the sleeping-dog strategy would cure this ill, and I will argue for this claim throughout the course of this paper. However, these robots suffer from a further problem which is not even addressed by the sleeping-dog strategy. Not only do they bother with the noneffects of their plans, but they also bother with many genuine effects which are obviously irrelevant to their goals, such as the number of revolutions of the wagon's wheels. The extra problem facing their programmers, then, is how to design systems which test plans without bothering with obviously irrelevant inferences.

This problem may be generalized in a straightforward way, since there are other kinds of goal-oriented searches besides plan testing. In order to generate a plan, for example, one may search for an inferential path from the initial conditions to the goal which requires performing some actions. In order to generate subgoals for a current goals, one may search for an inferential path to the goal which requires that certain subgoals be reached. From this general perspective, Dennett's problem becomes that of designing a system which finds inferential paths between initial conditions and goals without considering inferences which 'obviously' do not point in the right direction. I will call this the 'relevance problem'.

Relations to the Frame Problem of AI

Despite the similarities between the persistence and relevance problems, it is something of a mystery why, in Dennett's hands, the shift takes place. He seems to feel that the original frame problem is merely an instance of the more general relevance problem. Thus, he calls the relevance problem a 'broader' problem than the 'narrowly conceived' original frame problem (Dennett 1987, p. 43). Although this may have some initial appeal, I think it should be resisted.

First, consider what Dennett can say in defense of the claim that the persistence problem is an instance of the relevance problem. A first attempt might be to argue that the desirability of ignoring noneffects of an event follows from the desirabilty of ignoring all irrelevant knowledge. The situation is not so simple, however. Often, noneffects *are* highly relevant to one's goals. In Dennett's fable, for example, pulling the wagon does not change the fact that the battery is on the wagon, and this is directly relevant to the robot's goal. Therefore, the robot might need to access the knowledge that the battery will stay on the wagon.

Nevertheless, it is possible for Dennett to reply that, even if noneffects are often relevant to a system's goals, processing them with explicit frame axioms is irrelevant. However, this substitution of 'irrelevant processing' for 'irrelevant knowledge' forces an unwelcome shift in the construal of the relevance problem. What is 'irrelevant processing' supposed to mean? Useless processing? But if a robot needs to know about a certain (relevant) noneffect, a corresponding frame axiom might be very useful in supplying this knowledge. Of course, given that systems can use the sleeping-dog strategy instead of frame axioms, the latter are too costly. But being too costly is not the same as being irrelevant. If it were, *any* problem about processing costs would be a problem about irrelevant processing. On this view, for example, electrical engineers debating the relative processing virtues of various home computers would be discussing an 'instance' of the relevance problem! But then the relevance problem would no longer be Dennett's problem of accessing useful knowledge at the right time. Therefore, appealing to the irrelevance of processing noneffects fails to show that the persistence problem is an instance of Dennett's relevance problem.

There is a more direct reason not to assimilate the persistence problem to the relevance problem. The persistence problem arises completely independently of goals, planning, action, or problem-solving. It deals purely with causal reasoning – keeping track of change. In my fable, C3 and friends are 'pure predictors'; the only 'goal' they ever have is to report as much as they can about the effects of an event. As a result, *every* effect is 'relevant' to them, and no effect is irrelevant. Therefore, no instance of the relevance problem can arise for pure predictors like C3; there are no irrelevant effects to ignore. Since the persistence problem is present in its full force for C3, it cannot be an instance of the relevance problem. Nevertheless, the point remains that if there are ever to be smart robots such as R2D2, and C3P0, the relevance problem must be solved.

The Role of Bidirectional Search

The task facing the plan-tester is, as I have described it, that of searching for an inferential path from a plan and some initial conditions to a goal. In this respect it is rather like walking through a labyrinth, searching for an unobstructed path from the entrance to the exit. Now, compare three strategies for negotiating a labyrinth. First, there is 'forward search': starting at the entrance and walking around (marking one's path, of course) until one happens upon the exit. Second, there is 'backward search': starting at the exit and trying to make one's way to the entrance. Third, there is 'bidirectional search': searching forward while a partner searches backward until one finds a path marked by the other. Bidirectional search is clearly the more efficient strategy, in general (see Barr and Feigenbaum 1981, pp. 46–53).

From this perspective, it appears that a major defect of Dennett's robots is that they engage only in forward search. His robots start with their plan P and initial conditions I and keep making inferences from these (and from their consequences, and so on) until they happen upon their goal G (or its negation). As a result, they infer consequences more or less at random, with respect to the goal, and so suffer from the relevance problem. We can account for one aspect of R2D2's fabled perspicacity and real-time adroitness if we suppose that it uses bidirectional search instead. Supposing this, how would R2D2 test P?

We can imagine R2D2 first searching backward from G. The procedure is to look at some inference rules of the form 'IF ⟨condition⟩, THEN G', and to mark these conditions as plausible parts of paths from P to G. (Recall that G is the goal of saving the battery from the bomb.) This set of inference rules is likely to refer to the condition that the battery and the bomb are far apart, but is unlikely to refer to conditions regarding the number of revolutions of a wagon's wheel or the color of the walls.[2] So the locations of the battery and bomb would be marked as 'relevant' to G.

At this point, R2D2 can ask itself the question: what happens to the whereabouts of the battery and bomb if I roll the wagon out of the room? More precisely, R2D2 can let the details of this question guide its forward search from this plan. That is, instead of looking at all the rules of the form 'IF ... A WAGON ROLLS ..., THEN ⟨consequence⟩', it can look only at those with potential consequences for the positions of batteries and bombs. Presumably, it finds inference rules such as these:[3]

> IF A WAGON ROLLS, AND x IS IN THE WAY, THEN x IS PUSHED ALONG.
> IF A WAGON ROLLS, AND x IS ON THE WAGON, THEN x RIDES ALONG.

R2D2 therefore checks whether it believes that the battery and bomb satisfy x in the antecedents of these rules. It finds that, in fact, it does believe that the two are on the wagon, so it infers that the two will ride along, and will not be far apart. Finally, it infers that the battery will not be saved, and can try to find a better plan based on what went wrong with this one.

As I mentioned above, the relevance problem arises for tasks other than plan testing, such as subgoal generation and plan generation. Given that R2D2 can paint the wagon, draw the drapes, or pace up and down the room, what keeps it from considering these options in generating a plan to rescue its battery? Bidirectional search does. R2D2 can search backward from the goal, to find subgoals and actions most likely in general to lead to the goal. It can then direct its forward search from the initial conditions to determine which of these subgoals and actions are most likely to be suitable under these conditions. Other subgoals and actions should be considered only if none of these are suitable or if subsequent plan testing rules them out.

Although bidirectional search greatly reduces the computational costs of problem solving, it does not itself bring these costs to a minimum. In my illustration, I vaguely described R2D2 as looking at 'some' inference rules of the form 'IF ⟨condition⟩, THEN G'. But which? If it looks at them all, it is likely to bother with many irrelevancies. I discuss this problem in the next section in connection with 'relevance holism'. First, however, I want to discuss briefly another problem related to the relevance problem.

Although Dennett casts the relevance problem as a problem about finding knowledge relevant to one's current goals, it may be suspected that there is a deeper problem about how to make the right goals current at the right times. However, I am not aware of any attempts to show what the 'problem' is. We might suppose that some goals are always current in R2D2, e.g., the goal of staying out of danger, and that some goals are triggered by certain conditions, e.g., given that there is a potential danger, R2D2 can generate the goal of finding out if any valuables are in danger and removing them from the danger. Once R2D2 learns that there is a live bomb in the room (i.e., a potential danger), but that there is some time to work with (so R2D2 itself is not yet in danger), R2D2 can search for valuables near the bomb (i.e., in danger). We can imagine that it can discover that the battery is near the bomb either by quickly looking around the room, or else by being told this, as in Dennett's fable. Consequently, it can generate the goal of removing the danger and, as I have described, it can generate and test plans to meet this goal.

2. HOLISM AND THE FRAME PROBLEM

The Holism Problem

The second wise man, John Haugeland, construes the frame problem as arising from the fact that inferential relations in the real world are holistic: what is reasonable to infer from a given condition may depend on many other 'surrounding conditions'. First, virtually any inference can be warranted by virtually any condition, if the right surrounding conditions hold. From the premise that a wagon is pulled, for example, one may infer that a bomb moves (if there is one on the wagon), that one pulls a muscle (if the load is heavy), that the wheels will squeak (if they aren't oiled), that one will please a co-worker (if he has asked for the slab on the wagon), and so on. Second, virtually any inference can fail to be warranted by virtually any condition if the wrong surrounding conditions hold. As Haugeland points out, there are many possible situations in which pulling a wagon might fail to make a bomb ride along even though the bomb is on the wagon:

But what if [the bomb] is also tied to the doorknob with a string? Or what if, instead of [rolling], [the wagon] tips over? (Haugeland 1987, p. 85)

This holism leads to Haugeland's problem:

The so-called frame problem is how to 'notice' salient [inferences] without having to eliminate all of the other possibilities that might conceivably have occurred had the facts somehow been different. (Haugeland 1985, p. 204)

In other words, the problem is to come up with an efficient algorithm for respecting the fact that what may be inferred from a given condition may depend on virtually any surrounding condition. Such an algorithm would have to make tractable the number of surrounding conditions a system must check, without blinding it to the 'salient' ones. In order to distinguish this problem from others that have gone by the name 'frame problem', I will refer to it as the 'holism problem'.[4]

The holism problem intensifies the relevance problem. My illustration of bidirectional search in section 1 proceeds under the assumption that the inference rules associated with R2D2's goal of saving the battery from the bomb do not refer to the precise number of revolutions of a wagon's wheel, or the color of the walls, or any other 'obviously' irrelevant conditions. If, however, the bomb is activated by the squeaking of the wagon's wheels, the precise number of revolutions of the wheels may be of crucial relevance. Even the color of the walls may be relevant, if the room is painted in such a way as to camouflage the door. As a result of this holism, to deal with the real world R2D2 is likely to need inference rules to handle these possibilities, raising the combined 'relevance-holism' problem: how can a system know which knowledge is relevant to a goal in its particular situation, without having to think about a vast number of possibilities?

Relations to the Frame Problem of AI

As Haugeland points out, the sleeping-dog strategy (see the introduction) does not provide a solution to the holism problem. Of course, more than this is needed to show that something is wrong with the sleeping-dog strategy. (After all, the sleeping-dog strategy also 'fails' to solve the problem of world hunger.) Haugeland therefore makes a stronger claim to the effect that the sleeping-dog strategy *raises* the holism problem. The sleeping-dog strategy requires there to be 'positive indications' to the effect that certain facts are changed by an event, so that the system can focus only on these facts. These positive indications are provided by inference rules. Therefore, he concludes, it is the sleeping-dog strategy which 'raises formidable design questions about how to get the needed positive indications for all the important [inferences]', i.e., the holism problem (Haugeland 1985, p. 206). On closer inspection, however, it is easy to see that it's *not* the sleeping-dog strategy which raises the holism problem; the problem arises for *any* system which has to make inferences about the real world, whether or not it uses the sleeping-dog strategy. For example, in my introductory fable the computer C3 does not use the sleeping-dog strategy. Nevertheless, of course, it must make inferences, and these inferences must be sensitive to salient surrounding conditions, so it must face problems about inferential holism.

As a consequence, something more is needed to show that the sleeping-dog strategy is inadequate for the problem it's intended to solve, namely, the persistence problem (see the introduction). Perhaps Haugeland's idea is that the persistence problem cannot be solved without simultaneously solving the holism problem. Since he does not even attempt to provide reasons for bringing inferential holism into discussions of the frame problem, there is room for speculation about why he is tempted to do so. Perhaps the reasoning goes like this: to be a solution to the persistence problem, a system must ignore the facts which are not changed (by an event), so it must be able to tell which facts are changed, so it must respect the holism of change, and, more generally, the holism of inference. The problem with this argument is fairly subtle; to display it I must invoke a distinction between domain-general 'process-and-form' problems and domain-specific 'content' problems. I will devote more attention to this distinction than may at first appear necessary, because it will prove to be crucial later in this section in my defense of a solution to the holism problem.

Much research in AI proceeds on the assumption that there is a difference between being well-informed and being smart. Being well-informed has to do, roughly, with the content of one's representation – about their truth and the range of subjects they cover. Being smart, on the other hand, has to do with one's ability to process these representations and with packaging them in a form that allows them to be processed efficiently. The main theoretical concern of artificial intelligence research is to solve 'process-and-form' problems of finding processes and representational formats which can qualify a computer as being smart.

Of course, in order to build computers which can deal with the real world, we must also solve 'content' problems involving figuring out which particular representations computers should have, so that the computers qualify as being well-informed about a variety of domains. It is neither surprising nor worrisome that AI has not solved all these content problems, for they are not, in the first instance, AI's problems. One can make headway into process-and-form problems in the AI laboratory, but to make headway into content problems, one must incorporate empirical investigations in particular domains ranging from medical diagnosis to the mechanics of middle-sized objects to sociology to chess to laundromats to train stations. It seems a reasonable division of labor, then, for AI to pass domain-specific bucks to domain-specific sciences.[5]

Accordingly, the persistence problem is posed as a domain-general process-and-form problem. In other words, it is not about which particular facts a system should take to be unchanged by which events. Consider again the frame axiom proposal (see the introduction). Frame axioms turned out to be a bad idea, not because they didn't capture reliable information about nonchanges (we may suppose that they did), but because there were too many of them. The persistence problem therefore arises regardless of how reliable or unreliable a system is about which facts are unchanged. As a result, to solve it all we need to do is to design a system which has the capacity to ignore the facts which are not changed, if it knows which facts really are unchanged.

It is this fact which shows that the holism problem does not lurk behind the persistence problem. To be a solution to the persistence problem, a system only needs to ignore the facts it thinks are not changed by an event. But to do that, the system needn't be able to tell which facts really are changed. Since a solution to the persistence problem needn't insure that systems are right about which facts are changed, it needn't insure that systems have the capacity to keep track of the holism of change. So the sleeping-dog strategy can solve the persistence problem without solving the holism problem. Of course, I am not denying that we need to solve the holism problem in order to get intelligent machines that can deal reliably with the real world. In the rest of this section I focus on attempts in AI to solve this very problem. The point here is merely that the fate of this problem is irrelevant to the fate of the sleeping-dog strategy.

The Role of Heuristic Search

At root, the holism problem is this: for any set of conditions one wishes to make inferences from, there are always too many potentially applicable inference rules to consider, rules which may require one to check virtually any surrounding conditions. Returning to the labyrinth analogy, the problem is that from any fork there are so many paths that one can't follow them all. If one knows nothing about the particular labyrinth one is in, one must select a path more or less at random. This is called 'blind search' in AI. However, in some cases one can use specific information about the labyrinth to help one select the paths which are likely to be the best to follow. This is called 'heuristic search'. For example, one might know that the better paths in a certain garden tend to be wider, while those in another tend to be better lit. Such heuristics can help one to achieve better results than blind search (see Barr and Feigenbaum 1981, pp. 58–63).

Now, when a computer is searching for inferential paths, it can use similar heuristics to avoid blindly checking every inference rule. For example, associated with each inference rule might be some measure of its general reliability. The inference rule 'IF A WAGON IS PULLED, IT ROLLS' might, for instance, be deemed more reliable than 'IF A WAGON IS PULLED, THE COLOR OF THE WALLS CHANGES'. In addition, or instead, each inference rule might make reference to the antecedent probability that it will 'apply', that is, to the antecedent probability of the surrounding conditions it presupposes. Take the rule 'IF A WAGON ROLLS, AND x IS ON THE WAGON, THEN x RIDES ALONG'. As Haugeland says, this rule can fail if x is tied to the doorknob, but then the antecedent probability of such failure might be deemed to be very low.

Given some such metric, a computer can constrain searches by looking initially only at the set of rules with the best marks (the size of the set depends on how many rules can be processed at the same time). It can thereby focus on the rolling of the wagon rather than the potential change of color of the walls, and it can assume 'by default' that x is not tied to the doorknob.[6] If this set doesn't get it where it wants to go, it can try the next best set, and so on down the 'search hierarchy'.

If one's special concern is relevance holism, one might prefer (instead, or in addition) to use heuristics regarding the general usefulness of inference rules. For instance, the rule 'IF A WAGON ROLLS, AND x IS ON THE WAGON, THEN x RIDES ALONG' may be deemed to be generally more useful than the rule 'IF A WAGON ROLLS, THEN THE NUMBER OF REVOLUTIONS OF ITS WHEELS IS PROPORTIONAL TO THE DISTANCE'. This may be so even though the former is less reliable (since x might be tied to the doorknob) and less likely to be applicable (since the wagon might be empty).[7]

Although Haugeland doesn't discuss heuristics as an approach to the holism problem, Jerry Fodor, the third wise man, registers this complaint:

So far as I can tell, the usual assumption about the frame problem in AI is that it is somehow to be solved 'heuristically'. . . . Perhaps a bundle of such heuristics, properly coordinated and rapidly deployed, would suffice to make the central processes of a robot as [holistic] as yours, or mine, or the practicing scientist's ever actually succeed in being. Since there are, at present, no serious proposals about what heuristics might belong to such a bundle, it seems hardly worth arguing the point. (Fodor 1983, pp. 115–116)

Fodor appears to be insisting that the trouble with the idea of heuristic search is that it raises the hard question: *which* heuristics should be used to establish search hierarchies of inference rules?

It is unclear whether Fodor construes this as a domain-general process-and-form problem or as a domain-specific content problem. He seems to be asking for a domain-general answer when he calls for a 'principled solution to the frame problem' (Fodor 1983, p. 116), although he doesn't attempt to explain the difference between principled and unprincipled solutions. Looked at this way, however, 'serious proposals' about heuristics are a dime a dozen. I've just seriously proposed three principled heuristics, regarding the general reliability of an inference rule, its antecedent probability of applying, and its general usefulness. Of course, these principles leave open the various domain-specific problems about which inference rules are generally more reliable for dealing with the real world than which others, about which conditions in the real world are antecedently more likely to hold than which others, and about which inference rules are more likely to be useful than which others. Perhaps, then, Fodor is referring to the difficulty of these domain-specific 'hierarchy problems'.

How is a computer to establish the search hierarchies of inference rules necessary to solve hierarchy problems? Well, if we could set robots loose to gather data for themselves, they could rely on their own past experience, experience of which conditions have in fact obtained most often, or of which inference rules have in fact been most reliable and useful. But, as I mentioned above, we are not currently able to do this. Typically, then, a system must rely on the hierarchies we program into it. Can Fodor argue that the solution to the 'frame problem' escapes our grasp by swinging away on this loose end? After all, how do we know which hierarchies to program into a reasoning system? Alas, for many domains, we don't! Hierarchy problems are domain-specific content problems; to solve them, we have to do a lot of science. In this respect, hierarchy problems are no deeper than any other content problems, say, the 'shape problem': how are computers to know the shapes of objects in the real world? Well, we've got to tell them, since we can't very well turn them loose to find out for themselves. And for us to know, we've got to split up and do a lot of domain-specific investigations: you've got to find out about the shapes of wagons, I've got to find out about the shapes of bombs, etc. Similarly with hierarchy problems: you've got to find out how often wagons malfunction, I've got to find out how often bombs are put on wagons, etc. If AI is ever to build a well-informed computer, it must incorporate the findings of experts in wildly diverse domains. The important point is that AI's 'problems' of ranking conditions according to their relative probabilities, and of ranking rules according to their relative reliability and usefulness, are no more surprising or principled than its 'problem' with specifying the shapes of objects.

Summary

Before moving on, it may be helpful to summarize the main conclusions thus far. First, the relevance problem and the holism problem have nothing important to do with the frame problem as it is understood in AI, namely, the persistence problem. As a result, it is improper to use them in arguments against the sleeping-dog strategy. Second, the two problems, construed as domain-general problems, are easily solved by appeal to two familiar AI tools, bidirectional and heuristic search. Finally, although AI does not have a complete solution to certain domain-specific problems, the musings of the three wise men have not shown this to be a deep, epistemological problem; AI can simply incorporate the results of the domain-specific sciences.

3. KOOKINESS AND THE FRAME PROBLEM

The 'Fridgeon' Problem

The third wise man, Jerry Fodor, raises a novel and interesting objection to the sleeping-dog strategy based on the kooky predicate 'fridgeon', defined as follows: *x* is a fridgeon at *t* if *x* is a physical particle at
t and Fodor's fridge is on at *t*. Fodor points out that when he turns his
fridge on, he makes billions of changes – namely, he turns each particle
in the universe into a fridgeon. Therefore, he argues:

> If I let the facts about fridgeons into my database . . . , *pursuing the sleeping dog strategy*
> *will no longer solve the frame problem* . . . [A] strategy which says 'look just at the facts
> which change' will buy you nothing; it will commit you to looking at indefinitely many
> facts. (Fodor 1957, pp. 144–45; emphasis Fodor's)

The point is quite general. As Fodor explains, "There are arbitrarily
many kooky concepts which can be defined with the same apparatus
that you use to define perfectly kosher concepts", namely, the apparatus
of 'basic concepts' and 'logical syntax' (Fodor 1987, pp. 145–46). "So",
he continues, "the problem – viz., the FRAME problem – is to find a
RULE that will keep the kooky concepts out while letting the nonkooky
concepts in" (Fodor 1987, p. 146; emphasis Fodor's). But this would
be tantamount to 'a rigorous account of our commonsense estimate of
the world's taxonomic structure', which would require 'formalizing our
intuitions about inductive relevance' (Fodor 1987, pp. 147–48). It's no
wonder, then, that Fodor claims the frame problem is "too important
to leave to the hackers" (Fodor 1987, p. 148)![8]

Three Kinds of Memory

Before turning directly to Fodor's problem of formalizing inductive
kookiness, it will help to get clearer about what a system should do in
the face of kookiness. What I will argue is that a system should represent kooky facts implicitly in its representations of nonkooky facts. The
basic idea can be explained by reference to the way people (like your-
self) deal with the concept 'FRIDGEON'. If Fodor is right, then you
must keep representations of fridgeon facts out of your 'database'. But
this doesn't mean you must keep the definition of 'FRIDGEON' out

of your memory; if you did, you wouldn't even be able to understand Fodor's argument! On a natural view, then, you must have something like a mental dictionary in which you can store the definition of 'FRIDGEON'. (For simplicity, we can suppose that this dictionary is wholly separate from the database of 'facts', although it is not necessary for my purposes.) If (for some odd reason) you want to check whether Nancy-the-Neutron is a fridgeon, you must first find 'FRIDGEON' in your mental dictionary, and then check your database to determine whether Nancy satisfies the definition – that is, whether Nancy is a particle and whether Fodor's fridge is on. Given that 'FRIDGEON' appears in your mental dictionary, then, representations of fridgeon facts needn't appear in your database. So you don't need to update them when you discover that Fodor has turned his fridge on. The same is true for an AI system with both a dictionary and a database. When Fodor turns his fridge on, the system only needs to change *one* representation, namely, its representation of the state of Fodor's fridge.

The most obvious objection to this strategy is that even representations of fridgeon facts must sometimes be explicit. Otherwise, one could never use the concept 'FRIDGEON' as you are in thinking about Fodor's argument. In the example, once you find 'FRIDGEON' in your dictionary and check whether Nancy satisfies the definition, you still must infer explicitly that Nancy is a fridgeon. In other words, apparently, you must put the representation 'NANCY IS A FRIDGEON' in your database. Since this representation is explicit, however, it needs to be updated explicitly when Fodor turns his fridge on. It might seem, then, that the distinction between the dictionary and the database cuts no ice. The proper response to this objection is to appeal to a third kind of memory which cognitive scientists call 'working memory'. Working memory is a temporary storage space for representations which are being used at a given time. The importance of working memory for present purposes is that once representations in working memory are used, they can be erased. Now, while it is true that fridgeon facts sometimes need to be represented explicitly, they need only be explicit in working memory, not in the long-term database. Therefore, after generating and using the explicit representation 'NANCY IS A FRIDGEON', you can simply erase it, without worrying about updating it. The same is true for an AI system with a working memory.

But Fodor can also object to this. The situation is different when a system is *told* that Nancy is a fridgeon – that is, when this is new information. If the system simply erases this representation from working memory, it will lose the information about Nancy. So, apparently, it must first *copy* the representation into the database, in which case it needs to worry about updating the copy. The response to this objection is simple. If the system is to keep fridgeon facts out of the database, it must translate representations of them into nonkooky representations (using the dictionary), and copy these nonkooky representations into the database. So, when a system is told that Nancy is a fridgeon, it should put the representations 'NANCY IS A PARTICLE' and 'FODOR'S FRIDGE IS ON' into the database.

How to Rule out Kooky Concepts

Even given the viability of keeping kooky concepts in the dictionary and in working memory, the 'fridgeon' problem has not been addressed. For how does a system know which concepts to keep there and which to allow into the database? Mustn't it follow a rule which, as Fodor claims, codifies 'our intuitions about inductive relevance'? Not obviously. I agree with Fodor that no one knows how to formalize inductive kookiness, but I disagree with his claim that we need to do this in order to save the sleeping-dog strategy. As Fodor himself insists, kooky concepts are defined in terms of basic concepts, so representations involving kooky concepts can always be left implicit in representations involving only basic concepts. Suppose, then, that a system follows this rule: allow only *basic* concepts into the database, and keep all *defined* concepts in the dictionary and in working memory. Even though this rule does not formalize kookiness, it is generally applicable to any kooky concept Fodor chooses to define.

Call a system using this rule a 'basic system', since all of its inferential processes are carried out over representations involving only basic concepts. Although a basic system does not need to appeal to inductive relevance in order to exclude kooky predicates, if it is to count as well informed about the real world then it needs to know which particular 'basic representations' to infer from which particular others. Call this the 'basic learning problem'. It may appear that my appeal to basic systems simply begs Fodor's questions, since the basic learning problem is similar to Fodor's problem of formalizing inductive relevance.[9] If this *is* Fodor's question, however, it deserves begging, for it is deprived of any interest. Given the possibility of basic systems, Fodor cannot support his (interesting) claim that the sleeping-dog strategy raises special problems about kooky concepts. All he can claim, then, is that the sleeping-dog strategy must work hand-in-hand with a solution to the basic learning problem. But this is no surprise. The basic learning problem arises for *any* system which has to make inferences about the real world whether or not it uses the sleeping-dog strategy (compare the discussion of C3 in section 2). Therefore, the sleeping-dog strategy does not raise or intensify the problem. More importantly, Fodor has not shown any principled difficulties with solving the problem. If we want well-informed robots, then we must do two things: we must engage in lots of domain-specific scientific investigations about what may be inferred from what, and we must occupy ourselves with issues surrounding how machines can learn as children do. The basic learning problem is a familiar example of a domain-specific content problem (see section 2).

Another objection is that the rule which defines basic systems is a bit too strong. It not only keeps kooky concepts out of the database, but also excludes nonkooky defined concepts, like 'MY BULGARIAN GRANDMOTHER' and 'VEGETABLE CRISPER'. The problem is that if one often uses these concepts, one might need to have representations involving them at one's mental fingertips – that is, one might need to have them explicit in the database. In other words, it might take too much time and energy to deal with all the basic concepts each time one needs to use one of these complex concepts. Fair enough. The rule needs to be weakened in the following way: allow only representations involving basic concepts into the database except for representations (involving defined concepts) that are so useful that you need to have them at your fingertips. In other words, when a particular combination of basic concepts recurs very frequently in the course of problem solving, the system may introduce into the database an abbreviation for it (i.e., a complex concept). As amended, however, the rule needn't mention anything about 'our commensense estimate of the world's taxonomic structure'.

One last argument on behalf of Fodor: he can object that weakening the rule may allow fridgeon facts back into the database after all. If individual fridgeon facts were (somehow) vitally important to a system, it might indeed need to have fridgeon information at its fingertips, but then it would be forced to update many representations when Fodor turns on his fridge. This is true. For such a system, however, 'FRIDG-EON' would not be a kooky concept at all – at least, it would not be something the system *should* want to rule out of the database! A system with kooky enough needs *would* have to update indefinitely many beliefs; that's just tough kookies. The sleeping-dog strategy is not supposed to magically eliminate this possibility, but only to help minimize the number of updates, given a fixed set of needs. I conclude, then, that Fodor has not shown that the sleeping-dog strategy faces a problem about formalizing our intuitions about inductive kookiness.

Summary

In two respects, the 'fridgeon' problem shares the fate of the relevance problem and the holism problem. First, none of them are properly identified with the frame problem as it is understood in AI (i.e., with the persistence problem), and none of them weigh against the sleeping-dog strategy. Second, they are all easy to solve. Therefore, neither Dennett nor Haugeland nor Fodor succeeds in demonstrating a deep, difficult problem for AI. However, they are left with a deep, difficult problem of their *own*, namely, the problem of framing the frame problem: why should one suppose that what they are talking about is the *frame* problem, and why should one suppose that it's a *problem*?

NOTES

* I would like to thank Ned Block and Stephen White for reactions to an earlier draft of this paper.
[1] For a good introduction to the AI literature on 'search', see chapter II of Barr and Feigenbaum (eds.) 1981. The term 'operators' is standardly used for inference rules as well as other goal-reaching devices which do not concern me here.
[2] As I explain in section 2, 'relevance holism' creates a difficulty here, but one which can be solved.
[3] I omit nuances such as the temporal factors mentioned in the introduction and the exceptions discussed in section 2.
[4] In *The Modularity of Mind*, Fodor anticipates Haugeland's treatment of the frame problem as a problem about holism. He writes that one of the things that 'makes [the frame] problem so hard' is that 'which beliefs are up for grabs depends intimately upon which actions are performed and upon the context of the performances' (Fodor 1983, p. 114).
[5] Couldn't we avoid having to gather all of this information for the computers by designing them to investigate the world for themselves as children do? No, for two broad

reasons. First, setting computers loose in the world involves implanting them in robots; but we don't yet know how to build robots that can see, feel, hear, hop, skip, and jump well enough to cross a city street safely. Second, there is the 'blank slate' problem. It appears impossible to learn efficiently about a domain unless one already has some reliable information about what sorts of data to concentrate on, what sorts of hypotheses to try out, etc. Thus, building robot learners requires endowing them with considerable domain-specific innate knowledge, which requires us to engage in domain-specific investigations after all.

[6] Occasionally, when the stakes are high, it may be advantageous for a system to go into a more careful mode in which it avoids making some default assumptions, explicitly checking the surrounding conditions instead. I ignore this nicety here, since to the degree that a system needs to be careful, the holism problem is made less important. If the stakes are so high that a system needs explicitly to check surrounding conditions, it can hardly be faulted for doing so.

Incidentally, AI researchers have had mixed success in trying to develop a 'nonmonotonic logic' for reasoning with default assumptions (for a review of this literature, see Shoham 1988). From the perspective adopted here, however, default (or nonmonotonic) reasoning is an ordinary example of heuristic search, which is generally thought not to require the development of a corresponding 'logic'. This is one way of seeing that we may not need nonmonotonic logic (as opposed to nonmonotonic reasoning), so that the shortcomings of nonmonotonic logics may not be important. If some in AI have not appreciated this point, it is perhaps due to placing too much emphasis on the distinction between heuristics and 'epistemology' (i.e., inference) offered in McCarthy and Hayes 1969 (for an example of this, see Janlert 1987, pp. 2–3).

[7] A good illustration of this method is in Holland, et al. 1986. Their 'strength' parameters reflect the past usefulness of rules and are used to contain search.

[8] Readers familiar with Nelson Goodman's 'grue' problem (Goodman 1965) should resist any temptation to smuggle in projectability problems. Fodor's problem simply has nothing to do with projectibility, since 'fridgeon', unlike 'grue', is perfectly projectable. For if at least one particle is a fridgeon, it follows that Fodor's fridge is on, so it follows that all particles are fridgeons. Therefore, even if Fodor is right that the sleeping-dog strategy converts the frame problem into a serious problem about inductive relevance, it would not follow that the frame problem would include the problem of avoiding the projection of 'GRUE'-like concepts.

[9] I thank Joelle Proust for pressing this point.

REFERENCES

Barr, A. and E. Feigenbaum (eds): 1981, *The Handbook of Artificial Intelligence*, Vol. I, William Kaufmann, Inc., Los Altos, California.

Dennett, D.: 1987, 'Cognitive Wheels: the Frame Problem of AI', in Z. Pylyshyn (ed.), *The Robot's Dilemma: the Frame Problem in Artificial Intelligence*, Ablex, Norwood, New Jersey.

Fodor, J.: 1983, *The Modularity of Mind*, MIT Press, Cambridge, Massachusetts.

Fodor, J.: 1987, 'Modules, Frames, Fridgeons, Sleeping Dogs, and the Music of the

Spheres', in Z. Pylyshyn (ed.), *The Robot's Dilemma: the Frame Problem in Artificial Intelligence*, Ablex, Norwood, New Jersey.

Goodman, N.: 1965, *Fact, Fiction, and Forecast*, 2nd ed., Bobbs-Merrill, Indianapolis, Indiana.

Haugeland, J.: 1985, *Artificial Intelligence: the Very Idea*, MIT Press, Cambridge, Massachusetts.

Haugeland, J.: 1987, 'An Overview of the Frame Problem', in Z. Pylyshyn (ed.), *The Robot's Dilemma: the Frame Problem in Artificial Intelligence*, Ablex, Norwood, New Jersey.

Holland, J., K. Holyoak, R. Nisbett and P. Thagard: 1986, *Induction*, MIT Press, Cambridge, Massachusetts.

Janlert, L.: 1987, 'Modeling Change – The Frame Problem', in Z. Pylyshyn (ed.), *The Robot's Dilemma: the Frame Problem in Artificial Intelligence*, Ablex, New Jersey.

McCarthy, J. and P. Hayes: 1969, 'Some Philosophical Problems from the Standpoint of Artificial Intelligence', in B. Meltzer and D. Michie (eds.), *Machine Intelligence 4*, Edinburgh University Press, Edinburgh.

Pylyshyn, Z. (ed.): 1987, *The Robot's Dilemma: the Frame Problem in Artificial Intelligence*, Ablex, Norwood, New Jersey.

Shoham, Y.: 1988, *Reasoning about Change*, MIT Press, Cambridge, Massachusetts.

Department of Linguistics and Philosophy
Massachusetts Institute of Technology
Cambridge, MA 02139

INDEX OF NAMES

289

INDEX OF SUBJECTS

STUDIES IN COGNITIVE SYSTEMS

Series Editor: James H. Fetzer, *University of Minnesota*

1. J. H. Fetzer (ed.): *Aspects of Artificial Intelligence.* 1988
   ISBN Hb 1-55608-037-9; Pb 1-55608-038-7

2. J. Kulas, J.H. Fetzer and T.L. Rankin (eds.): *Philosophy, Language, and Artificial Intelligence.* 1988   ISBN 1-55608-073-5

3. D.J. Cole, J.H. Fetzer and T.L. Rankin (eds.): *Philosophy, Mind and Cognitive Inquiry.* Resources for Understanding Mental Processes. 1990
   ISBN 0-7923-0427-6

4. J.H. Fetzer: *Artificial Intelligence.* Its Scope and Limits. 1990
   ISBN Hb 0-7923-0505-1; Pb 0-7923-0548-5

5. H.E. Kyburg, Jr., R.P. Loui and G.N. Carlson (eds.): *Knowledge Representation and Defeasible Reasoning.* 1990   ISBN 0-7923-0677-5

6. J.H. Fetzer (ed.): *Epistemology and Cognition.* 1990 ISBN 0-7923-0892-1

7. E.C. Way: *Knowledge Representation and Metaphor.* 1991
   ISBN 0-7923-1005-5

KLUWER ACADEMIC PUBLISHERS – DORDRECHT / BOSTON / LONDON